With increasing medica[...] taken out of women's h[...] midwives there is now lit[...] or where babies are born and few women experience labour and birth without medical intervention. This has led to a situation where women seeking maternity care which enhances the natural physiological process have to question and challenge routine procedures.

This book takes a comprehensive and critical look at the issues surrounding the practices of modern childbirth — issues such as medicalisation, the use of drugs and technology, choice and safety in childbirth, the spiritual dimension. It offers a complete alternative guide for women who wish to accept responsibility for their own bodies and babies. Included is information on options and legal rights, nutrition, assertiveness, home birth, avoiding unnecessary episiotomy, the use of natural medicine, all of which will help reinforce women's confidence in their own abilities, knowledge and intuition. In the wider context, the book also explores the links between the way our children are born and the quality of future life on earth.

Birth Matters, a collection of writings by fourteen contributors, covers a broad range of topics and gives a new, wholistic perspective on childbirth. It contains articles by twelve women, all of whom have been involved, either as mothers or midwives, in working to improve women's maternity care and the quality of birth, in organisations such as The Birth Centre, The Association For Improvements In The Maternity Services and The Association Of Radical Midwives. Also included are articles by Marsden Wagner of the World Health Organisation and Michel Odent, famous for his pioneering work at Pithiviers.

BIRTH MATTERS

Issues and alternatives in childbirth

Edited by Ros Claxton

London
UNWIN PAPERBACKS
Boston   Sydney

First published in Great Britain by Unwin Paperbacks 1986.

UNWIN ® PAPERBACKS
40 Museum Street, London WC1A 1LU, UK

Unwin Paperbacks
Park Lane, Hemel Hempstead, Herts HP2 4TE, UK

Allen & Unwin Australia Pty Ltd
8 Napier Street, North Sydney, NSW 2060, Australia

Unwin Paperbacks with the
Port Nicholson Press
PO Box 11–838 Wellington, New Zealand

British Library Cataloguing in Publication Data

Birth matters: issues and alternatives in
childbirth.
1. Childbirth
I. Claxton, Ros
618.4   RG651
ISBN 0-04-612040-8

Set in 10 on 11½ point Palatino by Grove Graphics, Tring,
and printed in Great Britain by Guernsey Press Co. Ltd,
Guernsey, Channel Islands

Contents

We dedicate this book to our children
in the Spirit of Peace

Acknowledgements

My love and thanks go to all the people I worked with in the Birth Centre from whom I learned so much, in particular: Sophy Hoare, Kathy Hughes, Ros Mackenzie, Sheila Simmons, Gerlinde Wilberg and Liz Winkler.

My thanks to the following people who read manuscripts and gave much support, encouragement and valuable advice: Yvonne Baginsky, Beverley Beech, John Claxton, Sophy Hoare, Cate Lewis, Richard Stephens and Nancy Stewart.

Thanks to the practitioners who generously gave information for use in the chapter 'Natural healing — a wholistic approach to health': Michael McIntyre, Sarah Moon and Sue Turner.

My thanks to all the parents and midwives who contributed so readily and at such short notice to the chapter 'Keeping the home birth option alive'.

Thanks to Desmond Bardon for helping me realise why this book should be written and to Peter Leek for providing the possibility.

Thanks to Joanna Macy for permission to use 'The Shambhala Prophecy' which first appeared in *Yoga Journal*, January–February 1985.

And, finally, very special thanks go to my husband Johnny and our daughters Eve, Ruth and Hannah for all the patience and love given during the unusually long labour that produced this book.

Ros Claxton (*Editor*)

The contributors

BELINDA ACKERMAN

Belinda Ackerman holds nursing qualifications and trained as a midwife and health visitor. She has worked both as a domiciliary midwife and in hospitals. She is an active member of the Association of Radical Midwives and is particularly interested in promoting the role of the midwife and a woman's right to choose her place of birth and mode of delivery. She has two sons.

YVONNE BAGINSKY

Yvonne Baginsky holds a degree in politics from Edinburgh University and helped start Birth Rights, the childbirth information and support group for Scotland in 1978. In 1983 she and her husband Jack Shea made a film about home birth called *Home Truths*. She has two daughters, both born at home, and now works as a freelance journalist and writer.

BEVERLEY BEECH

Beverley Beech became involved with maternity care issues after the birth of her elder son in 1972. She has been the Hon. Chairwoman of the Association for Improvements in the Maternity Services since 1974 and is currently a lay advisor to the National Perinatal Epidemiology Unit in Oxford. In 1983 she published, with AIMS, the first booklet that identified breaches of parents' rights in maternity care, *Denial of Parents' Rights in Maternity Care*, and subsequently with Ros Claxton wrote *Health Rights Handbook for Maternity Care*. Since 1983, Beverley has been working as co-ordinator of the Community Rights Project in London. She lectures extensively both to lay and professional groups and is involved in the Birth Centre teachers' course. She has two sons.

CHRISTINE BEELS

Christine Beels became involved in childbirth issues through the births of her own three children. Between 1974 and 1981 she taught childbirth classes for the National Childbirth Trust and was Secretary for AIMS 1978–81. She is the author of *The Childbirth Book* (Granada), first published in 1979. She gradually became involved with assertiveness training as she came to see its relevance and application for women concerned with childbirth issues. She now works for the Health Education Council designing health education material for young people. She also works on the Birth Centre teachers' course.

ROS CLAXTON

Ros Claxton holds a degree in Sociology and has taught in schools, further education and as a home tutor to teenage mothers. She became involved with the Birth Centre London in 1977 and edited the *Birth Centre Newsletter* from 1977–82. In 1982 she helped found the Birth Centre teachers' course which she continues to be involved with. She has three daughters and now runs a yoga centre in Norfolk with her husband.

CAROLE ELLIOTT

Carole Elliott holds qualifications in acupuncture, homeopathy, hypnotherapy, psychotherapy and re-birthing. She started a self-support group called 'Birth and Beyond' at a rural community in New South Wales, Australia, where she also ran a healing centre and worked as a lay midwife. In between travelling round the world she works as a therapist in London, runs birth preparation classes for the Active Birth Movement and gives lectures about her work. She has four children and delivered two of her grandchildren.

INA MAY GASKIN

Ina May Gaskin holds BA and MA degrees in English. She worked with the Peace Corps in Malaysia 1963–5 and for the Office of Economic Opportunity in San Francisco teaching English to Hong Kong immigrants. In 1970, with her husband Stephen Gaskin, she founded The Farm, a rural community in Tennessee, USA, where she now lives and works as a lay midwife. She is also director of The Farm Midwives' Birth Centre and since 1975 has edited *The Practising Midwife*, a quarterly publication for midwives, physicians, nurses and childbirth educators. She is the author of *Spiritual Midwifery* (The Book Publishing Company) which documents the home births that have taken place at The Farm and *Babies, Breastfeeding and Bonding*. In 1982 she was elected vice-president of the Midwives' Alliance of North America (MANA). She has two sons and two daughters.

SOPHY HOARE

Sophy Hoare holds a degree in modern languages and worked in publishing and for the Design Council. She has been teaching yoga since 1976 and has written three books on the subject: *Yoga* (Macdonald Guidelines); *Tackle Yoga* (Stanley Paul) and *Yoga and Pregnancy* (Allen & Unwin). She became involved with the Birth Centre in 1979, edited the *Birth Centre Newsletter* from 1982–5 and also works on the teachers' course. She has three daughters and a son.

MICHEL ODENT

Michel Odent qualified as a general surgeon. He joined the hospital at Pithiviers in 1962 where he was in charge of general surgery, but became increasingly involved in the work of the maternity unit. He believes that his lack of training in obstetrics left him more open to learning through experience. His pioneering work at Pithiviers became known in this country when the BBC television film *Birth Re-Born* was shown in 1983. He is the author of *Entering the World* (Marion Boyars), *Birth Re-Born* (Souvenir Press) and *Primal Health* (Century Hutchinson). He lectures on childbirth throughout the world. He has three children.

CAROL RUDD

Carol Rudd studied psychology and philosophy at Manchester University and also holds qualfications in herbalism, irridology and nutrition. She trained as a polarity therapist in 1978–82 and is currently studying psychotherapy. She has three daughters and lives in Dorset where she teaches courses in the wholistic approach to health and also works as a therapist.

JOHANNA SQUIRE

Johanna Squire holds a BSc degree in Sociology. She became involved with the childbirth movement in 1979 when trying to arrange a home birth for her second child. In 1981 she helped found the Hull Birth Centre and since 1983 has been editor of the *AIMS Journal*. She has three sons.

NANCY STEWART

Nancy Stewart holds a BA in political science and a masters degree in education. She worked as a primary school teacher and health educator in a city health centre before moving to Britain from the USA. In this country she ran a pre-school kindergarten and is a past editor of the *AIMS Journal*. She helped found the Birth Centre teachers' course and is involved in working on the course and with AIMS. She is a freelance writer and also runs childbirth preparation groups at her home in Shropshire. She has four children, three sons and a daughter, all born at home.

SALLY STOCKLEY

Lives in East Anglia with her husband and two children. She has degrees in the history of Africa and has lived in or visited various parts of Africa, China and Europe. For the past four years she has been co-ordinator of a birth group meeting in the village in which she lives. Her experiences in this group, as well as those as a psychic and a mother, have augmented her awareness that there are more tools available for the maintenance of our own and our babies' health than many of us at present fully realise.

MARSDEN WAGNER

After qualifying in medicine, Marsden Wagner went on to specialise in paediatrics and epidemiology. He taught paediatrics and public health at the University of California before becoming director of Maternal and Child Health for the State of California. Since 1978 he has been Regional Officer for Maternal and Child Health at the European office of the World Health Organisation in Copenhagen. He is particularly interested in the humanisation of health services, especially those surrounding birth. He has four children.

Introduction

ROS CLAXTON

This book explores the issues surrounding childbirth today and takes a look at alternatives available to women. Birth is no longer an intimate event shared between the woman, her family and her midwife. The experience, taking place in large state institutions, has become fragmented. Investment in expensive drugs and machines form a necessary part of the scenario which often obscures the individual needs of the woman and her child. Modern childbirth is medicalised to such an extent that our concept of its very nature has been radically changed. Dealing with disease and pathology, the medical profession finds it difficult to have faith in the natural processes of pregnancy, labour and birth; in the medical view these processes can only be seen to be 'normal' in retrospect. Techniques which have been developed to help the minority who experience complications, have come to be used on almost everyone. Birth, according to the medical view, should only take place in hospital where help is close at hand; benefits of currently used drugs and technology outweigh risks; pain inevitably accompanies labour and can only be relieved by pharmacological means. The specialist training of the doctor makes him expert in all matters pertaining to pregnancy and, as a lay person, the mother's own knowledge and feelings cannot be taken seriously, nor is she able to participate in decision-making.

In contrast to these assumptions, the authors of this book share the view that birth is a normal, non-medical process for the majority of women. They believe that all medical interventions carry risks and should never be applied routinely. The obstetrician may be expert when it comes to abnormal cases, but it is the midwife whose art and skills should encourage and facilitate the natural process. The woman's own knowledge, feelings and intuition have the utmost validity and should therefore be treated with respect.

This book is written for women who believe birth to be a natural process and seek more from the experience than is currently on offer in most hospitals today. By extending their knowledge and awareness such women realise that they play an important part in the healthy outcome of their pregnancies and births. Women seeking maternity care which enhances the physiological process and minimises the amount of unnecessary interference, find that the institutionalisation and medicalisation of birth impose a conformity of treatment. This leads to a number of difficulties when they start to question or refuse certain procedures. Few obstetricians have faith in the physiological process (they rarely witness a natural birth) and midwives are expected, as part of the obstetric team, to play their part in carrying out hospital policy. It often takes great courage on the part of a woman to begin to challenge, perhaps for the first time in her life, the established system of 'experts'. Many women have been surprised at the clarity and strength of the maternal feelings aroused in them. Nevertheless, pregnancy is a sensitive time and it is important for both the mother and the baby that stress be minimised; realising that you are not alone in questioning established practices can help relieve anxiety and reinforce confidence in the woman's own knowledge and intuition. As a means of understanding the current situation, the first part of the book takes a look at the issues surrounding modern childbirth. With acceptance of responsibility for our own health during childbearing comes the realisation that we play a large part in making ourselves 'safe' and that 'safety' cannot always be provided by drugs and technology. Bearing this idea in mind, the second part of the book explores alternative possibilities. Viewing birth in its wider context, the third part of the book contains two personal statements for the future.

Much of the material included in this book has its origins in work carried out by several of the contributors, including myself, within a nationwide network of women known as 'The Birth Centre'. This experience, plus the births of our own children, has increased our awareness of the difficulties faced by women who seek a natural birth. The original Birth Centre was formed in London in 1977, when a group of women, mainly mothers, midwives and ante-natal teachers, dissatisfied with impersonal care, routine medical intervention and lack of choice, decided to offer information and support to other childbearing women. The 1970s were eventful years for those involved in childbirth issues and it is interesting here to note some of the events which preceded the formation of the Birth Centre. The medicalisation of birth had reached a zenith at the beginning of the seventies with, for example, labour being induced routinely in many hospitals in an attempt to minimise the number of births taking place at 'inconvenient' hours; the domiciliary service was being systematically dismantled and women were being told that home birth was no longer possible; other options, such as GP units and small maternity hospitals, were gradually being threatened or closed down to make way for large, centralised obstetric units; midwives were fast losing their independent status as they became part of the obstetric team under the direction of the obstetricians. The maternity services were beginning to fulfil the needs of those working within them rather than the needs of pregnant women. Not surprisingly, there was widespread discontent. Jean Robinson, then chairwoman of the Patients' Association, reported that there were more complaints about the maternity services than any other aspect of the National Health system. Together with such groups as the Association for Improvements in the Maternity Services and the National Childbirth Trust, she led the public debate on the issue of routine induction. Eventually, and for the first time in the field of obstetrics in this country, consumer pressure led to a subsequent drop in the induction rate in 1974–5. In spite of this, other improvements called for by parents were not forthcoming and the basic medical approach to pregnancy and birth remains unchanged.

Then in 1976, another perspective was added to the childbirth debate when Frederick Leboyer launched his book *Birth Without Violence* in this country. Up until then, ante-natal preparation focused on the mother and her experience of birth; this pioneering work helped increase awareness of the baby's sensitivity during and after birth. Many of his ideas, especially his contention that 'birth is not a medical matter but a poem', led his medical colleagues to dismiss him as a 'mystical romantic' or worse! Together with his accompanying film, *A Child Is Born*, he travelled around the country. It was in response to the interest that he aroused that the first Birth Centre was formed and the seeds were sown from which other centres evolved.

In 1976 midwives took a step forward towards reclaiming their profession when the Association of Radical Midwives was formed by a small group of students. Gradually, from 1977 onwards, other Birth Centres began to open all over the country and the network of like-minded individuals grew. Strong links were formed with the Radical Midwives and contact was made with similiar birth groups in countries such as the USA, Australia, New Zealand and Europe. We discovered we were part of an international movement which existed wherever birth had come to be dominated by modern obstetrics. In 1981, the London and Cambridge Birth Centres invited the French doctor, Michel Odent, to come and talk about his work. At his maternity unit in Pithiviers, no unnecessary medical interventions take place and the majority of women experience a natural birth. Here, midwives work in freedom within the true spirit of midwifery and women and their babies are treated with love and respect. This visit led to a BBC television film, *Birth Re-Born*, which had a tremendous impact when shown the following year and caused many more people to question the techniques of modern childbirth. In the same year, 5,000 people attended a 'Birth Rights' rally in London in protest against the interventionist approach to pregnancy and birth at the Royal Free Hospital and the refusal of a midwife there to deliver a woman in the squatting position.

The Birth Centre network continued (and continues) to provide women with information about options, legal rights, drugs and technology, natural medicine and so forth. However, we were becoming increasingly aware of the limitations of the conventional approach to ante-natal education: so many women attending classes which claim to prepare them for natural birth end up with medical intervention and are left with a strong sense of failure or guilt. The problem seemed to us to lie not only with the interventionist policies of the hospitals, but with the inadequacy of current childbirth education to deal with this situation. Not only do women need information about the use of drugs and technology, they also need the confidence to challenge the system if necessary. Ante-natal education may cover the former (not always as critically as we would like to see), but it rarely provides help with the latter. Teachers, on the whole, concentrate on the physiology of labour and birth, giving a set of breathing and relaxation techniques to help cope with labour. The woman then goes into hospital and finds that she is expected to submit to certain routine procedures and the cycle of interventions is set into motion. Her breathing techniques alienate her from her bodily sensations, she cannot relax in the hospital environment and staff are unable to provide the comfort, emotional support and atmosphere necessary to see a woman through a natural birth. In addition to this, the husband or partner is often left bewildered or at a loss to know how to help.

In response to increasing criticism of current ante-natal classes, the Birth Centre decided in 1982 to set up a new birth teachers' training course (none of us are happy with the use of the word 'teacher' in this context, 'facilitator' is nearer the mark but much clumsier to say!). On this course, the 'teachers' learn to use assertiveness training to help give women the confidence to ask for and be firm about what they want; they encourage women to believe in the validity of their own intuitive feelings and they prepare women for labour by working with the body as well as the mind, trying to integrate and harmonise all aspects of being. Much of the material included in the second part of the book is drawn from work experienced during these birth teachers' courses.

The need for information contained in a book such as this arises from the inability of the obstetric profession to take a critical look at its procedures and to let go of its paternalistic attitudes towards women. Our Birth Centre work has led us to realise that change will not be initiated from within the medical profession itself. Even those sympathetic to our needs have a hard time trying to enlighten their colleagues. Change has been, and will continue to be, brought about by women being clear about what they want and what they are prepared to accept. Neither will information on options and legal rights come from the profession. So, it is up to women themselves to provide each other with such knowledge. One of the most encouraging aspects of our Birth Centre work has been the discovery that when women are informed and have the support of a partner, friends or a birth group, they usually manage to get what they want. Obviously not all women are able to have a natural birth, but those that end up with medical intervention should be able to give their informed consent to what they know is a truly necessary procedure.

Looking back over our work since the Birth Centre was first formed, I see that what we have been working towards is a 'wholistic' approach to pregnancy and birth. Many of our problems, in this and other spheres of life, arise from the way we perceive the world and our place within it. Our culture is dominated by the reductionist view that can only understand the whole by breaking it down into its component parts. We then objectify the world, detach ourselves from it and lose sight of our interconnectedness with it and with each other. We separate mind from body and, seduced by the brilliance and power of conceptual thinking, consider our minds to be superior to our bodies. From here it is but a short step towards the belief that we are capable of controlling, rather than co-operating with, the forces of nature.

Having isolated our minds in this way, we develop and value the functions of the left side of our brains, that is intellect, analytic abilities, mathematical and verbal skills, to the exclusion of the functions of the right side of the brain which cover intuition, creative expression, dreaming and so on. The scientific approach, upon which Western medicine is based, is rooted in this mechanistic, left-brain way of thinking and any expression which does not fit this paradigm is ignored or scorned. Pregnancy and birth are experiences very much grounded in the functions of the right side of the brain; confusion and conflict occur when women find themselves subjected to a medical approach which hardly recognises, and indeed considers itself superior to, this other mode of being.

During the last decade, a number of movements exploring personal growth and development have emerged; there has been a resurgence of interest in the spiritual aspect of life. Much of what is happening is based on a new wholistic awareness which includes what Marilyn Ferguson, in her book *The Aquarian Conspiracy*, called 'whole-brain knowing'. This approach attempts to develop and bring into a state of balance the functions of both sides of the brain. In particular it gives attention to the under-valued aspects of the right brain by recognising the validity of our own experience and the primacy of our own perception as a source of 'knowing'. This approach recognises intuitive insights, the life and symbols of the unconscious and the fact that the body has an intelligence of its own. Unfortunately, these ideas have had little impact so far on modern medicine and obstetrics and those sympathetic to such a perspective must try to realise it in the face of ignorance or even hostility.

Tuning in to a wholistic approach means healing the split between mind and body. Only then can we heal the split between ourselves and the world and experience our deep inter-connectedness with each other. In a world overshadowed by the threat of nuclear extinction, it is no longer possible to consider the way we give birth in isolation. Inter-connected as we are, every action, however small it may seem, has its repercussions on the whole. By giving birth to our children in a harmonious and loving way we make a positive contribution to their future and to the creation of a peaceful world.

PART ONE

The Issues

We live in a society bent on unilateral control, whether it be of the Russians, the gypsy moths, or the second stage of labour.

Elizabeth Noble

The medicalisation of birth

MARSDEN WAGNER

There is a quiet revolution taking place at the present time in health care around the world. Up until a hundred years ago, medical care combined about 90 per cent art with 10 per cent 'technology'. Then medical care attached itself to the rising star of science. This was at that magic time in history when physics was leading the way and classic mechanical physics helped launch the industrial revolution. The view of the world was mechanistic, based on the dichotomous split which goes back to ancient Greek times. This split has become deeply ingrained in our modern way of thought; we take it as a given implicit assumption and it colours everything we do. The split may be seen as follows:

Art	Science
Quality	Quantity
Subjective	Objective
Feminine	Masculine
Intuition	Logic
Mind (Emotion)	Body

Descartes, at the beginning of the modern era, argued persuasively that the only path to knowledge was via the scientific (objective, logical, mechanistic) side of the dichotomy and that we must ignore and/or control the art (quality, subjective, intuitive, emotional) side.

This limited, one-sided mechanistic view was then applied to the field of medicine and the body and disease processes were all seen in these terms. Interestingly enough, this approach has been applied to the disease process, less so to the treatment process and not at all to the system of health care services. (In fact, in our so-called 'scientific medicine', somewhere between only 10 to 20 per cent of routine procedures have ever been evaluated with clinical control trials.)[1] The mechanistic view began with looking at the body as a machine and then gradually focused on smaller and smaller aspects, looking next at the organs as separate machines, then sub-organ level until today we are down to the molecular level. This approach produced many 'miracles' such that everybody believed it was only a matter of time until it would be possible to understand the human body and the disease processes perfectly. This approach reached its peak in the 1960s and is certainly still very strong.

Then, about ten years ago, something began to go wrong. People like Ivan Illich[2] began to show the very serious problems with regard to iatrogenesis in modern medicine. Others, like Cochran[3] and McKeown,[4] showed the fact that modern medical care was not really correlated with the level of health of the people. This and other writings made it more and more clear that there might be some limitations to the scientific, mechanistic approach to human health. Ironically, about seventy-five years ago the very same thing was happening in physics. Classic physics had also performed miracles during the nineteenth century, but more and more data suggested that something was wrong with its approach and at the beginning of the twentieth century, Einstein, Bohr and friends showed that mechanistic physics has limitations. Indeed, they demonstrated that there were vast areas where these laws held not at all and an entirely new system had to be developed. They also showed something most fascinating, which is that you can't keep the observer out of the equation — a fact which now began to threaten the sacred, one-sided dichotomy. So a battle was launched in physics and is still raging today. Incredibly, this battle has been one of the best-kept secrets of the twentieth century. Indeed, in the 1950s when I was an undergraduate student at the University of California, I was required to take courses in physics where I was taught pure, classical physics and was never once told that there were any kind of limitations to this approach. Meanwhile, other disciplines such as psychology and medicine continued to build on the mechanistic approach based on this one-sided, dichotomous view of the world.

Then, in the 1970s, Capra,[5] Pirsig[6] and others brought this battle out of the closet. And what did we find out? We found out that the physicists had clearly demonstrated that the subjective/objective split can no longer exist in science. We found out that the state of consciousness of the observer must always be in the equation in science. We found out that the hypothesis, which is fundamental to the entire scientific method, comes from subjective intuition and that hypothesis generation has no objectivity in it. We found that most of the important fundamental discoveries of modern science were the result of an intuitive flash of a scientific mind which was at the moment of the flash not even thinking about science, but was, for example, drawing up a shopping list of groceries for the day. We found out that science can tell us nothing about the quality of life and has nothing to say about good and bad. We found out that science cannot guide us because it is entirely retrospective: it proves what we have already made some educated guess about. These very serious limitations of science may be out of the closet but they are unfortunately not yet widespread in the other disciplines which have followed physics in taking up the mechanistic, scientific approach. It can only be a matter of time before the news spreads.

What is now beginning to happen in the 1980s is that all of these observations with regard to the limits of medicine and science are being applied to the current medical care crisis and what we are discovering is the following: the current crisis in health care is, at root, the result of the dichotomous assumptions underlying the scientific, mechanistic approach to health. Health is subjective, yet because of the dichotomy we have been trying to apply a purely, so-called objective approach, thereby denying its essential subjectivity. The solution to this crisis clearly must lie in the rejection of the current imbalance which arises out of the dichotomous view of the world. This will produce two fundamental changes in modern medicine: bringing 'art' back into medical care and bringing the observer back into medical science. Future health care will therefore be the result of these solutions and will have wide ramifications and implications.

All this can be illustrated clearly as we look at the phenomenon of birth. Birth is not a disease nor is it a pathological process or even a health problem. Birth is a biosocial process which is, by its very nature, a feminine process and a sexual process. In order for medical science and medical care to take over birth it was necessary to medicalise it; to make it pathological, to put it into hospital under the control of male physicians, to take over and control midwifery and to deny the feminine and sexual characteristics of birthing. That is to say, what was necessary was to move birth from the realm of art (quality, subjectivity, intuitive, female) to the realm of science (quantitative, objective, masculine, logical, body mechanics).

This medicalisation of birth has several key aspects. Firstly it leads to the mechanisation of birth: the woman is seen and treated as a reproductive machine to which other machines can be attached. The consequent uncontrolled proliferation of invasive technology is now at its peak in the United Kingdom. In England and Wales, one out of every five births (20.6 per cent) has an operative intervention (forceps, vacuum extraction or caesarean section). This is higher than the eight continental countries where data is available and is exceeded only by Scotland (23.7 per cent). The induction of labour, a significant proportion of which falls into the category sometimes called 'daylight obstetrics', is according to the best estimates between 20 per cent and 30 per cent of all births in England and Wales, while in the rest of Europe it is between 10 per cent and 20 per cent.[7] Finally, between 30 per cent and 90 per cent of all delivering women in Western Europe and North America have their vaginal opening cut with scissors during birth, in spite of the fact that a careful review of the literature concludes that the highest reasonable rate is no more than 20 per cent and in some hospitals in the European region the episiotomy rate is 1 per cent with less than 5 per cent natural tears.[8]

This then is what women face and the most important and insidious aspect of all is that it is out of their control. Social scientists have long talked about 'the power of definition'. This means that those who define the problem control the solution: it is the male obstetricians who are defining birth and who control the interventions; the male obstetricians decide who is at risk and what the desirable outcome should be. The opposite of such control by the medical establishment is, of course, freedom of individual choice: thus choice becomes the key issue in all aspects of birth. The World Health Organisation commissioned a study of routine medical procedures carried out during pregnancy and childbirth.[9] The study showed that many procedures have never undergone scientific evaluation while having significant undesirable psychological and social effects. Neither are women given a choice about these procedures. In a survey of twenty-three countries in Europe, the women had a choice about what was done to them during delivery as follows:

Women could sometimes choose whether or not to be shaved in 5 out of 23 countries.

Women could sometimes choose who would be present in 10 out of 23 countries.

Women could sometimes choose whether or not to have routine electronic fetal monitoring in 5 out of 23 countries.

Women sometimes had a choice (in normal delivery) concerning anaesthesia in 10 out of 23 countries.

Women sometimes had a choice about episiotomy in 1 out of 23 countries.

Women sometimes had a choice about delivery position in 3 out of 23 countries.

So women have almost no choice about what is happening to their own bodies during childbearing.

Another key aspect of the medicalisation of birth is the suppression of the midwife's role. Three developments in particular have eroded the autonomy of midwives: one, the classification of higher and higher percentages of pregnancies as high risk; two, the growing concentration of birth in hospitals; three, the increase, especially over the last fifteen years, in the technological component of ante-natal care which has come to be more and more a hospital-based service in many countries. Midwifery was historically an independent profession. Nursing has always been subject to the control of physicians. By insisting that midwives be trained first as nurses, the doctors killed two flies with one swat. The students are first trained to comply in a subservient profession. And since basic nursing focuses on the care of the ill, the students are at the same time trained to see the world in pathological terms. The result? Midwives are medicalised into nurse-midwives and women lose control of birthing. There are, of course, exceptional nurses and exceptional nurse-midwives who struggle for independence, but they are swimming upstream in their professions. This decline in the status and power of the midwife is to be found all over the developed world. It means that childbearing women have increasingly been deprived of those skills traditionally offered by midwives — skills which include a priori an emphasis on the normality of child-bearing, continuity of care and sensitivity to psycho-social as well as clinical needs.

'Safety' is a central tenet of medicalised birth and is the other side of the coin of 'unsafe' or 'risk'. 'Risk' is the bludgeon which is used to scare, not only women, but politicians and health care providers. 'Unsafe' or 'risk' is a concept not a fact and is based on the premise that all births are pathological or potentially pathological. The antithetical premise that all births are normal, or potentially normal, is much more valid since around 90 per cent of births, if reasonably managed, turn out to be normal. Which of these two premises is used profoundly influences the kind of care a woman receives. If the pathological premise is used, care then consists of the unrelenting pursuit of pathology. Because it is unrelenting, doctors are bound, sooner or later, to find something which they will define as unsafe or high risk. Screening becomes a means of recruiting people into the health care system and the percentage of pregnant women labelled high risk goes up and up. Equally important, the pursuit itself may in a number of instances create and/or enhance the potential for complications and thus unsafe or risk becomes a self-fulfilling concept.

The concept of 'unsafe' has also been promoted by the manipulation of statistics, a favourite ploy being to lump all home births, planned and unplanned, together. Since a large number of unplanned, out of hospital births are precipitous and/or premature, the complication rate is high and any value of planned, normal home birth is submerged by pathology of the unplanned and made to look unsafe. I am frankly amused by the desperate efforts of the obstetrical profession to explain away the fact (not concept) that the one country in Western Europe (Holland) which still has over one-third of all births at home also has one of the very best safety records in terms of both the mother and baby. The truth is that it has never been shown scientifically that, for normal pregnant women, hospital births are safer than home births.

Thus the last hundred years has seen the unfolding of an obstetrical drama. The first act of the drama is the story of the medicalisation of birth as briefly reviewed above and could well be summarised by saying: the male physician has written the obstetrical drama so that he is the star rather than the woman. With the second act of the drama comes the good news. There are places in the world where the medicalisation of birth is counter-balanced by strong traditions which have held. For example, two years ago in China, I watched a caesarean section birth using one acupuncture needle in one earlobe while the woman lay wide awake chatting with the staff. On The Farm in Tennessee, USA, a rural community founded by Ina May Gaskin and her husband in 1970, lay midwives combine traditional methods and modern basic techniques in a way that nearly eliminates medicalisation.

The second piece of good news is that where tradition has succumbed to medicalisation, a reaction is setting in. I suspect that one thing the medical establishment was not prepared to reckon with was the Women's Movement. This international movement has more recently given high priority to reclaiming health and illness as the rightful property of individuals rather than medical professionals and is demanding greater control by women over the conditions of their own lives. Women have already taken the vaginal speculum in their own hands and with regard to birthing, women are beginning to demand to be in control of their own birth and to listen to their own bodies and to choose their own birthing positions and to choose who will be with them during this important experience. So we see the emergence of alternative perinatal (i.e. surrounding birth) services.

In those countries where the official medical system provides little choice as to type and place of care, personnel providing care and the element of continuity, the women begin seeking alternative services. Recently, the World Health Organisation decided to take a look at these services and recruited a Danish midwife, who had been active in providing and evaluating alternative services, and an English sociologist to conduct this study.[10] These are some of their findings. Alternative perinatal services form an international movement with two characteristic themes in the ten countries in Europe and North America where we have looked so far. These themes firstly focus on the desire of service users to choose a form of care appropriate to their own personal needs, and secondly see the character of childbearing as a social rather than a purely medical event. Thus, despite differences between countries, the alternative perinatal services form an international movement with a sense of common aims and strategies amongst users and providers.

Another finding of this study was the relation of these alternative services to traditional care. Over most of the world and throughout history, the health care of women and children has resided with the female community. It has been provided by experienced lay members of this community in the context of an informal system that has stressed both continuity of care and health as a social product. Its knowledge base has been empirical rather than scientific. Some of the modern alternative perinatal practices represent the preservation of the vestiges of this older system. It is on this framework of indigenous lay female-controlled health care that most modern medical health systems have been grafted. There are many ways in which these modern alternatives are not really alternatives at all but represent a return to beliefs and practices predating the emergence of modern obstetric medicine. In this way, modern official perinatal care can be seen as the real interruption or real alternative in a deep-rooted human tradition of lay health care. Indeed, many axioms of modern alternative care are just a normal way of doing things in many of today's known cultures. Upright delivery positions, ambulation in labour, delayed cutting of the cord, post-natal closeness between mother and infant and a patient attitude to the removal of the placenta are some examples of normal practices in much of the Third World today.

One of the most important findings of the alternative perinatal service is that it is not simply a repository of herbal remedies and enthusiastic home deliveries, nor is it an attempt simply to fill in some of the gaps that are missing in the official services. It is rather an alternative model or a completely different way of providing care to people. Essential to this alternative model is a move away from the medical paradigm of childbearing with its emphasis on risks and its division of pregnant women into those for whom childbirth is somehow intrinsically risky and those for whom it is not expected to be so. It is also a move away from the medical paradigm of childbearing which sees 'normal' birth as an event that takes place in hospital and measures all normalcy in the framework of a hospital-based, obstetrician-controlled situation. Alternative providers are finding from their own experience that they are establishing importantly different parameters for 'normal' childbearing than those currently accepted within the official system. For example, the dictate that a normal first labour does not last more than 18 hours, or that a second stage taking more than one hour is abnormal, are being shown to be generalisations derived from populations whose biological normality is essentially altered by these institutional settings and levels of medical intervention. Perhaps the main message of the alternative movement is thus the one about non-separation of body and mind. The emotional comfort of childbearing women is, in this view, more than a luxury demanded by a vociferous minority consumer movement: it is held to be the basic prerequisite of physical safety itself. Another characteristic of this alternative model is a moving away from the hierarchy separating user from provider which is built into the official health care system of most developed countries today, towards shared decision-making.

The alternative perinatal services give great prominence to the role of the female midwife and to the way in which her autonomy as the manager of normal childbearing has been diluted over the years. The role midwives play in alternative services reflects their role in the official system. On the whole, the weaker the position of midwives in the official services, the more pronounced their role in the alternative services. Even in those European countries with a comparatively strong tradition of midwifery as an autonomous profession, there is a tendency for midwives within or attached to hospital obstetrics to become 'doctor's assistants' and to be replaced by nurses who are cheaper. The study found that midwives working within the hospital-based official system perform a range of activities and undertake a degree of responsibility that is less than that legally allowed, while working outside the system the responsibilities and activities often exceed the legally permissible limit. Thus, the lesson to be learned from the midwifery of these alternative services is that the most effective challenge possible to the male hegemony of the modern, technological medical world, lies in the domain of independent domiciliary practice.

The study found that more and more women are demanding home birth or non-medicalised options. As I travel around Europe talking and giving lectures, I have discovered that I can say all manner of crazy things but if I mention home birth to a medical audience everyone reacts emotionally, most commonly with anger. Why? Because a doctor, to be in control and to be in power, must be in his own shop. Look at the reaction of the medical profession to home birth. They come up with ambulatory birth where the woman is still in hospital for the moment of truth. In the United Kingdom, the obstetricians have proposed to give more control to the general practitioners (but never, of course, to the midwives). They have tried to make the hospital birthing unit more like home by hanging up curtains and bringing in a television set (this reminds me of the sign in the bakery shop that says 'we sell home-baked bread'!) Such well-meaning attempts completely miss the point about the difference between hospital and home. The home is the nest or cave which surrounds the woman with a familiar physical, emotional and social environment which gives a feeling of relaxation and security which facilitates a smooth birth and which can never be duplicated outside the home. It is, of course, essential that the woman can also choose a hospital birth and so we are beginning to see more and more meaningful alternatives in the hospital setting. For example, in one hospital in London, locks have been put on the *inside of* the door to the labour room. This means the woman can have control over who is present — a real switch from the past.

What then do I see to be the important trends for the future? Firstly, a combining of the non-allopathic approaches to health care with the allopathic approaches — that is to say, the melding of both sides of our dichotomy. I mentioned earlier the caesarean birth in China using acupuncture. Such non-allopathic approaches from the East are becoming more accepted in the West — indeed I have a friend in Paris who had a caesarean section using acupuncture. We are realising more and more that with regard to traditional and alternative health care possibilities we threw the baby out with the bath water. It is clear that we need both approaches and the European Office of the World Health Organisation is forming a new programme that focuses on these alternative health care possibilities.

A second trend will be to focus more on health as a positive component of a fulfilling daily life and not just the absence of disease or other negative conditions. This, in other words, will be an honouring of the art side of the dichotomy as important and essential in life. With birthing, this means not only an accepting but a celebrating of the intuitive, feminine, sexual nature of the birth process. In doing this, however, we must be very careful that modern medicine, rooted in science which only recognises linear thinking and so-called objectivity, does not take over and attempt to 'objectify' these aspects of birthing.

Birthing will not be returned to its proper female territory until women themselves take control, not only of their bodies and of childbearing, but also of the movement for this control. Our study of alternatives found that midwives and childbearing women have an underlying coalition of interests in the way in which childbearing is managed now and in the future. Those branches of the alternative movement in which mothers and midwives have recognised this underlying coalition and have organised together have been the most successful in securing change. Women are re-writing the obstetrical scenario so that birth is no longer an obstetric drama but a human drama.

REFERENCES

1 *Acta Obstetrica et Gynecologica Scandinavia*, supplement 117, published by the Scandinavian Association of Obstetricians and Gynaecologists, 1983.
2 Ivan Illich, *Medical Nemesis*, Marion Boyars, 1976.
3 A. L. Cochran, *Effectiveness and Efficiency: Random Reflections on Health Services*, London Nuffield Provincial Hospital Trust, 1972.
4 T. McKeown, *The Role of Medicine — Dream, Mirage or Nemesis*, Oxford Blackwells, 1980.
5 F. Capra, *The Tao of Physics*, Wildwood House, 1975.
6 R. Pirsig, *Zen and the Art of Motorcycle Maintenance*, Corgi, 1976.

7 Bergsjo, Schmidt and Pusch, 'Differences in the reported frequencies of some obstetrical interventions in Europe', *British Journal of Obstetrics and Gynaecology*, vol. 90, pp. 628–32, July 1983.

8 S. B. Thacker and H. D. Banta, 'Benefits and risks of episiotomy: an interpretative review of the English language literature 1860–1920', *Obstetrical and Gynaecological Survey*, vol. 38, issue 6, pp. 322–38, 1983.

9 *Acta Obstetrica et Gynecologica Scandinavia, op. cit.*

10 *Alternative Perinatal Services in Europe and North America*, World Health Organisation, 1982.

Obstetric drugs and technology

NANCY STEWART

More than one woman, on declining some form of medical intervention in her pregnancy or labour, has been advised by an indignant doctor to go have her baby under a bush. She probably quite safely could. But though the great majority of labours will produce a healthy child with no medical assistance at all, the list of medical procedures and drugs routinely employed in normal childbirth is already long and continues to grow. Most of these innovations have never been properly evaluated to determine their benefits and risks, either before they were introduced or after becoming the norm for routine care. They are in fact of questionable safety, may be adopted at immense cost to the health service, and are often in direct opposition to a labouring woman's need for freedom to respond to her particular labour as it unfolds.

Why, then, is there such uncritical dispersal of obstetric techniques beyond the few who might benefit, to routine application? It has been suggested that dispersal of innovations can be explained by three factors, none of which centres on the well-being of mothers and babies: specifically, on the structure of the organisation of maternity care, on the role of interest groups, and on the established paradigm.

We can see the operation of these three factors by considering an integral part of most obstetric practice — the use of drugs for relief of pain in labour. The organisational structure has had clear influences on the readiness with which new drugs and methods of administering drugs have been adopted. Had the traditional midwife, attending birth in the woman's home, remained the centre of maternity care provision, anaesthesia and analgesia for childbirth would have remained available only to the minority who encountered medical complications and so were referred to the care of a doctor. But since doctors have become the most powerful figures in setting standards of care, and since medicine is largely a pharmacological discipline, the use of drugs in labour has become routine. Similarly, the rapid hospitalisation of birth made possible the advent of epidural anaesthesia, which is appropriate only in a large hospital setting where specialist anaesthetists are readily available. It is possible, too, that the division of labour in the hospital structure — with different groups of care providers working in ante-natal clinics, admission, labour and delivery, and post-natal areas — precludes the personal care and attention that can minimise the need for drugs.

The influence of interest groups in drugs for childbirth is not one to be taken lightly. The pharmaceutical industry is a powerful lobby, actively promoting its lucrative business. With one full-time drug company representative for every five GPs, the drug manufacturers provide information about their products to doctors who often don't have time to seek information from more neutral sources. And along with the information come other benefits for the medical audience, ranging from pens and desk-pads emblazoned with the drug logo, to lavish luncheons, expensive gifts and even holidays. The General Medical Council, concerned with reported excesses in drug companies' courting of medical favour, has called for stricter limits on such gifts. They also initiated an investigation of standards of advertising in medical journals and drug company leaflets — in which un-founded claims may be made for drugs, or side-effects not men-tioned — and the common practice of drug companies paying doctors to prescribe a drug as part of the clinical trials testing its safety and effectiveness.

The testing of drugs for use in pregnancy and obstetrics is largely under the influence of drug manufacturers. Since the thalidomide disaster of the 1960s, there is greater awareness that standard tests on other animals and on adults may not disclose the dangers for a human fetus. Yet many doctors still consider a drug that is not specifically contraindicated in pregnancy to be 'safe', or will prescribe drugs after the first trimester of organ and limb development — apparently oblivious to the fact that central nervous system development is most rapid in later pregnancy. But contrary to the assumption that drugs prescribed in pregnancy or used for pain relief in labour have been proved safe, the US Federal Drug Administration has stated that there is *no* drug, prescription or over-the-counter, which has been proved safe for the unborn child exposed in the womb. The World Health Organisation has complained that the drug testing requirements amount to a 'trial-and-error' approach to drug safety for children and fetuses — it is only after problems are reported in the use of the drug that it may be thoroughly investigated, as no systematic follow-up studies are currently required.

In determining the relative safety of drug products, it is the manufacturers who design the studies, obtain and analyse the data, and arrange for clinical trials. The regulatory agency considers the drug company's data, but rarely investigates it fully. In the present arrangement between the pharmaceutical industry and the NHS, the drug companies are encouraged to research and develop new drugs by a large guaranteed profit margin each year: whatever is spent on developing drugs, we will pay through adjustments of drug prices to ensure a healthy profit for the companies. One representative of the pharmaceutical industry even suggested we should go further to introduce a no-fault compensation scheme to encourage new drugs, so that increases in drug prices would pay for any compensation for drug damage, without penalty to the company.

Of the drugs used in obstetrics, the measures considered to demonstrate 'safety' are relatively insensitive indicators of only immediate outcomes. For instance, a drug may be approved if it does not lower Apgar scores by more than two points. But two points of an Apgar score (rating newborn respiration, heart rate, colour, muscle tone, and response to stimulus) may make a significant difference to a small or weak baby. And such a rating cannot detect any subtle neurologic damage such as learning difficulties, minimal brain dysfunction, or hyperactivity. Dr Yvonne Brackbill, whose research found significant effects from obstetric drugs in children at age 7 years in such areas as language skills and fine motor tasks, explained to an investigatory hearing that drugs approved as safe for medical use have not been tested on infants, and have not been tested for *behavioural* effects.

'Blood gas parameters do not predict reading achievement,' she said. 'Apgar scores do not predict language skills. Respiration rate does not predict motor skills.' Because the brain is developing most rapidly around the time of birth, it could be that drugs affecting the newborn central nervous system could have permanent effects.

But it is not only the influence of vested interests in encouraging drug use that has made 'pain relief' almost synonymous with medication. There is also a receptive market for drugs, determined by the paradigm under which the services operate. In the dominant paradigm, childbirth is seen as a medical condition to be actively — usually pharmacologically — treated. In any other medical condition, a doctor will prescribe a drug to relieve symptoms, so it comes quite naturally to do the same with birth. This view disregards the possibility of creative pain that a woman can work with and through in giving birth, but sees pain as a totally negative symptom that should be eradicated. Hence the enthusiasm for epidural anaesthesia, promising pain-free birth ('Tell them they can be sitting up, manicured and reading *Vogue*').

Women may not actually want a pain-free birth, as a recent study of women's responses to drugs in labour showed.[1] Those women who had epidurals reported the greatest degree of pain relief, but also had the highest levels of dissatisfaction with their experience both immediately after the birth and a year later, while the women who had no drugs reported the most pain, but the greatest degree of satisfaction. Although only 8 per cent of the women in the study had no drugs in labour, a year later 45 per cent of the women felt that pain was a necessary part of the emotional experience of childbirth, and 61 per cent thought that a sympathetic midwife was of more value than all treatment for pain relief.[2] This contrasts with a survey of obstetricians, 89 per cent of whom felt that epidural anaesthesia allowed women the best experience of childbirth, and with the current trend towards encouraging midwives to be more involved in the technological side of maternity care. One doctor praised the move towards having midwives top up epidurals, claiming that it was 'satisfying for the midwives who at last can give some really effective pain relief'.

The medical view pays scant attention to the importance of the emotional environment on a woman's perception of pain. Dismissing preparation classes as promoting reliance on 'mere relaxation', a consultant explained, 'I think the relaxation sessions are very valuable to help her before she actually gets her epidural.' One obstetrician said that he would rather deal with a drugged baby than a very agitated and tense mother, illustrating the medical assumption that a tense mother's need for help must be met with a drug rather than with human support — comforting arms, a massage, a change of position, and above all constant confidence in the labouring woman's ability to give birth. Such human demands on the birth attendant are not covered in the medical paradigm of birth, and so they are rejected in favour of a drug which may at least make the woman quieter and more easily handled, allowing attendants to feel that she is more comfortable and that they have given the necessary assistance. We might wonder if giving a drug to a labouring woman does not largely serve to dispel the attendants' fears about pain in labour, or embarrassment about the intimacy of offering emotional support at this powerful time. The woman's own ability to cope with pain through secretion of endorphins — which may actually be disturbed by pain-relieving drugs — is ignored because this does not fall comfortably within the medical paradigm.

So the vast majority of women giving birth in Britain receive drugs in labour. They may be given routinely, a prescribed amount at a prescribed stage of labour. Sometimes they are given because a woman asks for help in coping with her labour, and she or her attendants or both turn to a drug when help is needed. And sometimes they are used because a woman is experiencing a labour that is complicated in some way, and drugs may be required to cope with the extra pain or stress.

A drug administered in labour will rapidly reach the baby through the placenta. Often a drug will remain in the baby's circulation in measurable doses for days after birth, as the newborn's immature liver is not able to break the drug down and eliminate it efficiently.

The most common obstetric drug is pethidine, a synthetic narcotic. Pethidine does not remove sensation, but is supposed to provide relief from pain, and perhaps aid relaxation. It is not very effective in relieving pain: the manufacturers recommend 100 milligrams as a maximum dose, but at that level its pain relief can hardly be distinguished from a placebo. Even at 150 milligrams, only 50–60 per cent of women report satisfactory pain relief. Side-effects sometimes include nausea and vomiting, drowsiness and an uncomfortable feeling of being removed from reality. It does not relax a tense cervix, as is sometimes claimed, but does in some cases slow down labour. It is impossible to predict whether these effects will occur in a particular mother.

Pethidine given in labour can depress a newborn's respiration, make the baby sleepy, and interfere with the sucking ability. It also affects the baby's ability to habituate (learn to ignore an irrelevant stimulus), and may cause the baby to change state frequently, and to cry and be unable to quiet itself. Many of these effects have been observed to last for at least six weeks or two months, and could potentially affect the feeding relationship and the mother's attitude towards her child. It is commonly thought that giving the pethidine 4 hours before the birth will minimise effects on the baby, but recent evidence shows that this may in fact be the worst time, as the concentration of the drug builds up in the baby's system for several hours, and the by-products are also potentially harmful.[3] In any case, it is impossible to determine accurately when birth will occur.

Pethidine is often combined with an anti-nausea drug (Fentuzin or Phenergan) to combat the side-effect of nausea in the mother, or with a narcotic antagonist (levallorphan). Both these additional drugs increase the sedative and depressive effects on the baby.

Tranquillisers such as Valium (diazepam) and Sparine (promazine) are often used to reduce anxiety, and sometimes in an attempt to lower blood pressure or combat pethidine's nauseant effect. These drugs may seriously affect the baby's ability to maintain its body temperature, reduce muscle tone and the ability to suck, and depress breathing. These effects may last for days or weeks. Valium is actually contra-indicated for use in infants, so the willingness of doctors to prescribe it for the mother-and-baby unit shortly before the birth is hard to understand.

Inhalation analgesia, most commonly a mixture of nitrous oxide and oxygen (Entonox, or 'gas and air'), is often used towards the end of the first stage of labour, or during the second stage. It is self-administered with a face mask that the woman can use as she feels a contraction begin. Entonox is rapidly excreted from the lungs, so the effect is short-lived and must be timed to coincide with contractions, but the majority of women find it helpful and it has the advantage that a woman can control its use. There have been no direct studies of the effects of inhalation analgesia alone on the baby, but Entonox appears to have no measurable effects. Sally Inch, in her book *Birthrights*, suggests that Entonox is an undervalued analgesic. Exposure of operating-room personnel to anaesthetic gases of this type, however, has resulted in infertility, miscarriage, congenital malformations, and decreased cognitive behaviour, and anaesthetic levels of nitrous oxide (higher than those used in Entonox) in pregnant rats proved a cause of malformations; so even though Entonox appears to be relatively safe for use in labour perhaps we should not take its safety entirely for granted. Another gas sometimes used in inhalation analgesia is Penthrane, which stays in the blood longer, making it easier to obtain adequate analgesia. Its by-products, however, result in a measurable increase in fluoride in the baby's urine, which could at high levels cause kidney damage, though this is considered unlikely at the levels found.

Lumbar epidural anaesthesia involves the introduction of a local anaesthetic (most commonly bupivicaine, but lignocaine and others are also used) into the epidural space, located just inside the bone of the vertebral column but outside the membrane (dura) surrounding the spinal cord. The drug is administered through a catheter that has been threaded through a hollow needle into the epidural space; the needle is then removed, but the catheter left taped in position so that further doses of the anaesthetic can be given as the effects wear off, after about one and a half to two hours. When administered properly, the epidural should remove all sensation of the labouring uterus, although there are instances of a partial or completely failed block. Unlike pethidine, an epidural does not affect the woman's alertness. It may be useful in cases of serious heart or respiratory disease, or in diabetic women, as it reduces the respiratory work and muscular activity of labour. It is sometimes used to lower very high blood pressure, to slow a precipitate delivery, particularly if the baby is malpositioned or preterm, or for elective caesarean section instead of general anaesthesia, enabling the mother to be awake and receive her baby.

The disadvantages for the mother include a rapid fall in blood pressure, which can reach dangerous levels and has been responsible for maternal deaths. The routine installation of an intravenous drip to administer fluids is required to counteract the fall in blood pressure. The woman is also immobilised, usually asked to lie on her left side. In administering the epidural, there is a possibility of the needle puncturing the dura, with a resulting leak of cerebrospinal fluid that causes a severe headache for a few days after the birth. Rarely, the anaesthetic is injected directly past the dura, which is a life-threatening emergency since the anaesthetic then paralyses much of the body including the muscles of respiration so that artificial ventilation becomes necessary. Longer term neurological complications, such as numbness in the legs or weakness or continued headaches, can also occur. Cases of permanent paralysis were reported twenty years ago as a result of infection from faulty aseptic technique, and more recently because of the accidental injection of the wrong drug.

A well-recognised effect of epidural anaesthesia is a large increase in the rate of forceps delivery, by about two to three times. In some surveys, the forceps rate with epidurals has been as high as 60–70 per cent for first-time mothers, and 40 per cent of later births.[4] This high rate can be reduced by allowing the anaesthetic to wear off during the second stage of labour so that the woman can feel the urge to push, but it is still higher than if epidurals are not used. This may be a result of the epidural decreasing the muscle tone of the pelvic floor, so that the baby's descending head does not meet the resistance it needs to guide it to rotate properly. An epidural block may also slow uterine contractions so that labour is longer.

In addition to any greater risk of being pulled into the world by the metal blades of forceps, the baby faces other effects of epidural anaesthesia. The mother's lowered blood pressure can reduce the circulation to the placenta, with a resulting reduction in oxygen available to the baby and slowing of the baby's heart rate; this effect is particularly strong when oxytocin is also being used, as it frequently is to counteract the epidural's slowing effect on the labour. But the baby also faces direct influences from the drug, which is absorbed into the mother's bloodstream and transferred to the baby within minutes. Some drugs used in epidurals can affect the baby's heart rate, and cause poor muscle tone. With bupivicaine, one study found that when women had higher amounts of the drug in labour effects on the babies persisted through the six-week study period. The babies were more likely to be cyanotic and unresponsive to their surroundings. Visual skills, alertness, motor organisation, and response to stress were also adversely affected, while muscle tone alone appeared to improve with high levels of the drug.[5]

There is an interesting footnote illustrating the power of a paradigm in these matters: Some obstetricians administer adrenaline to the labouring woman along with an epidural, because this slows the rate at which the drug is passed along to the baby. The disadvantage, however, is that adrenaline also slows the progress of the first stage of labour. They appear never to consider that adrenaline — the 'fight or flight' hormone — is the exact opposite of what labour is all about. It interferes with production of natural oxytocin and endorphins — the body's own opiates that could make epidurals unnecessary — and allies with the stress hormones to cut down circulation to the uterus and the baby. It's the same hormonal pattern that makes the red deer capable of stopping her labour when danger threatens, and causes mice to experience longer labours with greater mortality when disturbed in labour.

Few women given obstetric drugs in labour, as Yvonne Brackbill's research has shown, know even the name of the drug, let alone the side-effects or recommended conditions surrounding its use.[6] They may accept the suggestion of a drug with little question, assuming that since it is offered it must be in the best interests of both mother and child. But in fact the suggestion of medication may come from what Doris Haire has termed 'a misguided kindness' in offering the mother a few hours' comfort, at the same time exposing her to the possibility of a lifetime's anguish should the drug's risks prove damaging to her baby. Or it may come from interests unrelated to the welfare of mother and child: 'Just as a pain-free, non-squirming, relaxed patient enabled dentists to perform their tasks smoothly, so did an epidural give rise to a relaxed, manageable and accessible mother', as an obstetric anaesthetist explained.

Pain-killing drugs are merely addressing a 'symptom' of labour, and might be seen to be optional. But the same lack of agreement and lack of evidence about benefits and risks applies to many obstetric interventions that are supposedly undertaken for clinical indications, and that extend throughout pregnancy and birth.

Most pregnant women today will undergo an ultrasound scan. The rapid escalation of this technology over the past decade has seen a change from scanning as an unusual procedure for pregnancies where some problem was suspected, to a routine practice in some areas involving scanning every pregnancy at least three times. This change has proceeded in the face of warnings from researchers that animal, test-tube and human experiments have shown a range of effects from ultrasound exposure, including chromosome damage, DNA changes, immune system changes, red blood cell changes, and premature ovulation after ultrasound exposure of the ovaries. While the US Food and Drug Administration warned that ultrasound should be used with caution in pregnancy until more was known about its effects, most doctors continued to assure women that it was completely harmless. A recent study of exposed children has found low birthweight and dyslexia to be associated with ante-natal exposure to ultrasound, although because of the study design and small numbers involved this is not conclusive.[7, 8] The call for caution by the World Health Organisation and others is just beginning to be heeded, as Denmark, Canada, and Japan have taken steps to minimise exposure with equipment standards and guidelines for use, and the British health minister has responded to pressure from the Association for Improvements in the Maternity Services by stating that ultrasound should not be used routinely in pregnancy. There is a lack of long-term studies to determine whether there is a risk, but in the meantime many thousands of unborn babies have been subjected to this unknown quantity.

There is also little evidence that ultrasound scans do much good. In some cases — such as diagnosing placenta praevia, or guiding a needle for amniocentesis, or establishing maturity when a medical induction is necessary — ultrasound can be a valuable tool. But its routine use is less impressive. It is often employed to determine gestational age, knowledge of dubious benefit, as will be discussed under inductions. Routine ultrasound is also intended to detect small-for-gestational-age (SGA, or growth retarded) babies. One study found that routine scanning did detect a larger proportion of SGA babies than scanning only when indicated by clinical examination.[9] But the detection rate was still only 57 per cent after three routine scans, and there was a high false positive rate: 94 per cent of the women told they had a small baby in fact did not. And even though more of the SGA babies were identified before birth, this made no difference to the outcomes in terms of health of the babies or prevention of growth retardation. Treatment consisted of more scans and monitoring, bedrest, and encouragement to eat a 'well-balanced' diet that was below the calorie level most often recommended for pregnancy. Diagnosis alone clearly will not prevent problems; yet obstetrics continues to employ expensive, untested techniques to search for problems, while ignoring the possibility of primary prevention through maternal nutrition.

A woman who is undernourished for pregnancy is more likely to have a premature labour. The drug companies have taken up the challenge not of preventing but merely suppressing premature labour by producing and aggressively marketing the b-sympatho-mimetic drugs (tocolytic drugs such as Ritodrine). These drugs in some cases suppress uterine activity, and may allow the pregnancy to continue long enough for steroid therapy to hasten fetal lung maturity. But so far their rapidly increasing use has not been matched with improved rates of perinatal survival, and women and babies are being exposed to their considerable risks. Several maternal deaths have been associated with this therapy, which can cause pulmonary oedema, severe cardiac problems, cerebral vasospasm, a fall in blood pressure, and various metabolic alterations. The possible long-term effects on the baby have not been studied. The *British Medical Journal* described the use of drugs in preterm labour as 'usually unnecessary, frequently ineffective, and occasionally harmful', but a doctor writing in a popular baby magazine claimed great success for Ritodrine, 'with no damaging effect on mother or baby', and this group of drugs is a fast-growing product range.

If, on the other hand, labour is 'late' there are other drugs which can be employed. Prolonged pregnancy is the most common reason given for induction of labour. Other medical reasons include pre-eclampsia, hypertension, renal disease, or Rhesus isoimmunisation, but in these instances it is debatable whether subjecting a compromised fetus to the prolonged stress of an oxytocin-induced labour is preferable to an elective caesarean section. 'Prolonged pregnancy', which is varyingly defined as anywhere from a few days to two weeks or more past the 40-week mark, is associated with an increased risk of mortality, although compared with births an equivalent amount preterm the risk is still very small. In an effort to prevent this mortality, some centres have advocated a liberal induction policy, but several studies have found no evidence of improvements in perinatal mortality through widespread induction. One study at Dulwich Hospital involved randomly allocating women at 42 weeks gestation to either routine induction, or ante-natal tests until labour began spontaneously (in all cases by 44 weeks). There was no difference in mortality, but the induced group had much higher rates of caesarean section, and the induced babies had lower initial Apgar scores. The authors conclude that routine induction beyond 42 weeks does not improve outcomes, and should be abandoned.[10] Instead, many workers agree that unnecessary inductions may be avoided by considering individual cases, based on the results of tests of placental function such as oxytocin challenge tests, amnioscopy to look for meconium staining of the amniotic fluid, or fetal movement counting.

Labour may be induced by rupture of the membranes, with the disadvantages of removing the protective cushion of waters from the baby's head and umbilical cord; causing stronger and more frequent contractions that may require more analgesia; and introducing the risk of infection which some doctors feel commits them to delivery within a certain number of hours. Rupture of membranes alone may not be sufficient to induce labour. Sometimes prostaglandins are used in vaginal pessary form to ripen a cervix that is not ready for labour, or to induce labour. They are fairly effective and may eliminate the need for an intravenous drip, but have the disadvantage that the level of prostaglandin cannot be easily regulated. When given orally or intravenously, there are side-effects of nausea and diarrhoea. Little is known about the disadvantages of prostaglandins, but there have been reported cases of uterine rupture and fetal and maternal death associated with their use.

Oxytocin infusion is the most common form of induction of labour, and it is also used to accelerate labour. Oxytocin, with the resulting frequent and strong contractions of a different quality than physiological contractions, results in a greater need for analgesia. Hypertonus — when the uterus contracts too strongly — can interfere with circulation to the placenta causing fetal distress, and has caused uterine rupture. There is also an increase in forceps and caesarean deliveries when oxytocin is used, sometimes related to the higher rates of fetal distress. Postpartum haemorrhage is more likely following oxytocin administration, and babies are more likely to require intubation for respiratory depression and to develop jaundice.

Other more conservative methods of accelerating labour have been demonstrated. For instance, nipple stimulation (preferably by a loving partner, but even a breast pump will do!) stimulates the flow of natural oxytocin. Ambulation in labour was shown in one study to immediately increase uterine activity in cases of uterine inertia to levels not reached in an oxytocin drip group for two hours; the ambulatory group made slightly better labour progress than the oxytocin group, and reported much less pain.[11] We may look again to the medical paradigm of labour that favours an intravenous drip over such other alternatives.

Oxytocin infusion provides a useful example of the phenomenon Sally Inch has aptly termed the 'cascade of intervention', in which one intervention has consequences that lead to others, which in turn lead to still others. Labour is essentially a finely tuned physiological process of interactions of both maternal and fetal hormones, nervous system, and muscular action which is still very little understood; a spanner thrown into the works at any point can have effects far beyond the point of entry. For administration of oxytocin, an intravenous drip must be set up. Beyond the serious dangers of intravenous fluid overload on the metabolic processes of both mother and baby (which can include cerebral oedema, convulsions, coma, and brain damage as well as newborn respiratory problems and feeding difficulties), the drip itself necessarily restricts the mother's ability to move about in labour. An induced labour will probably be electronically monitored, either by an external monitor which further restricts mobility and may lead to fetal distress because of the supine position, or with a scalp electrode which also restricts movement and which can introduce infection into the uterus or subject the baby to scalp abscess or haemorrhage; and which requires the breaking of the waters with the attendant risks of that procedure. Fetal monitoring has not been shown to be more effective than frequent auscultation with a stethoscope in preventing fetal mortality or morbidity, but it does result in a much higher caesarean section rate, probably because as many as two-thirds of the abnormal tracings are false alarms. Because of the increased possibility that caesarean section under a general anaesthetic will follow an induced labour, it is common to deny women food and drink to prevent the life-threatening complications of inhaling vomit while anaesthetised. Without sustenance, the labour slows down and ketosis builds up — so a glucose drip is used. Along with the other problems of fluid overload and immobility, a glucose infusion exposes the baby to the possibility of hypoglycaemia in the newborn period, which in severe cases can lead to brain damage. The higher drug levels used in induced or accelerated labours, together with the extra stress of the labour itself, can cause respiratory depression in babies, particularly if the birth has mistakenly been induced prematurely. But ultrasound will attempt to prevent that by establishing gestational age, and amniocentesis can check for lung maturity. The greater likelihood of postpartum haemorrhage will reinforce medical ideas about the need for active management of the third stage of labour, with injection of the drug syntometrine which has serious side-effects and increases the risk of retained placenta. Active third-stage management also requires the early cutting of the umbilical cord which deprives the baby of the full quota of its blood and may contribute to respiratory distress in premature babies . . . and so it goes round and round, one intervention linked to another.

For all these interventions, medical journals debate the risks and benefits and methods. From one hospital to another, or from one doctor to another within the same hospital, the rates of interventions often vary enormously. But this disagreement is not communicated to women. Surveys of women's reactions to their care have indicated that the majority of women are satisfied with their medical treatment, though this satisfaction decreases over time, so that months later they may be more critical of interventions which they were grateful for immediately after the birth. Yet it is not surprising that a demand for medical innovations exists: these drugs and techniques are seen as representing the furthest progress of medical care. The doctor is assumed to be an expert with the neutrality of science as his guiding principle. If no side-effects of drugs or treatment are mentioned, it is assumed that there are none. And so the demand reflects the cultural image of medicine. It is only when we begin to see the operation of the medical paradigm of childbirth that we understand that the medical choices that affect our care are not neutral, and are not always even rationally based.

For a woman during pregnancy or labour, it may not be easy to weigh up the options open to her about her medical care — and even less so to insist on an option which has not been presented to her. Her best ally is information, linked with her own intuitive feelings of what is right for her. Any intervention has its benefits and risks, and the weight of these alters in different circumstances. Dutch obstetrician G. J. Kloosterman has said that 'the great and admirable improvement in obstetric care is only important in the handling of pathology; in no way can we improve a normal pregnancy and labour in a healthy woman — we can only change it, but not for the better'. How is a woman to know when she has entered the range of difficulty where the benefits of an intervention will outweigh the risks of changing the course of her labour?

She can ask a few key questions that will help her in making this assessment. *What* exactly is being proposed? *Why* is this intervention necessary in her particular case (to distinguish it from routine intervention)? If it is a diagnostic procedure, what specifically will be learned and what difference will this knowledge make to her care? What are the *risks and benefits* of this treatment? What *alternatives* are there? What would happen if *no treatment* were used?

She may not always be given such full information — the doctor may not know what alternatives are available, for instance. So it helps if she has already read to inform herself. If she has time to consider the intervention she can contact childbirth groups for more information; she can ask to see the package insert of a drug that gives detailed information about its use; she can ask for a second opinion from another midwife or obstetrician, or paediatrician concerning the possible effects on her baby. During labour, she can have a well-informed partner who can help her sort out the pros and cons. And she makes her decision. If she accepts an intervention because, based on accurate information, she believes it is necessary, she is less likely to later resent the intrusion on her natural labour, and is more likely to be satisfied with the appropriate partnership between woman and provider which meant that help was there when it was needed, but not thrust upon her when it was not.

REFERENCES

1   B. Morgan *et al*, 'Analgesia and satisfaction in childbirth (The Queen Charlotte's 1000 Mother Survey)', *Lancet*, vol. 9, no. 10; pp. 808–10, 1982.

2   B. Morgan *et al*, 'The consumers' attitude to obstetric care', *British Journal of Obstetrics and Gynaecology*, vol. 91, pp. 624–8, 1984.

3   B. R. Kuhnert *et al*, 'Meperidine and normeperidine levels following meperidine administration during labour', *American Journal of Obstetrics and Gynaecology*, vol. 133, pp. 909–14, 1979.

4   I. J. Hoult *et al*, *British Medical Journal*, no. 1, pp. 14–16, 1977.

5   D. Rosenblatt *et al*, 'The influence of maternal analgesia on neonatal behaviour: II. Epidural Bupivicaine', *British Journal of Obstetrics and Gynaecology*, vol. 88, pp. 407–13, 1981.

6   L. Woodward *et al*, 'Exposure to drugs with possible adverse effects during pregnancy and birth', *BIRTH*, vol. 9, no. 3 pp. 165–71, 1982.

7   Stark *et al*, 'Short and long-term risks after exposure to diagnostic ultrasound in utero', *Obstetrics and Gynaecology*, vol. 63, no. 2, 1984.

8   Moore *et al*, 'Ultrasound exposure during gestation and birthweight', paper presented at the Meeting of the Society for Epidemiologic Research, 1982.

9   M. Hughey, 'Routine ultrasound for detection and management of

the small-for-gestational-age fetus, *Obstetrics and Gynaecology*, vol. 64, no. 1, pp. 101–7, 1984.

10 Studd, *British Journal of Obstetrics and Gynaecology*, 4. 89, pp. 292–5, 1982.

11 *American Journal of Obstetrics and Gynaecology*, 15 March, 1981.

The issues of choice and safety

JOHANNA SQUIRE

'Choice' has become a password in progressive maternity care. Women having babies today could be said to have a far wider choice than ever before with the implementation of schemes such as 'domino' deliveries and the use of 'birth plans'. Giving birth could also be said to be safer than ever before: the perinatal mortality rate has declined steadily since the 1930s and maternal mortality is thought of as something belonging to the dark ages. (A glance through the *Confidential Enquiries into Maternal Deaths* might persuade one otherwise.[1]) But how much real choice is there? Is the professed aim of making childbirth ever safer for both mother and baby really being achieved? Examining one basic change in the structure of Britain's maternity service will shed much light on both questions.

In the 1930s the majority of births took place at home. By 1958, 49 per cent of all births took place in consultant hospitals; by 1970, this had risen to 66 per cent; 1975 to 88 per cent; 1981 to 94.2 per cent. Medical and political policies have combined in pursuit of two related ends: the centralisation of maternity services into large obstetric hospitals and for *all* births to take place in such hospitals. The stated rationale behind this mass hospitalisation was, and still is, greater safety for both mother and child. Obstetric medical advisors gradually gained govern-ment backing for increasing hospitalisation for birth, as successive reports on the health service reflect. Of particular note was their recommendation to the Peel Committee[2] in 1970 that 100 per cent of births should take place in hospital. Despite the revelation since that there was no evidence to support this recommendation, it was accepted and has become the corner-stone of the structure of Britain's maternity service. In 1980, the Short Committee[3] reiterated the commitment to achieve 100 per cent hospital births, and again it was stated that this was in the interests of increased safety and welfare of mothers and children, and yet again no evidence was produced to support this position, neither did the committee request any. By 1980 there was a wealth of evidence available to the committee which showed that increasing the percentage of births taking place in obstetric units was *not* enhancing the safety and welfare of mothers or their children; if anything, it was putting the majority in jeopardy. The increase in hospitalisation after 1967, when the rate was around 75 per cent, had already been shown to have been counter productive in terms of reducing the perinatal mortality rate,[4] if the proportions of births taking place in general practitioner (GP) units and at home had not been further reduced, the perinatal mortality rate would have fallen faster than it did[5] and would probably be lower than the current figure of around 10/1,000.

Obstetricians have always seen increased safety in terms of increased monitoring and control of the pregnancy and, more particularly, the birth. They have applied an ever lengthening line of technological innovations to women and their babies in their attempt to make all pregnancies and births conform to their own definition of normal. Women have been over-ruled: mothers' instinctive feelings as to what is 'right'; midwives' training and long experience in normal pregnancy and birth, have been superseded by men, machines and medication. An individual experience, unique to each mother/child/couple, an essentially feminine, creative, emotional and very finely balanced natural process, has been distorted and confined to a series of model stages in the attempt to analyse and define an ideal type, to be used as a yardstick for all. As a result, truly normal birth has virtually been extinguished. The search for pathological or potentially pathological conditions throughout pregnancy and labour is relentless. As the frontiers of medicine are pushed forward, more techniques for detecting a wider range of abnormality at earlier and earlier stages of pregnancy are discovered. More and more women are being categorised as being 'at risk'; no birth is now considered to be safe until it is over.

Women's confidence has been undermined to such an extent that we scarcely believe we are capable of carrying and giving birth to our child, let alone able to take an active part in making arrangements for our care. We have relinquished responsibility for ourselves and our children to those who have convinced us of our inadequacy. We have naively believed that 'they' know what is best; they are, after all, at the top of their profession and through long years of experience should have been able to evaluate their practices, discarding those not found to be beneficial and encouraging those shown to be of value. The overriding value on which obstetricians have built their practice is that of safety. The greater safety of mother and child is the only reason that has been advanced for the herding together of women in hospitals for birth; the well-being of the baby is the only reason given for subjecting women and their unborn children to the battery of tests and examinations that are euphemistically termed 'care'. Our choice is no longer relevant: the only essential choice is the safety of our children, and for that, the obstetrician has assumed total responsibility. He has taken over. Around 98 per cent of births now take place in hospital.

But obstetricians are not the experts in normal pregnancy and birth; many of the techniques and technologies they have introduced have never been thoroughly evaluated before being put into routine use and too many have subsequently been shown to be more harmful than helpful. But their use is so entrenched it takes many years for such practices to be abandoned. There is no evidence — and there never has been any — to support the contention that the increased use of technological interventions has contributed significantly to the reduction of perinatal mortality or morbidity. Despite the rigorous search for abnormality, 80–90 per cent of pregnancies and births could proceed normally and not require specialised assistance. That they do not proceed normally has far more to do with the medicalisation of maternity care and its transfer into hospitals then with women's inadequacy for childbirth. Equally, there is no evidence to support the policy of 100 per cent hospital birth. As Norman Fowler, Secretary of State for Social Services, has stated recently, 'No analysis of perinatal mortality so far conducted supports the argument that all mothers should give birth in hospital.'[6]

In determining standards and practices for maternity care, scientific objectivity has long since been lost, although doctors still rely on their scientific aura. The basis of scientific evaluation lies with the postulation of a likely hypothesis, its rigorous testing and its rejection if the evidence does not bear it out; this standard of evaluation has too often been ignored. Admittedly there are many aspects of maternity care that do not lend themselves to the scientific method; in these instances, where mothers'/parents' experience and feelings should act as guidelines, they too are ignored. By assuming responsibility for us and our babies, obstetricians completely sidestep their responsibilities *towards* us, to provide us with information on the risks, benefits and alternatives, to offer their opinion, but finally, to stand by the individual's decision. Instead they deny us access to the information we need to be able to make informed choices about our care and too often override us when we do attempt to assert our wishes. We have no access to our medical notes and so are unable to discover what is on record — for example, the reason for a previous forceps or caesarean delivery or for an episiotomy being performed — and whether the record is accurate. It is one thing to give an oral 'reason', quite another to commit it to paper. Our notes also often contain personal comments which may adversely affect any future relationship with other medical personnel. Obstetricians control access to techniques and technology which they can deny us if we do not accept their method of administration along with any additional measures that they consider necessary. Midwives, too, are often pressured into carrying out policies against their better judgement, otherwise it becomes intolerable for them to continue to work under the obstetrician who decreed the policy. GPs are also under constraint — to send all their prospective mothers to be vetted by a hospital consultant who will then proscribe in which unit each should be delivered. It is not unknown for a consultant to threaten a GP with refusal to accept women referred from him unless he discontinues his practice of providing back-up for home births. Obstetricians have a monopoly in maternity care: it is their advice that formulates the basic structuring of the service; their policies that are enforced. It is their refusal to consider alternatives and to acknowledge evidence that questions or even discredits their theories that prevents real changes and improvements being made.

The issue has become that of the obstetrician's controlling power over the maternity services: it is largely they who determine how the services are structured, what type of care is offered and where and even what practices that care should include. It is argued that the maternity services were set up for the benefit of women and their babies. However, it is becoming evident that our benefit is no longer a priority — that the service now exists to enable those in control to further their own knowledge of how pregnancy and birth occur and how best to control the process. Obstetricians argue that in order to be able to help women who have difficulties, maybe in being able to conceive or carry a baby to term, they must continue to do all they can to discover more about the complex mechanisms of pregnancy and birth. But their methods seem to be aimed at isolating, controlling or treating one aspect of the process without an appreciation of the very fine balance of the whole. The choice of aspect also reflects areas of highest potential prestige if success is obtained. Methods are chosen that give the obstetrician complete control; he assumes total responsibility, the mother and child total dependency. Approaches that would engender confidence, self-help and self-responsibility in the parents, that could lead to positive, truly preventive, health promotion tend to be ignored; they are time consuming and non-prestigious and they do not generate wealth. The concentration of resources and equipment in special and intensive care baby units, rather than ensuring that so many babies are not born in such a precarious state of health, is one example. Some women and babies do need specialist care, but whether it is always geared primarily to their interests or to the doctors' is debatable. Are some of the experimental techniques used in neo-natal medicine and beginning to be used in prenatal medicine really for the benefit of the child? Or is it an opportunity for doctors to demonstrate their skills, to further their knowledge and see exactly how far they can carry their achievements? Is the search for the 'perfect' baby, our search or theirs?

There is much knowledge already in existence that would greatly benefit both women, babies and families, but it has been suppressed or ignored. Recognition of that knowledge would remove the obstetricians' monopoly of control because it shows that, for the vast majority of women and babies, high-technology hospital care is not only unnecessary but positively harmful. We must gain knowledge for ourselves, take responsibility for ourselves by exercising the choices that we have to the full, so that the obstetricians' power is dissolved before it becomes absolute and our choices non-existent.

It has been argued that, by historic tradition, obstetricians and to a lesser extent midwives, are the state's licensed guardians of the welfare of its inheritants — the babies born to its citizens — to protect them and give them the optimum start in life. It is further argued that legislation concerning the practice of midwifery which limited who might practise and restricted the use of certain instruments and techniques to doctors, should be seen as being in the interests of child — and to a lesser extent, mother — protection. The fact that such legislation also created a male medical monopoly is argued to be only a subsidiary effect.[7] But traditionally childbirth was 'women's business'. With the introduction of mechanical 'aids', notably forceps, male doctors successfuly invaded this hitherto female territory. Midwives were forbidden to practise with instruments and as doctors more frequently attended the higher social classes, doctor-care came to be regarded as superior; midwives did not have access to so many resources, although their knowledge and experience were far greater. In 1763, Elizabeth Nihill, a midwife, wrote that she considered that 'the man-midwife used instruments unnecessarily to hasten the birth and save his own time'; worse still, adding insult to injury, 'he was adept at concealing his errors with a cloud of hard words and scientific jargon'.[8] It is a tragedy that her words are still valid today and the myth of superior doctor-care persists in the maternity service. Concentrated in hospitals, consultant doctor care is thought by many to be the best. The 'doctor knows best' and the more qualified and higher ranking in his speciality he is, the better. This might apply in general medicine but not in relation to 'normal' pregnancy and birth. Consultants are not trained in normality but in pathology; it is midwives who are the experts in normal pregnancy and birth. Their training equips them to give care, on their own respon-sibility, during the ante-natal and post-natal periods; 'care' includes the detection of abnormal conditions at which point she is expected to obtain medical assistance. In international surveys it has been shown that countries with the greater numbers of midwives achieve better outcomes than countries with greater numbers of doctors.[9] Midwives are supposed to be independent practitioners in their own right, yet in all but a few of the situations to which their practice is now confined, they come under the direction of consultant obstetricians and their professional opinion can be over-ruled by consultant policy.

A fundamental choice in maternity care is one which many women do not realise they are making; choosing the sort of care they wish to receive. Nor do many women realise that they have any choice, so the type of care they receive becomes largely dictated by the choice of the place of birth: hospital consultant unit, GP unit (which may be attached to the consultant unit or separate) or home. The majority of women are not offered a choice as to the place of birth and, unaware of the implications of their 'booking', are 'guided' by their doctor's advice. If the GP is active in maternity care and practises close enough to a GP unit, a woman may be offered a GP unit booking. If not, it is standard practice for her to be booked into the nearest consultant unit, regardless of whether she actually requires specialist care because of some departure from normal in her pregnancy. Home birth has to be requested, even insisted upon, and GPs and midwives in many areas are under pressure to phase out this aspect of their practice. With the closure of separate GP units, this option is also becoming difficult to obtain. GP obstetricians find that their practice is too far away from the combined GP unit at the hospital — if it has one at all — and therefore they cannot undertake full care. Also, in utilising a combined unit, GPs come under the jurisdiction of the hospital consultants who claim responsibility for all women booked into the hospital, regardless of which unit. Women are often vetted by the consultants to determine their suitability for delivery in the GP unit, a practice which undermines the professional opinion of the GP. Slowly but surely, the desired target of 100 per cent hospital births is being achieved by a gradual reduction in the alternatives; alternatives in which birth was accepted as a natural, physiological event; in which midwives could practise autonomously and in which mothers shared the planning of their care. It is vital that women exercise their right to choose, to maintain the options that are still left; the right to choose where they wish to give birth, including home, and to choose how they wish to give birth.

But to choose other than a hospital consultant unit birth and their drug- and technology-orientated policies, is running counter to the prevailing medical philosophy: that birth outside such a unit with every resource on tap 24 hours a day, is at best dangerous and, at worst, potentially lethal to the mother and, more particularly, her child. This philosophy has as its major premise, 'birth is extremely hazardous': labour is considered to be so inefficient that every aid must be immediately to hand in case it 'goes wrong' — the implication being that it will. Ante-natal care, far from promoting good health and confidence in prospective mothers, is a relentless search for pathological conditions, almost an attempt to prove that women are inadequate for pregnancy, which is reinforced by their preparation for labour which stresses all the medical assistance they will require. If women attempt to stand up to this intimidation, the medical advisors and consultant obstetricians have come up with the ultimate threat: ignore our advice and care and your baby will die or at least be born severely handicapped. We need to be very sure of our ground and ourselves to be able to say, 'I do not think your policy of care is appropriate to my needs or the needs of my child; I do not think it enhances our health and welfare so I will not agree to it.' Despite the dogged determination of shroud-waving doctors, more women are finding the courage to say it and more will do so because the evidence is incontrovertible. The majority of births are still categorised as 'normal' despite the interventions of misguided doctors — and some midwives. It is likely that the majority of these, without intervention, could be truly normal births. Why, then, have so many people been convinced of the inherent danger of birth?

'Pariophobia — fear of giving birth. An iatrogenic disorder common amongst women from 16 to 35 years of age. Originating from around 1930, currently an epidemic.' From government committees to obstetricians to parents, almost everyone believes that there are intrinsic dangers in being pregnant and, more particularly, in giving birth. Pregnancy has been removed from the continuum of women's general health and is regarded as an abnormal state. The line between abnormal and pathological is very thin and because women have to use the conventional medical system to obtain maternity care, they tend to be regarded as ill. Most of pregnancy is spent watching, waiting and testing for every possible pathology. During the birth, the vigilance is even more emphatic. Obstetricians have barely begun to fully understand the intricacies of either healthy, normal pregnancy or natural birth. They have been unable to break the processes down into qualifiable, manageable 'bits' which, reassembled in the correct order, will produce the same result. Despite this they attempt to direct and control the whole process so that it conforms to their construction of normal. In so doing they destroy the equilibrium of truly normal birth so that further intervention is required to try and correct the imbalance. Their prophecies become self-fulfilling: the way in which the majority of women are now made to give birth, under obstetric control, is indeed fraught with danger, and mothers and babies end up in need of being 'rescued' from potentially lethal situations. What parents fail to realise is that many of the standard practices of what is termed 'care' are the cause of the initial imbalance which precipitates the 'cascade of intervention'.[10] Some practices are now so routine that they are no longer recognised as interventions but part of 'normal' progress which, more and more, consists of manipulation along an approximate course by those who know least about the way. Other interventions, especially those in pregnancy, are made in attempts to correct symptomatic problems, the causes of which are either not understood or are simply ignored. The mass of complications arising from poor nutrition in pregnancy is an excellent example. Doctors know surprisingly little about good nutrition; their business is sickness, so the foundation of good health seems not to concern them. Good nutrition during pregnancy could protect the health and welfare of many women and babies and even save lives. But its use is neither prestigious, nor an opportunity to demonstrate obstetric skills, particularly innovative ones, so it does not rank very highly in the priorities. Drug- and technology-orientated interventions should be being used only as last resorts; instead they have become a first line of defence. The fact that doctors do manage to rescue some babies from potentially lethal situations is used as justification for the extension of their activities, whereas the fact that more and more babies seem to end up in need of 'rescuing' should indicate an urgent need to look at the origins of such disastrous conditions. Nature is not stupid; lethal systems of reproduction simply do not evolve, they have been created. The disparities between the mortality rates for different social classes have persisted for so long that low class status is now a recognised pregnancy risk factor. It may be that smaller and sicker babies can be saved through improved technology and techniques, but despite this, the mortality rate for babies born into social classes IV and V remains consistently higher than the rate for social classes I and II babies, mainly because of a refusal by politicians to tackle the socio-economic problems of this group in general and refusal by the medical profession to attempt to compensate through the provision of care, with particular attention to nutrition. The medical profession could recommend that more work and resources be put into health promotional care to the benefit of the whole population and with especial benefits to the pregnant population. But they have consistently favoured resources being put into mechanical aids to monitor deficiencies once they have occurred and into rescue remedies. Is their interest really in helping women and babies to have safer, healthier pregnancies and births? Or is it primarily in promoting their own practices? If their motives are in doubt or if their practices cannot be shown to be in our interests, should we continue, without question, to accept their advice?

Obstetricians have long claimed that a fully equipped hospital is the safest place in which to give birth — not a small general practitioner hospital (usually termed an 'isolated' unit), but a large general hospital with an obstetric department or a fully fledged maternity hospital, with 24-hour consultant obstetric, paediatric and anaesthetic cover, and all facilities, or as many as possible known to medicine. Such is their faith in labour as a natural physiological process that its onset is greeted with an array of technology more appropriate to an accident and emergency department. Birth is as feared as death; as one doctor has even commented, 'Birth is about as natural as death is.' Perhaps he is right; we have to fight about as hard to achieve a natural death as we do to achieve a natural birth. Birth is viewed in terms of its potential for death, judged by the league tables of mortality and morbidity rates. It seems it is rarely celebrated as the creation of new life and hope.

All over the country small general practitioner maternity (and other) units are being closed, the rationale being that they are uneconomical. In fact the closures and concurrent dismantling of the domiciliary midwifery service (which have been steadily progressing since 1974) have far more to do with the centralisation of maternity services and the medical view that GP unit and home births are dangerous. There appear to be adequate funds for the extension of unevaluated technological procedures — the purchase of ever more sophisticated ultrasound scanners, fetal monitoring equipment, including the latest telemetric models — and for the increasingly large quantities of pharmaceuticals consumed in obstetric maternity units. In 1979, comparative costings showed that public sector costs for a GP unit delivery were 10 per cent less than for a consultant unit delivery; GP unit delivery costs in turn were 10 per cent higher than those for home deliveries.[11]

Blanket obstetric practices such as routine monitoring, routine episiotomies, routine scanning and even routine booking for hospital delivery, all began in much the same way. Having found that a small number of women benefited, the argument 'what is good for a few must be even better for many' came into play and procedures were introduced wholesale with no proper evaluation of their efficacy for whole populations. If birth in hospital under obstetric management is indeed safer, it should be demonstrably so; if the separate GP units are so dangerous, their figures should reflect it; if giving birth at home equates with a return to the maternal and perinatal mortality rates of the 1930s, the records should reflect this.

Data from two national perinatal surveys, carried out under the auspice of the Royal College of Obstetricians and Gynaecologists in 1958[12a] and 1970,[12b] have contributed greatly towards reliably quantifying the association of pregnancy outcome with most maternal characteristics and complications of pregnancy and also with infant birthweight and gestational age. The association of outcome with medical care, ante-natal or intra-partum, has not been examined with the same enthusiasm, even though it is the assumed association between increased hospital obstetric care and lowered perinatal mortality that has shaped the entire structuring of the maternity services. Marjorie Tew, a research statistician, is the only person to have thoroughly analysed the figures available and attempted to make them public knowledge.[13] To date, no one has been able to refute her work but several have refused to publish it because it undermines the wisdom of the policy of 100 per cent hospital birth and refutes the obstetricians' claims that hospital birth is safest and that 'isolated' GP units and home births are dangerous and should be withdrawn.

The 1958 survey was designed specifically 'to provide inform-ation of value upon a number of aspects relating to the safety and health of mother and infant, including the possible effects of place of confinement'. The analysis did not eventually include this last objective, however, despite the fact that the data revealed the crude perinatal mortality rate (PNMR) to be 2.5 times as high in consultant hospitals as in GP units and at home. Only limited data from the survey were published, but this was sufficient to show that the hospitals' excess mortality could not be explained either by their excess of births at high pre-delivery risk — arising from selection procedures and transfer of women from other places (GP units and home) — or by their excess of births of low weight and short gestation.[14] The results of the 1958 survey thus did not support the increasing numbers of deliveries being carried out in hospital on the assumption that obstetric management was beneficial. But the trend towards hospitalisation continued. In 1977 Marjorie Tew published an article[15] which demonstrated that the official stillbirth statistics also contradicted claims that birth in hospital was always safest. As this raised other questions, she requested access to unpublished figures from the 1958 survey; this she was denied. Instead, Dr Jean Golding (later known as Dr Jean Fedrick), the effective custodian of the data, carried out some of her own analyses and eventually published a paper in March 1978,[16] which showed that for two small sub-groups, which made up only 6 per cent of all births in the survey, the PNMR by place of *booking* was lower in hospital. All other statistical evidence pointed in the opposite direction, including the PNMR by place of *delivery* which was higher in hospital. Dr Golding's paper was the only evidence in support of hospital confinement, but the policy continued to be encouraged and the rate to rise.

In 1970 the Peel Committee recommended 100 per cent hospital births; in the same year the second national survey was conducted. The results were not available until late 1978 and again only limited data were published. The disparity between the perinatal mortality rate in hospitals and in GP units had doubled: 27.8/1,000 births in consultant units to 5.4/1,000 in GP units and 4.3/1,000 at home. This was passed over without comment. Marjorie Tew drew attention to it in a further article.[17] Dr Golding again carried out her own analyses of unpublished data, presumably hoping to find some small groups with which to promote the case for hospital confinement. But in April 1981, she wrote to Mrs Tew stating that her findings had not supported her result from the 1958 data. Were there no groups for which hospital birth was safer?

The analysts of the 1970 survey had constructed a Labour Prediction Score which incorporated all risks up to and including the first stage of labour. All births in the survey were classified according to this score. But the PNMR for each level of predicted risk, although recorded by place of birth, had only been published for all births at that risk level, effectively preventing any comparison of outcomes by place of birth. From other published data it was virtually certain that the excess hospital mortality was not due to an overwhelming excess of 'at risk' births and may well have had something to do with the increased exposure to unnecessary intervention in hospital, i.e. hospital confinement itself becoming a risk factor.[18]

In May 1981 Tew requested access to the PNMRs for each place of confinement in order to thoroughly investigate her growing suspicion. She was informed that the information had not been retained on tape and that she would have to pay a minimum of £150 to obtain it. However, Dr Golding later informed her that, due to certain pressures, they had carried out the analysis themselves. Surprisingly it did not appear anywhere in print. It is almost certain that had Dr Golding's results shown hospital birth to be in any degree safer, the results would have been given the widest possible publicity. In July 1981, through her continued efforts, Marjorie Tew was given official permission to receive the comparative PNMR data she had requested; despite this, for two years she was unable to obtain it from Dr Golding. With a grant from the Scientific Foundation Board of the Royal College of General Practitioners to pay the £150 tabulation fee, the figures were finally released in November 1983. Marjorie Tew's analysis produced the following results:

Labour prediction score	*Perinatal mortality rate per 1000 births*	
	Hospital	GP/Midwife
Very low risk	8.0	3.9
Low risk	17.9	5.2
Moderate risk	32.2	3.8
High risk	53.2	15.5
Very high risk	162.6	133.3
All risks	28.0	5.4

(The values for GP units and home births are combined as they are very similar.)

At every level of risk the PNMR in hospital is much higher and, in all but the very high risk group, very unlikely to have occurred by chance. (The small number of births in the very high risk group under GP/midwife care (15) does make it possible that this result alone occurred by chance.)

No one denies that technology and skilled obstetric intervention in individual cases can be life-saving; but as a blanket policy it is clear that it is not. The figures not only discredit the claim that birth in hospital is safer, but also the claim that the higher the pre-delivery risk, the greater the benefit of obstetric care. Thus the entire basis of our maternity service has been called into question by an obstetricians' survey using an obstetricians' instrument for analysis; yet the obstetric profession is refusing to recognise Marjorie Tew's findings. They have not been able to dispute them in print nor produce any evidence to the contrary, but the two leading medical journals, the *British Medical Journal* and the *Lancet*, have both refused to publish the findings (on the grounds 'that they were not of general interest'), thus denying them the authority and recognition that would arise from public scrutiny by the medical profession. The profession largely controls what appears in their own journals. Research material that is not published is not counted as recognised or accredited;

it does not get listed in the archives or mentioned in literature searches, so many are totally unaware that evidence disputing obstetricians' claims of hospital safety and the benefits of obstetric management even exists. It is vital that Marjorie Tew's findings become public knowledge and the only way, so far, seems to be through informing parents, midwives and individual doctors who are prepared to listen — perhaps our GPs whose obstetric practices are under threat of extinction.

Recently it has been well publicised that, during 1975–7, the perinatal mortality rate apparently increased among babies born at home, even rising above the rate for those born in hospital obstetric units. This prompted more recommendations, notably by the Short Committee in 1980, that home birth should be further phased out, with no examination of any other data, or even a detailed look at the reasons for the increase. A closer look reveals clearly that the mortality rate for home births as a total rose because the previous majority of *planned* home births had become a minority, leaving the majority of unplanned births to dominate the figures. Unplanned births include those who, although booked for hospital delivery, go into labour prematurely and/or delivery precipitately and those who have received no ante-natal care and are not booked anywhere. A study of home births documented in the Cardiff Births Survey (1980)[19] showed that there were nearly twice as many *un*planned as planned deliveries; four out of five women who delivered at home without planning to do so were booked for hospital delivery and the others were not booked at all. The incidence of death among the unplanned births was over ten times that of babies of planned home births. This and other differences between the groups were striking, notably that mothers planning home births received a greater intensity of ante-natal care than the reference population and 96.7 per cent had a professional attendant at the birth whereas the vast majority of unplanned births were unattended. From this evidence it is argued that home birth per se is not safe; no one has ever contended that it is. But hospital birth per se is not safe either, yet the whole service is based on this erroneous contention. What the home births evidence does indicate is that those perhaps most in need of help from the maternity services are still not receiving it and that, whatever official policy is, some births will unavoidably take place at home. Thus the low level of planned home births is not sufficient reason to run down essential services like the flying squads which, rarely called to planned home births, are vital to the unplanned majority. It might further be argued that, since this service must be maintained for the unplanned births, its expense and the depletion of hospital staff when it is called out are not valid reasons for discouraging planned home births.

The proportion of births taking place in hospital is now even higher than in 1970, probably around 98 per cent. The question of home v. hospital birth is a very big one, but equally important are the choices we make about the type of care we receive, whether at home or in hospital. Whilst our choice of the place of birth at present has quite a significant effect on our care, we should not have to stay at home in order to receive the quality of care we are looking for; it is essential that hospitals are made to improve their standards of care and the way in which it is made available to women. Just as some women will unavoidably give birth at home, so others must give birth within reach of vital hospital services. Just as some women choose to give birth at home, so others choose a hospital booking. All these choices must be given equal validity. All women must be given the opportunity to choose, the information in order to make informed choices and the acceptance of our decisions without recriminations. This requires recognition of our integrity as people worthy of being given truthful reasons, facts not assumptions, and able to understand and make decisions on the basis of available evidence. Thus it is vital that all the evidence is presented, not just that which suits the self-interest of some empire-building medical professionals.

Britain has the highest rates of some interventions — forceps, induction of labour and episiotomy among them — in Europe.[20] Our caesarean section rate has risen rapidly in recent years; but none of these interventions has been found to be causally related to the continuing decline in our perinatal mortality rate. On the contrary, some are associated with increases in mortality and morbidity. Doubts are being raised about the efficacy of some procedures but their overuse persists and new technologies are added, invariably without benefit of thorough evaluative studies.

In 1984 another national survey was undertaken[21] concentrating on examining facilities — manpower (sic), equipment and services — at each place of birth. Unless such an examination has a concurrent evaluation of the effects of such facilities on infant/maternal outcome the survey may well amount to little more than a basic documentation of the very facilities that enable the proliferation of unevaluated medical practices. Whilst an impressive inventory of equipment, services, staffing numbers and their seniority may make obstetricians feel their service is superior, a growing number of parents know from experience that it is not, and a growing body of evidence is accumulating to demonstrate this point.

Even so, it is difficult to be totally rational about such an emotional issue. The facts and figures may give us the inform-ation necessary to make an informed choice, it may free us from certain fears, but there is another more subtle fear at work; that of standing up and making the choice for ourselves; fear of being a whole, competent, active, responsible person — and responsible for our child and its welfare as well as our own. Women, particularly, tend to be brought up and encouraged to be passive, even submissive, in need of being 'looked after'. We defer our own needs and wants to those of others, especially when we perceive those others as being in positions of authority. When the things we may feel are right for us are portrayed as putting someone else at risk — in the case of birth, our own child — then we are even more likely to try to put aside our feelings and undergo whatever is deemed necessary. We feel powerless to challenge authoritative opinion, because we lack confidence in ourselves and our knowledge and sometimes lack the knowledge itself and feel unable to raise questions on other less tangible, more emotive grounds even though such feelings can be as valid. But our feelings in childbirth are not lightly put aside; our instinctive, emotional senses resent the intrusions and disturb-ances. Afterwards we are left feeling drained, emotionally and physically battered, barely able to care for ourselves let alone a helpless baby.

Some women have recounted that, when it came to making decisions about how their baby was to be born, especially when previous pregnancies had been managed for them, for the first time in their lives they felt they had to stand up for what they felt to be right. They had to take the responsibility for those decisions and not passively accept the prevailing standard practice that was offered. For those who do make such a stand, there seems to follow a great feeling of relief, accompanied by a growing strength of recognition of their own worth as capable individuals.

Perhaps we are also afraid of giving ourselves to the very strong physical and emotional demands of childbirth. We have sought to control and regulate so much of our lives that, whilst the actual risks of living have become marginalised, we have concurrently become more afraid of those aspects of life that defy rational explanation and control. Being born and giving birth are perhaps the foundation stones of the vital functions of our lives. If we can fully experience birth as self-responsible, creative, capable individuals and give the joy of that experience to our child, how much more able we shall be to take responsibility for shaping and determining the rest of our lives and for defending and supporting our children's rights, so that they grow up in the strength and knowledge that they are responsible individuals, as respectful of their own worth as they are of others!

Men, although traditional 'responsibility bearers' for the family, are sometimes particularly afraid of such intimate involvement and personal responsibility.[22] The male model of 'being' advocates objectivity, being rational (rather than emotional), and, above all, in control. Afraid of the strength of emotion it may awaken in them, men attempt to distance themselves from the experience. The biological fact that giving birth is something men cannot do themselves may also drive them to discount women's experience of it and yet, at the same time, make them desirous of having control over it. Years ago, and still in traditional societies, childbearing was women's business, but it was not belittled as it is in modern society. Pregnant, parturient women were acknowledged as having great strength, sometimes even a malevolent power, and many rituals and taboos surrounded pregnancy and birth — some for the protection of mother and child, others simply showing respect for women's ability to bear the children on which the future of the people depended. Perhaps it is such potential strength that men recognise and feel inadequate beside. Obstetricians, particularly, will cover their feelings of inadequacy with activity designed to demonstrate their control and superiority; activities which reduce the woman's strength and make her submissive and dependent. Their medical training specifically prohibits emotional involvement, so feelings, emotions have no place in a medical view of childbirth. Such obstetricians find a willing ally in fathers afraid to become involved, and the fathers find a welcome refuge in the obstetricians' assumed omnipotence.

The control is, of course, claimed only on medical grounds — assumed to be scientifically proven — thus men, fathers and obstetricians, collude in the man-made myth of the safety of obstetric management and confinement in hospital, leaving the woman isolated in her views, struggling to balance her feelings with their apparent rationality. Once in the hospital she may feel more alien to herself than before. Hospitals are for sick people who have something wrong with them; is there then something wrong with her? The doctors are there to do their best for you, to help you, but their 'help' seems totally inappropriate to our needs. We have been trapped.

It is vital that we confront the issues of choice, personal choice as well as more concrete choices between different options, and the issue of the safety of our choices and we must do it now. All the time options are being closed to us. In 1980 in evidence to the Short Committee it was suggested that legislation might be introduced to prevent women from making decisions which might (in the eyes of the medical profession) damage their babies. (This was brought up during discussion on women who chose home births.) GP obstetrics is under threat of extinction, not only because of difficulties in the numbers of training posts, but because GP units around the country are being closed and maternity services centralised so that many GPs are prevented from practising by sheer distance. The draft of the new Midwives Rules and Code of Conduct[23] suggests that with respect to home deliveries, midwives should be bound by decisions of the local supervisor of midwives and by the policy of the local supervising authority (usually the Regional Health Authority). A legal paper from Wolfson College Oxford,[24] is even more disturbing: the authors argue that, as a matter of some urgency, the law should be changed to 'restore' medical professionals to their position as 'child protectors'. In other words, to give obstetricians the legal authority to over-rule a mother's wishes if they consider that intervention is necessary in the interests of the child, but the mother will not consent to it. In America women have already been ordered by law to undergo caesarean sections and other treatment to which they have declined to consent to.[25] In this country neonates have been made wards of court in order that operations can be performed on them when their parents have refused to consent. How long will it take to extend this position back to birth and, with the advent of inter-uterine surgery, before?

We are strong; we are capable; we are right. We have the information and, so far, we retain the right to insist on what we not only feel but can very often prove is best for ourselves and our children. All we need is the courage to use it. Each time we do, we grow in strength and that strength will encourage others. Our choices now affect not only ourselves and our children, but them as parents and their children and how they will be 'allowed' to give birth and be born. Let us choose for our children to be born in the safety of strength and joy, rather than in the danger of passivity and fear.

REFERENCES

1   *Confidential Enquiries into Maternal Deaths in England and Wales, 1976–78*, HMSO, 1982.
    Maternal mortality rate (excluding abortion) was 11.9/100,000 to total births, ranging from 5.4 to 18.0 in different regions. Although the figure is low, 59 per cent of deaths had 'avoidable' factors, i.e. some aspect of care could have been improved. 40.6 per cent of 'avoidable' deaths were attributed to consultant unit staff; 1.7 per cent to midwives, an astounding achievement considering that a midwife is the most senior person present in about 75 per cent of all births.

2   Peel Committee Report, Standing Maternity and Midwifery Advisory Committee, HMSO, 1970.

3   Social Services Committee, *Perinatal and Neonatal Mortality*, 2nd Report; House of Commons Paper 1979–80, 663/1. London, HMSO, 1980.

4 J. G. Fryer and J. R. Ashford, *British Journal of Preventive and Social Medicine*, vol. 26, 1972.

5 M. Tew, 'Home v. hospital confinement: the statistics', *Update*, vol. 18, 1979.

6 Communication to Dr David Owen, 8 July, 1984.

7 J. M. Eekelaar and R. W. J. Dingwall, 'Some legal issues in obstetric practice', *Journal of Social Welfare Law*, September 1984.

8 Elizabeth Nihill, *A Treatise on the Art of Midwifery*, 1763.

9 David Stewart, '*The five standards for safe childbearing*', NAPSAC International, 1981.

10 Sally Inch, *Birthrights: A Parents' Guide to Modern Childbirth*, Hutchinson, 1982.

11 J. A. Stilwen, *British Medical Journal*, no. 2, 1979.

12 (a) 1958: N. R. Butler and D. G. Bonham, *Perinatal Mortality*, Churchill Livingstone, 1963.
   (b) 1970: G. Chamberlain, *et al*, *British Births 1970*, vol. 2, Heinemann, 1978.

13 I am indebted to Marjorie Tew's work for information in the following section; without her unfailing efforts the invalid figures and false explanations of medical advisors would be all that is on record in this vital debate.

14 M. Tew, 'Obstetric hospitals and general practitioner maternity units — the statistical record', *Journal of the Royal College of General Practitioners*, 27 November, 1977 and M. Tew, 'The case against hospital deliveries: the statistical evidence'; in S. Kitzinger and J. A. Davis (eds), *The Place of Birth*, Oxford University Press, 1978.

15 M. Tew, 'Where to be born?' *New Society*, 27 January, 1977.

16 J. Fedrick, and N. R. Butler, 'Intended place of delivery and perinatal outcome', *British Medical Journal*, 25 March, 1978.

17 M. Tew, 'Is home a safer place?' *Health and Social Service Journal*, 12 September, 1980.

18 M. Tew, 'The safest place of birth — further evidence', *Lancet*, 30 June, 1979.

19 J. F. Murphy, M. Dauncey, O. P. Gray, I. Chalmers, 'Planned and unplanned deliveries at home: implications of a changing ratio', *British Medical Journal*, vol. 288, 12 May, 1984.

20 Bergsjo, Schmidt and Pusch, 'Differences in the reported frequencies of some obstetrical interventions in Europe', *British Journal of Obstetrics and Gynaecology*. vol. 90, pp. 628–32, July 1983.

21 Prof. G. Chamberlain, Director, National Birthday Trust Fund, 57 Lower Belgrave Street, London SW1 for further information.

22 Barry Collins, unpublished paper on men's attitudes about, and fears of, home birth, explores this subject in more detail.

23 The United Kingdom Central Council for Nursing, Midwifery and Health Visiting, 'New midwives rules and code of practice', a consultation paper, 1 May, 1984.

24 J. M. Eekelaar and R. W. J. Dingwall, *op cit*.

25 Yvonne Brackbill, June Rice, Diony Young, *Birth Trap — the Legal Low Down on High-tech Obstetrics*, The Mosby Press, 1984.

Midwives — past, present and future

BELINDA ACKERMAN

Midwifery is one of the oldest occupations known in history, dating back as early as the Book of Genesis. Exclusively a woman's profession until the mid-eighteenth century, it was frequently taken up by women as an extension to their domestic role as mothers. Traditionally, it incorporated healing and midwives were mainly used by the poorer classes.

The control exerted by men in midwifery began in the sixteenth century when midwives were tried as witches because of their unorthodox methods of healing with herbal and other remedies. Midwives also experienced hostility because they were not university educated as were their medical conterparts and their status was not deemed worthy of full recognition; in fact, there was no official training for midwives until it was formulated in 1902 by the Midwives' Act. In 1616, Peter Chamberlen first proposed training but it was rejected by the Royal College of Physicians.[1] Midwives were publicly abused by physicians during this time; Thomas Sydenham, for example, said 'they infested the sacred of medicine'. In 1763, William Hunter, an English physician, was appointed Physician Extraordinary to Queen Charlotte and it was he who made midwifery a respectable profession for men to enter. Women at this time did not challenge male expertise or status as this would have been considered 'improper' and so gradually they ceased to become healers, a role increasingly seen as a threat to their husbands' position.

As a result, during the eighteenth century, wealthy women opted for professional male practitioners when they needed a doctor and this in turn extended to childbirth. Doctors, striving for professional recognition, became increasingly scientific in their approach to healing and expanded their practice amongst the higher social classes for financial gain, leaving midwives to tend the poorer social classes.

After the Crimean War, Florence Nightingale's work made it respectable for middle-class women to take up 'nursing', but midwifery was still regarded as an ignorant and unhygienic profession. The character of Sairey Gamp in Charles Dickens' *Martin Chuzzlewit* published in 1844 provided a lasting public image of the squalor of home confinements and, by extension, of the ignorance of midwives. The Victorian social structure, adept at limiting the role of women in general, was equally effective in maintaining male dominance of midwifery. A move for change came in 1872 when the Obstetrical Society of London set up its own board of examiners and issued a certificate of competency to midwives, known as the L.O.S. after the society's initials. This set a trend and midwives united in their efforts to raise the level of maternity services and the status of their profession. The Midwives' Institute (which later became the Royal College of Midwives) was founded by Louisa M. Hubbard in 1881[2]; it pressed for the registration and training of midwives, stating that every mother should be entitled to the services of a trained midwife.[3] Even so, the 'handywoman' still existed and a select committee of the House of Commons found varying standards of care when they reported on the work of midwives in 1892.[4]

Finally, in 1902, the Midwives' Act was passed which was to regulate and control the practice of midwifery and the registration of all midwives. But as American lay midwife, Ina May Gaskin, has pointed out, 'the disrespect of midwives was really built into the British system with the Midwives' Act of 1902 which put midwives lower than doctors in the medical hierarchy by placing doctors on the board that oversaw midwives. There are no midwives serving on the boards that oversaw physicians.'[5] Under the rules of the Central Midwives' Board, the midwife was only asked to attend straightforward cases and was duty bound to call a doctor when the birth became difficult or deviated from the norm.

Meanwhile, in America, female midwifery was almost completely phased out by the 1920s. It was only much later that the link between midwifery and lower mortality and morbidity was realised and by then the interventionist approach of doctors was entrenched. In the 1930s, in this country, the demand for hospitalised childbirth grew out of the misguided medical belief that birth was dangerous and likely to end in tragedy at any time. This myth, created by the medical profession, helped increase doctors' prosperity and prestige. The hospital was their domain and independent midwifery practices fell into decline. Hospitalised childbirth coincided with the fall in the birth rate during the depression and led to the under-cutting of salaried domiciliary midwives. The Minister of Health gave hospitals grants in order to train midwives, which meant that they no longer had to pay for their own courses and training schools mushroomed throughout the country. Doctors urged more and more women to use hospitals and by 1933 one in three births took place there with charges at roughly 30 shillings per week. This undercut the domiciliary midwife by half and encouraged the takeover by doctors. The working classes who claimed public assistance had their maternity fees paid by the local authorities, but gradually in some areas the independent midwife was refused any recompense on the grounds that a mother could go to the municipal hospital free.

The 1936 Midwives' Act created a salaried staff under the local health authorities, virtually eliminating the independent midwife. However, the act placed a duty on local supervisory authorities to provide an adequate domiciliary service (a duty which still holds till this day although in many areas it is less than adequate). The act also included a mandatory refresher course for midwives to attend every five years.[6]

In 1946, the National Health Service Act came into force, enabling every pregnant woman to have free the services of a doctor and a midwife during her pregnancy and confinement. It also established obstetric flying squads and emergency blood transfusion services. Hospital births gradually rose from 52.8 per cent in 1947 to 65 per cent in 1961, although the numbers of hospital beds could not keep pace with the increase. The Cranbrook Committee, set up in 1956 to examine the administration of maternity services, advocated a 70 per cent hospital confinement rate and the integration of hospitals, GP units and community services. The Royal College of Midwives

(RCM) issued a statement saying that 'every mother should be delivered in a place where expert help is immediately available in an emergency'. The RCM thereby cast a shadow of doubt on the competence of midwives and their ability to seek medical aid promptly should the need arise. This helped further undermine the midwife's role as an independent practitioner.

The Peel Report of 1970 then recommended hospital confinement for all women on the grounds of increased safety for mother and child. However, it contained no evidence to substantiate the claim. The 1974 reorganisation of the NHS brought about the integration of hospital and community midwifery services. Hospital confinement rates leapt to 96 per cent and home birth became practically impossible in many areas. Consequently, midwives training from the early 1970s onwards had very little experience at all in domiciliary births. The Central Midwives' Board (the majority of whom were doctors) watched the decline without comment. This further demoted the midwives' role giving almost full control of birth to the medical profession. Most women coming into hospital to be delivered were unaware of the subtle consequences of these decisions.

In 1972, the Committee of Nursing published a report chaired by Professor Asa Briggs. There then followed seven years of debate which resulted in the 1979 Nurses', Midwives' and Health Visitors' Act which abolished the General Nursing Council, the Central Midwives' Board and the Council for the Education and Training of Health Visitors. In their place came the United Kingdom Central Council (UKCC) with a National Board for England, Scotland and N. Ireland and special midwifery committees democratically elected and for the first time formed solely of midwives. The Sex Discrimination Act of 1976 made it possible for men to train as midwives and training schools have been made available to men throughout the country, although so far the take-up rate is low.

It was in response to all these changes that the Association of Radical Midwives was formed in 1976 by a small group of direct-entry student midwives. They were frustrated and disillusioned with the type of care women received in the maternity service and the lack of concern shown within the midwifery profession itself. Their overall aim was to restore the role of the midwife for the benefit of the childbearing woman and her baby and:

- to re-establish the confidence of the midwife in her own skills
- to share ideas, skills and information
- to encourage midwives in their support of a woman's active participation in childbirth
- to reaffirm the need for midwives to provide continuity of care
- to explore alternative patterns of care
- to encourage evaluation of development in the field of midwifery.

The movement grew rapidly and regional groups were soon set up throughout the country. The group meets nationally every six to eight weeks and liaises closely with consumer groups such as the National Childbirth Trust, the Association for Improvements in the Maternity Services and the Birth Centre. The association lobbied MPs when the 1979 Nurses', Midwives' and Health Visitors' Act was going through parliament in order to get a better deal for midwives, and succeeded in getting three of their members elected to the English National Board. They have since spent many sessions discussing the re-establishment of the role of the midwife and providing much needed support amongst their members.

By the end of 1977 the shortage of midwives had reached chronic proportions. Some members of the midwifery profession expressed their concern that many midwives were working in situations in which they were unable to use their skills and knowledge to the full, primarily because of the increasing involvement of medical staff in the management of normal childbirth. The Royal College of Midwives expressed the view[7] that a study was required which would analyse the role of the midwife and develop the curriculum for midwifery training in view of the fact that the Central Midwives' Board had decided to extend the course from one year to eighteen months for state registered nurses and from two to three years for direct entrants. The Department of Health and Social Security produced a discussion paper on the future role of the midwife[8] and followed this by commissioning the Nursing Education Research Unit of

Chelsea College, London, to undertake a study of the role and education of the midwife. The research team made it their objective to find out the degree of responsibility and decision-making carried out by midwives. They concluded that a number of factors prevented midwives from fulfilling the role for which they are trained, namely the intervention by hospital obstetricians and GPs especially during the ante-natal period.[9] They deplored the shortage of midwifery staff and found there to be a disproportionate number of medical practitioners in the field of childbirth. As a consequence, they felt that an inadequate service was being provided to childbearing women.

In 1980, the Preliminary Select Committee on Social Services, chaired by Renee Short,[10] suggested that midwifery staffing levels should be increased, although the report referred to the doctor as having overall responsibility for the 'supervision' of the pregnant woman. The report suggested the setting up of Maternity Services Committees in each local health authority and a Maternity Services Advisory Committee was set up to look at how these could be established. Again, it was recommended that a majority of medical practitioners sit on the committee with a token number of midwives and mothers. The report produced an angry response from the consumer organisations who were not consulted when it was being written. There was little comment from the midwives' union, the Royal College of Midwives.

The rapid increase in the use of technology and the greater medicalisation of childbirth in the 1970s led to increasing dissatisfaction amongst midwives; mothers too were dissatisfied with the inhumane treatment often received as a result of these obstetric policies. Midwives are rarely treated as equals within the 'primary health care team', although they have built up a hierarchy in the same way as doctors. Even a Senior Midwifery Officer is dictated to by the consultant obstetrician in the hospital hierarchy. This is seen less in the community, where GPs and midwives are often able to form better working relationships. Doctors advise District Health Authorities with regard to policy-making and midwives, who are employees of the DHAs, are beholden to their policies. This creates a 'catch-22' situation: on the one hand, midwives are independent practitioners with their own rules and code of practice but, as employees of the NHS, they find their allegiance to childbearing women undermined by district policy.

Compared with doctors, midwives tend to be low achievers academically as they do not embark on a degree course as part of their training. They usually come from a lower socio-economic background and, in doing so, look to the doctors for guidance. Midwives need to become more autonomous and assertive, undertaking their own research instead of using doctors' textbooks to enhance their knowledge. A midwife has all the knowledge necessary to enable women to cope in labour unlike the obstetrician who sees childbirth as normal only in retrospect. By imposing routine technology and treating all women as problem cases, they take away a woman's confidence in her own abilities: it then becomes the obstetrician's needs that are met and not the woman's. Elvenreich and English[11] argue that male medical hostility to women is based on fear of female procreative power; a conflict has grown up between the 'reproducer as expert', and the 'doctor as expert' resulting in opposition between male medical knowledge and women's bodies and women's own knowledge about their bodies.

The midwife, in law, is a practitioner of normal childbirth and is therefore able to exercise clinical judgement. Thus it is the midwife and mother together who should share responsibility whilst the pregnancy remains uncomplicated, not the doctor. Midwives must realise that their profession will be eroded to that of obstetric nurse if they continue to accept that they hold no value unless they incorporate 'technology' as part of their routine work. So far, the Association of Radical Midwives has been the only midwifery group to recognise that the profession should align itself with women and their needs and not with doctors and their machines.

Midwives have let women down by letting junior doctors loose amongst labouring mothers. Instead, they should look to their own senior midwives for guidance rather than using them in menial tasks as they near retirement age. Doctors remain in the field of clinical practice as they move up through their professional career and as a reward are offered professorships. Many consultant obstetricians are only in their early thirties, whilst midwives are not usually offered Director of Midwifery

Service or District Midwifery Officer positions until they near retirement age.

The roots of the present-day midwife's passive behaviour lie in her training and in the fact that women are not expected to assert themselves in our society. The majority of midwives are first and foremost nurse-trained, which results in submissive behaviour towards doctors, an apolitical outlook and a tendency to spend a limited period of time within the profession. Direct-entry midwives, in contrast, are very often more mature women prior to training, have no preconceived ideas about taking orders from the medical establishment and are more likely to remain in the profession for a longer period of time. The Association of Radical Midwives has submitted suggestions for the new direct-entry course and is campaigning for an increase in the number of direct-entry training schools. Many of these schools were closed down all over the country when it was agreed to increase training from two years to three. The three-year course, brought about by EEC regulations, officially started in September 1981 and the only two hospitals providing it are Derby City and Edgware General, although applications are overwhelming. For example, in 1983, 230 requests were received by Derby but no places were available and 300 were received by Edgware, again none were accepted for training.[12] So far, midwifery schools have concentrated on providing the new eighteen-month training for SRNs throughout the country (159 had been approved by March 1983), despite the fact that a further one-year's post-qualification experience is required before these midwives are allowed to practise in EEC countries. Yet the three-year direct-entrant may practise immediately. It is quite obvious that the UKCC, dominated by male medical pressure, has succumbed to over-provision of midwifery schools for SRNs.

In a *Nursing Times* editorial in July 1983,[13] it was said that 'the most effective way in which the UKCC could demonstrate its good faith would be to encourage the expansion of courses providing direct-entry training into midwifery'. It went on to say that it is 'anomalous that midwives should undergo a three-year SRN training centred on ill-health before beginning midwifery training where the focus is on the healthy person'. Midwifery training needs to change dramatically in order to teach students about normal childbirth within the family setting. So much practice in maternity units has become technical and routine and it is midwives who can help to change this by encouraging women's faith in their own bodies. Provision of continuity of care and support by midwives throughout labour can reduce risks of medical intervention. A Royal College of Obstetricians and Gynaecologists' report on ante-natal and intra-partum care published in September 1982,[14] stated that midwives 'should play a greater part in the provision of ante-natal care' and that an 'increase in midwives should be made in the care of normal pregnant women'. They also recommended that midwives should be attached to all general practices where obstetric care is given. At the same time they suggested that women should be seen by hospital consultants for their first booking appointments!

Part 1 of *Maternity Care in Action*, compiled by the Maternity Services Advisory Committee, was also published in 1982.[15] It concentrated on ante-natal care and acknowledged the midwife as a practitioner in her own right. It suggested an increase in the number of district midwives in order to provide more community-based care; district midwives, it stated, should have direct contact with hospital obstetricians where the GP is not involved and should also have access to diagnostic equipment for use in the clinics. In Part 2, published in 1984,[16] the committee suggested minimum standards in staffing on labour wards and called for an end to routine procedures such as shaves, enemas and episiotomies. This is encouraging although, of course, many units still continue to enforce these interventions routinely.

The future of midwives and their ability to fulfil an independent role lies in education, research and the provision of continuity of care. Midwives should listen to the voice of their ally, the mother. Kate Newson, Director of Midwifery Services at the London Hospital, has said, 'We must change our attitude with regards to pregnant women and allow her to take increasing responsibility for her own care.'[17] She suggests that women could at least check their own weight and urine at the ante-natal clinic, possibly measure their own fundal height and count fetal movements prior to attending clinics. She points out that 'it may be as a result of our education system that midwives have failed to appreciate the importance of research and on-going education as essential parts of good midwifery practice.' Very few midwives ever audit their own practices, such as bothering to note how many times they carry out shaves and episiotomies.

Midwives, at last, are beginning to carry out their own research. For example, Mona Romney, a midwifery sister, carried out two studies recently, one into pre-delivery shaving and one into routine use of enemas in the labour ward.[18, 19] She concluded that shaves and enemas had no part in routine use for all women and may actually cause harm by increasing infection rates. Jennifer Sleep, midwifery tutor at the Royal Berkshire Hospital, carried out a randomised controlled trial into the use of episiotomies and concluded that routine episiotomies were unnecessary and should only be used in emergency cases.[20] Such studies show how midwifery practice can be changed to benefit childbearing women if a little effort is put into research. Midwives cannot continue to justify carrying out certain practices without first informing themselves of the reasons behind them.

Another area of concern is that of 'continuity of care' within the NHS system. The present lack of continuity is probably the most dissatisfying part of pregnancy for the majority of mothers. Over the past ten years, several midwives have turned to independent practice in order to provide women with total continuity of care and to avoid having to carry out routine obstetric policies. The women who opt for home birth in this way can be sure of seeing only two midwives and possibly one GP throughout the whole of their pregnancy. They can build up trust in these midwives which goes a long way to creating a relaxed and peaceful atmosphere during the actual delivery. It is a lonely existence for the midwife, though, with her only support coming from her one colleague and the local Supervisor of Midwives, but she reaps her reward from the knowledge that she has provided a complete and total service for which she is trained.

One way in which midwives can re-establish total continuity of care within the hospital, is being looked at by Caroline Flint, midwifery sister at St George's Hospital, Tooting, London. She set up a 'know your midwife' scheme in April 1983 which has a total of four midwives providing care to 200 women throughout the ante-natal period, delivery and puerperium. It was hoped to complete the experiment by August 1985 with the aim of showing that mothers will fare no worse than in the regular system of hospital care and that the whole experience is more satisfying for mothers. In the final analysis, it should be seen that there is less interference in the normal process of birth, thereby improving perinatal and neo-natal outcome. The object would then be to have this scheme adopted nationally.

The fact that continuity of care is a key issue in promoting the health of mothers and babies is shown by the Sighthill ante-natal scheme which was carried out in a community clinic as early as 1976.[21] This has dramatically reduced the perinatal mortality rate by using continuity of care by midwives. Perinatal mortality has dropped from 27 per 1,000 to 8 per 1,000 and has continued to fall subsequently. This compares with a rate of 20 per 1,000 for Sighthill mothers outside the scheme. The Sighthill experiment has shown that by following up high-risk women at home and in their local health clinic, the staff have received co-operation and trust in return. The midwives and GPs perform all the necessary tests in the clinics including ultrasonic scans, fetal cardiotocography, blood tests and the making of clinical decisions. They liaise closely with health vistors and this has helped local people recognise the midwife's special role instead of just seeing her as a nurse working within a hospital.

At long last two units which are run by midwives have emerged in England. The new Hinchingbrooke Hospital in Huntingdon prides itself on the high number of normal deliveries since its opening in September 1983. The maternity unit is run entirely by midwives, with senior obstetricians used only in emergencies. There are no junior doctors or students. Women keep their own records and attend local ante-natal clinics if that is more convenient for them. As a result, waiting times in the hospital clinic have been reduced dramatically. A midwives' unit is also in operation at the Park Hospital, Davyhulme in Manchester, run by Jean Towler, Director of Midwifery Services. Here women are offered the use of a birthing room complete with birth chair and bean bags. The midwives aim to give women more control over their own labours and this policy has improved the Apgar score of babies delivered and reduced the number of episiotomies and post-partum haemorrhages.

It has been shown over and over again that there are fewer

fatalities and a higher outcome of normal deliveries when the midwife is the provider of care during childbirth. For example, *World Medicine* reported in 1983[22] that a wide regional variation still existed in Britain with regard to maternal mortality ranging from 5.4 per 100,000 in Wessex to 18 per 100,000 in North East Thames (1976–8). This was not due to inequality of consultant establishments, as in Wessex there were 920 in one year per consultant, compared with 700 in North East Thames. More than half the deaths were deemed avoidable: 23 per cent attributed to the patient, 15 per cent to the anaesthetic team, 40 per cent to the consultant obstetric unit and *only 1.7 per cent to the midwife*.

Midwives must continue to work towards flexibility in caring for childbearing women and accept accountability for the provision of a total service which includes continuity of care. The art of midwifery is in being 'with' women rather than in being obstetric hand-maidens. Committed midwives will gradually reduce the demand for obstetric skills if they re-establish their role. Many have already gathered strength from the Association of Radical Midwives and feel able to take a stand over issues which ultimately affect the well-being of mothers and babies. The Association is constantly searching for ways to re-unite the midwifery profession which has long since drifted from its true path. The midwife, as defined by the World Health Organisation, is a 'properly trained person who must be able to give the necessary supervision, care and advice to women during pregnancy, labour and the post-partum period, to conduct deliveries on her own responsibility and to care for the newborn infant . . .' She should take up partnership with the woman whose care she is providing and strive once again to become the true guardian of normal childbirth.

REFERENCES

1 Walter Radcliffe, *Milestones in Midwifery*, John Weight & Sons, 1967.

2 Margaret Farrer, 'The Royal College of Midwives 1881–1981', *Midwife Health Visitor and Community Nurse*, Vol. 17, no. 7, July 1981.

3 Ann R. Ward, 'The passing of the Midwives' Act 1902', *Midwives' Chronicle*, July 1981.

4 Brian Abel-Smith, *A History of the Nursing Profession*, Heinemann, 1960.

5 Ina May Gaskin, 'Across the water', *The Practising Midwife*, vol. 1, no. 17, Autumn, 1982.

6 Midwives' Institute, *The Midwife in Independent Practice Today*, 1936.

7 Royal College of Midwives, 'Evidence to the Royal Commission on the National Health Service', 1977.

8 Department of Health and Social Security, 'The future role of the midwife', CNO 20, 1976.

9 S. Robinson, J. Golden and S. Bradley, *A Study of the Role and Responsibilities of the Midwife*, Nursing Education Research Unit, London University, 1983.

10 Social Services Committee, 'Perinatal and neo-natal mortality', second report, a Commons Paper 1979–80, 663/1 HMSO, London, 1980.

11 B. Elvenreich and D. English, *Witches, Midwives and Nurses*, Writers and Readers Publishing Co-operative, 1973.

12 Association of Radical Midwives Information Sheet, 'Midwifery training', 1983.

13 *Nursing Times*, editorial, 10 July, 1983.

14 Royal College of Obstetricians and Gynaecologists, 'Report of the RCOG Working Party on ante-natal and intra-partum care', September 1982.

15 First Report of the Maternity Services Advisory Committee, *Maternity Care in Action: Part 1*, HMSO, London, 1982.

16 Second Report of the Maternity Services Advisory Committee, *Maternity Care in Action: Part 2*, HMSO, London, 1984.

17 Kate Newson, 'The future of midwifery', *Midwife, Health Visitor and Community Nurse*, vol. 18, December 1982, no. 12.

18 Mona L. Romney, 'Pre-delivery shaving: an unjustified assault?', *Journal of Obstetrics and Gynaecology*, no. 1, pp. 33–5, 1980.

19 Mona L. Romney and H. Gordon, 'Is your enema really necessary?', *British Medical Journal*, vol. 282, 18 April, 1981.

20 Jennifer Sleep, 'The East Berkshire Episiotomy Trial', Research and the Midwife Conference Proceedings, pp. 81–95, Manchester, 1983.

21 Dr Kenneth Boddy, 'The Sighthill Ante-Natal Scheme', *Johnson's Baby Newsline*, Autumn 1983.

22 *World Medicine*, editorial, 5 February, 1983.

Psychic and spiritual aspects of pregnancy, birth and life

SALLY STOCKLEY

In England, and indeed in large parts of the world today, we live in a society dominated by the classical Western European scientific world-view, a world-view in which psychic abilities are often dismissed entirely, and certainly poorly understood by the majority of us. And yet, if a question is put to many people about the validity of psychic phenomena, or about their own personal experience in that field, they will often say, 'Yes, I'm sure there's something in it' or 'Yes, I have had an experience something like that', very often adding, 'but I don't understand it'. It seems that latent awareness of abilities and understanding that historically have been squeezed out of our lives for too long is nevertheless still very much with us.

My purpose in this chapter is to suggest not only that our world as a whole would benefit enormously from a greater understanding and use of psychic or non-material faculties, but that it can be particularly useful to think about such matters during pregnancy. I have observed that expectant mothers, in the birth group with which I am associated and elsewhere, are often especially intuitive if 'allowed' to be so. Expectant fathers often are too. This I regard as nature's plan and the plan of the world of spirit to ensure the very best in nurturing, understanding and health for the person shortly to be born into our world. Also, the time of birth and when the child is very young is often one in which much adjustment is needed within the family and there is a particular need for sensitivity and intuitive understanding. Thus it is often an opportunity for parents to make changes within themselves. An understanding of what is best for one's baby's health and safety brings clearly into focus the need for the *parents* to be fully involved in decisions made about pregnancy and birth, especially if their intuition is to be acted upon. Thus this time is also one in which a greater understanding of personal responsibility can come about, and it is this which is central to any psychic and spiritual development.

When using the word 'psychic' here I am referring to a whole range of abilities and phenomena which are produced by the action of the 'psyche' or soul (see also p. 82). Examples are intuition, telepathy, precognition, physical mediumship such as materialisation (production of ectoplasm) or psychokinesis (the moving of objects by mental remote control), mental mediumship, such as clairvoyance (literally 'clear seeing': the seeing of people or things not of this earth or place or time) or clairaudience (similarly 'clear hearing'), trance mediumship, automatic writing, psychic diagnosis, psychic healing, psychic surgery, out-of-the-body experiences, and memory of previous incarnations. These phenomena are difficult to weigh or measure by the methods with which most of us are familiar, operate independently of time and space as we know them, and cannot be understood within a purely material reality. Some of these abilities operate within the limits of this earth, while others involve communication with the world of spirit. To say that someone is 'psychic' is not necessarily to imply that he or she is 'spiritual' in the sense of being spiritually aware or mature. However, the employment of psychic abilities can greatly help to increase spiritual expansion and since I am only prepared to consider their use in a spiritual direction, in the service of love, I use the words together.

If we are to understand psychic abilities and take them seriously it is important that we realise that the classical Western European scientific world-view is not the only possible or logical one. Indeed historically speaking it is a very recent innovation and has developed somewhat arbitrarily.[1] In other periods of history than our own, and even in some parts of the world today, quite different world-views exist or have existed. Joan Grant[2] describes a lifetime of hers in Egypt about 3000 years BC. At this time, she says, the temples were not so much places of worship, but more like universities or teaching hospitals in which students studied various forms of psychic ability (including far memory, as well as hypnosis). This was not romantic dabbling, but useful productive work such as psychic diagnosis, psychic healing, and anaesthesia without modern drugs, and was considered perfectly normal in the world-view of the time. Imagine going to a government university today to do a practical course in psychic development!

Furthermore, today's materialistic, mechanistic, reductionist approach to reality, stemming from the seventeenth-century scientific revolution and classical Newtonian nineteenth-century physics, is, to put it mildly, rather a limited one, and unable to accommodate psychic phenomena such as those mentioned above. Lord Kelvin, the great nineteenth-century physicist and chemist, said that unless you could show him a mechanical model of a theory he found it impossible to believe it. As a lay person, I have always found this type of approach extraordinary. After all, it seems to me that the whole point of 'science' in the broadest sense of the word is to find out or explain that which has not yet been found out or explained, and we all know there is plenty of that. Before the 'discovery' of electricity, it was not the phenomenon which did not exist, but simply our knowledge of and ability to make use of it.

Electricity fitted reasonably happily into the mechanical model. Psychic phenomena, however, do not. Nevertheless we now have at our disposal an increasing body of data and research which shows us that psychic phenomena definitely exist. Some of this data is the result of laboratory experiments acceptable to modern scientific method.[3] In addition, many of the ideas upon which psychics and psychic researchers insisted and were ridiculed for, sometimes a hundred years or more ago, have later come to be accepted by science.[4] If our current view of the world cannot explain or help us to use psychic experiences and phenomena then we need a more comprehensive view, and I believe that our hope for the future lies in this direction. Clearly our materialist assumptions are not serving us well enough and we need to evolve new ways of seeing things and a broader understanding of the nature of man. This should help us towards ensuring a more emotionally secure, better fed and much healthier population; changing our institutions; and ending the nuclear arms race, to name but a few things.

Dr Gardner Murphy, a past president of both the American Psychological Association and the American Society for Psychical Research, has observed: 'If there were one-tenth of the evidence in any other field of science that there is in parapsychology, it would be accepted beyond question.'[5] What is fascinating is the lengths to which scientists have gone to be able not to admit the evidence, reminiscent of the determined opposition to Galileo's ideas in the seventeenth century.[6] Science itself has quietly accepted many glaring gaps in its own theory; for example, the existence of gravity, a phenomenon which pre-supposes action-at-a-distance and did not fit into the mechanistic viewpoint at all, was unexplained for two hundred years until Einstein's theory of relativity. Incidentally, psychics had always said that action-at-a-distance was possible. Similarly, we have no more idea of how the brain translates thought into action than we have of how information passes from one person's mind to another without physical communication, yet only the latter is called 'paranormal'. I would like to suggest that it is because the implications of psychical research are more threatening to the individual (What is the nature of man? Does man live after death, if so, why? Should I therefore change myself or my ideas?) than those of orthodox science, that the gaps in the former have been so frantically criticised while those in the latter have very often been allowed to slide.

What is that non-mechanistic and non-quantifiable part of man which thinks and loves and makes decisions, and in many cases can act intuitively, or receive messages across the world without any material aid, or see 'dead' people? What is consciousness and what are the different levels, types or aspects of consciousness? Why is man here? Modern science has not only restricted itself to consideration of certain types of phenomena, but also to certain questions, e.g. 'how?' but not 'why?' The two great developments of twentieth-century physics, quantum mechanics and relativity, have already shown us, in their failure to fit the mechanistic mould, that we cannot understand reality with just one explanatory model of the universe (this fact has not yet been accepted by mainstream science). Having recognised therefore that we need several explanatory systems to deal with different aspects of our experience, and that these will not be contradictory, we will be able to research the realms into which psychic and spiritual matters fall more fruitfully.[7] We shall perhaps cease trying to subject these matters to repeatable laboratory experiments (the methods of science) into which many of the most important obviously do not fit. Lawrence LeShan has suggested that until scientists in their own field can make a perpetual motion machine let alone a falling-in-love machine or a psychic-phenomena producing machine, they should stop criticising psychic researchers in their field for not doing enough repeatable experiments.[8] Following this, we can perhaps begin to understand better the uses to which psychic abilities should be put, and in this chapter I shall make some tentative suggestions. It is my belief that an understanding of psychic abilities is more likely to lead us to a spiritual conclusion than an understanding of science, although both are a part of the whole.

I have implied above that I am convinced by some of the psychical research which has been done. But even more important is the fact that I now have a body of experience in my own life using my own abilities and closely observing those of others when they have directly affected me, which has convinced me beyond any reasonable doubt that there is a psychic and spiritual reality and that it works and is worth using. Each of us can only provide 'proof' for ourselves because there is a part of the body of evidence which will never be available through 'objective' research but only through personal experience. We must ask ourselves, 'What do *I* think about it? Does it work for me?' More important, since an investigation into psychic abilities can provide an opportunity for spiritual growth, the very nature of this is that it must be a personal journey.

What follows now are some considerations which, bearing in mind the existence of a psychic reality, may help us to bring into the world babies who are more truly safe and healthy, in the spiritual and mental as well as physical meaning of health. Fundamental to all that I have to say is an understanding that mind and soul influence body and that what may appear to be 'purely mental' or 'purely spiritual' considerations can actually directly affect the physical health of ourselves and our babies. While some of what I have to say will have been scientifically validated, some of it stems from my own personal experience, and that of others, and is offered to the reader for his or her own evaluation in the spirit of proof outlined above. It comes from someone who first trained in psychic development (a training of course which cannot be described as completed) before giving birth to her first baby. I suddenly realised that here was a whole area which I had hitherto never thought about in 'psychic' terms. I began to realise that there might be things I had learnt which could be useful in finding out more about my baby, or helping her in some way, or helping us, the parents, to prepare for her. Furthermore, I began to wonder whether the psychic development which I had undertaken from my late twenties might not have been a little easier if I had been brought up in a somewhat different way. After all, why is extra-sensory perception common or at least possible in some societies and less so or not at all in others?

If we accept a psychic and spiritual reality, we accept that the mind or consciousness can be independent from the body and is not created by the brain. This, incidentally, is one of the things which psychical science has always said and which classical nineteenth-century science denied. However, major modern neurophysiologists, such as Wilder Penfield and Charles Sherrington, are now coming to precisely that view.[9] This immediately leads us to ask what happens to the consciousness when the body and its brain have died and also to ask where the consciousness comes from in a new baby.

There are not all that many people who would regard a newborn baby, still less a fetus, as a fully aware, feeling, thinking person with a memory and ability to interpret language. However, in his exciting book first published in 1981 Thomas Verny has collected together some of the most recent scientific evidence to show without doubt that, at least in the last three months of life in the womb, the baby is a feeling, remembering, aware being, who can learn and respond.[10] This evidence comes from 'properly controlled' studies and shows the immense importance of the mother's feelings during pregnancy. Lack of love towards her child has been clearly demonstrated to adversely affect that child's personality in later life and his or her physical health during pregnancy, labour and later life. While it is easy enough to see how stress hormones, reaching the fetal circulation from the mother's bloodstream via the placenta, can cause emotional and physical ill-effects in the baby,[11] Verny identifies two other ways in which the pregnant mother and her baby may communicate: behavioural (for example, the baby kicks when uncomfortable or anxious) and sympathetic. It is this last method, in which he includes the mother communicating her love for her unborn child, which Verny finds the hardest to define or explain. Similarly, when discussing memories of events during life in the womb, derived from hypnosis, drugs, dreams or other sources, he acknowledges that there appears to be evidence for 'extraneurological' memory. This goes back before the time in pregnancy at which we know that neurological memory (i.e. that made possible by the maturing brain and nervous system) exists.

Both Verny's 'sympathetic' communication and his 'extraneurological' memory are immediately better understood if the idea that consciousness is not purely physical or biological is accepted. Even more so if it is understood that a soul or consciousness can and does live in a world of spirit, before incarnating or reincarnating into a physical body. Those who understand or accept reincarnation usually also understand that the physical body may be entered again and again in this way in order that a particular consciousness may acquire certain experiences or the ability to deal with certain situations in a way which leads towards spiritual growth and enlightenment. My own understanding of reincarnation comes mainly from information given to me by spirit people whom I have learnt to trust through long association and previous verification. The main sources are those people such as Joan Grant who can remember previous lifetimes; experience of previous lifetimes provided by hypnotic regression (while under hypnosis a person regresses as far back as the womb or a previous life); and dreams. Some of this evidence is certainly impressive and has been corroborated by historical research after it was produced by the individual concerned, but of course there are others anxious to disprove this. (There are many books on the subject for anyone who wishes to make up their own mind.[12])

Evidence for survival of death has, of course, been provided to many individuals through mediums using various forms of communication; I am speaking here of reference by the spirit person, communicating through the medium, to matters or facts or objects unknown to the medium and to anyone except the sitter. Again, this type of evidence can usually only be acquired with any degree of certainty for oneself, and indeed is often startlingly convincing, but it is all too easy to dismiss or disprove someone else's experience should you wish to do so. Near-death experiences are less easy to come by in the personal sense, but are beginning to be written down. Accounts of life in the world of spirit, communicated through mediums and written down are also interesting, and often very inspiring in the spiritual sense.[13] Any certainty about survival of death may come from a variety of sources, therefore, but in the final analysis the most important is usually that inner judgement or knowledge, the use of which is open to all of us if we will investigate it within ourselves.

The question of when the consciousness enters the physical body is one which cannot be settled here and now. It may however be useful to draw a distinction between the formation of human personality (which some still say does not begin until birth, but which Verny suggests begins some time before birth) and the time at which the already existing soul, or psyche, enters the physical body. At times I have used the word 'consciousness' to cover both the soul, which itself may contain various levels of consciousness, and the human personality. As far as Verny's work is concerned, we may suggest that it can be either the personality or the soul which may be affected by what happens during the period of gestation, and of course the soul will affect the formation of human personality both before and after birth.

Although it allows that the psyche or soul may enter the body before the formation of human personality, the distinction drawn above does not solve the problem of exactly when the psyche, at whatever level of consciousness, enters the body. Views on the matter vary enormously: the consciousness entering at the moment of conception, at the time of quickening (first movements of the baby in the womb), at the time of birth, 'hovering' in and out of the fetus, or a final commitment not really being made until some weeks or even months after birth. My own view is that the soul or consciousness clothes itself in its physical body at different times, in different forms and even at different rates, and many pregnant mothers have reported sensing someone near but not actually within them, or a moment when they felt the new consciousness solidly there. It is the higher consciousness or higher self which carries within it the sum of our previous experience and our intimate connection with the wisdom of the world of spirit. During our life on earth it is this aspect of our consciousness, in its relationship to our human consciousness, which will enable us to develop spiritually. Even when the emerging personality is affected, as Verny shows, by stressful conditions or lack of love in the mother, there is always the possibility of the higher consciousness working on the resulting aspect of personality in later life and changing, enhancing or using it in some way. (I am not venturing here into the realms of 'evil' or 'possession'. I do not wish to imply that they do not exist, but the purpose of this chapter is to outline some of the things we can do to enhance the health of our babies, who are usually exceptionally well protected, psychically and spiritually speaking, in the womb.)

Enriched with an understanding of reincarnation and of psychic communication, the possibilities for providing a healthy environment for a child in the womb seem to me to increase spectacularly. Starting simply with an awareness of such matters will already bring benefit to yourselves and your baby; you don't need to be a qualified medium! We can see birth, then, as a shift in consciousness. Of course we experience different types of consciousness while on earth: our ordinary waking consciousness, the intuitive state, our dream state, and out-of-the-body and mediumistic experiences if we have them, for example. But birth and death are very big shifts. We can understand then that the person we are welcoming into the world is not necessarily a 'new' one and could have wisdom and knowledge of his or her own, perhaps even more than ourselves! There is evidence that at least some souls actually choose the parents to whom they shall be born, and certainly in the Tibetan tradition this is the understanding.[14] The value of choosing his or her circumstances in life is in my view dependent on what opportunities are thereby offered to undergo the experiences a person may need. In some cases a bargain may be struck between mother and 'baby' before either are born into this lifetime.

As well as allowing themselves to be aware of these possibilities, aspiring parents may consider whether the time at which *they* decide it is right to have a child is suitable to the other party. If there is a problem in conceiving or carrying the baby, it may simply be due to a lack of good nutrition or some other physical cause, but otherwise perhaps the time is not right and it would be wise to wait a little longer or look at one's life to see whether any changes in attitude or circumstances need to be made.[15] Very often physical and spiritual factors work together, i.e. a cause can be seen in either terms. It is important for any reader to use the remarks made here at whatever level is most useful to them. Above all, guilt is an unnecessary and inhibiting emotion and any pregnant mother should try to be understanding of herself as well as her baby. Sometimes managing to let go of one's own most desperate desires may make it possible for the incoming soul to have a better chance of realising some of his or hers. It is my view that one can talk and listen to a 'baby' before conception as well as afterwards.

A miscarriage may occur when a mother does not want her baby, but equally well may result from the fact that a particular soul needs to experience this earth for only a very short time in order to fulfil its requirements. While all thinking and caring people must regard abortion as something to be avoided if at all possible, it may be that in times of great need parents too can have the choice to refuse to carry on with the pregnancy, and that this may not be a total disaster for the incoming soul as another chance may be available at a later time with a different or even the same family.

It will be apparent by now that my own contention is that the baby at birth and in the womb is far more sensitive than even Thomas Verny would suggest. The baby therefore requires enormous respect and sensitive treatment at this time and for some time after birth, until he or she has become strong enough in the ways of the world to work out ways of living in it with his or her security and goodwill intact. In the birth and pregnancy group of which I am now a member, we encourage pregnant mothers to make use of that intuition to which we referred at the beginning of this chapter, and which of course comes under the heading of psychic abilities. We are not talking here about anything special or extraordinary but about an ability which most mothers find quite normal. We often have a 'quiet time' during our meeting in which parents may take time off from their busy lives to talk and listen to their babies and convey their love, thereby increasing the baby's health, as Verny says. Our aim is to provide the support and 'permission' sometimes needed to use these faculties when living in a society which on the whole denies their existence. We realised, during the setting up and development of our group, that spiritual nutrition is as vitally important to the baby's growth and development as biological nutrition.

Furthermore, we realised that there can be great value in intuitive diagnosis during pregnancy. Many of the devices currently used by the medical profession to discover the state of health of the fetus or to forestall any possible problems during pregnancy or labour either have not been adequately investigated or are known to have positively harmful effects. Nor are they always infallibly reliable. It therefore seems sensible to employ in diagnosis a tool which does not have harmful side-effects and which is extremely accurate if properly used: the mother's intuition. The process is one in which she responds to that inner voice which we all have if we will listen to it: an inner voice of certainty.

Given the society in which we live, it is necessary, once again, for most women to be provided with support and 'allowed' to trust their intuition. It is best of course if she is already well acquainted with this method of working, but it is a practice which in many women is enhanced, and can certainly be sharpened up, during pregnancy. As with all tools, the way to learn to use this one is through practice. Listen to your innner voice, act accordingly and see when you are right. You will soon learn which is the 'correct' voice. Naturally I am not suggesting that you 'experiment' with your baby. It is no good confronting a pregnant woman, who is unfamiliar with her intuition, with a sceptical or derisive member of the medical profession and expecting her to come up with some miraculous 'certainty' (although this *could* happen). Most of us need time, to quietly 'feel' how our child is, and to be amongst people who respect and understand this way of working. If she then feels a certainty, or feels strongly, a woman can act upon that; if not, or she is unsure about what she feels, she can of course take medical advice. Furthermore, this process of intuitive diagnosis is not something which should be set in opposition to medical advice. It may be that it is often necessary to refuse some intervention, which carries potentially harmful side-effects, on the strength of it, but very often, too, medical advice may coincide with a woman's intuition. Many doctors are naturally intuitive and would admit to using intuition in their consulting rooms, and a good midwife is often particularly intuitive about a pregnant or labouring woman, and respects that woman's intuition too. I have often heard a midwife say that a mother 'usually knows if something is wrong'.

I do not know if there are any scientific studies comparing the use of a pregnant mother's intuition with a machine or medical device and, along with what I have indicated above, I think this would be, though important, of only limited relevance. Using intuition is a skill, one which practically all of us have innately within us, and which we can learn to use, like walking! A necessary part of the use of this skill, like most skills, is that the user thinks that it can work: this is essentially different from the use of a machine, and each individual woman can only find out for herself whether her own intuition works or not. The great advantage which a mother (and indeed many fathers) have, is 'continuity of care'. It is the view of some people that almost the greatest single improvement towards a safe and healthy outcome to pregnancy would be the provision of continuity of care in the ante-natal service. In other words the same midwife listening to and feeling the same baby month by month or week by week will be better able to notice changes and abnormalities. A mother of course can feel and sense her baby all the time if she so wishes. As well as this, if she is responding intuitively, she will respond to the spiritual and emotional as well as physical state of the baby's health and therefore will have a more complete and accurate picture.

The use of intuition in pregnancy is one of those things of which I have direct experience, but which I have also seen at work in others and which I know can be startlingly correct if properly used. Over and over again in our birth group we have seen a mother's intuition proved correct. One mother, having given birth to her first two children at home, and having planned a third delivery at home, felt all along, without knowing the reason why, that she might have to go to hospital for this one, which indeed she did in the end, owing to a low blood count (the birth was perfectly straightforward, however). Another mother asked constantly for information about a retained placenta. She was not a nervous mother and had had no problems with her first baby (this was her second). She had a normal delivery but a retained placenta, with no other complications and no untoward results. (To the sceptical, of course, it may appear that the mother's interest in a retained placenta caused her to have one, but knowing the mother as I do, I am satisfied that this was not the case.) Another mother, living a lifestyle which might have suggested a home delivery, and sharing a house with other pregnant women who gave birth at home, nevertheless booked herself with quiet certainty into hospital: she ended up with an unexpected caesarean (this was a necessary caesarean, not one which was forced upon her through ignorance). I can very clearly remember, too, knowing that I must not take a particularly strong drug for migraine, and resisting the desire to do so, without knowing the reason why, until I discovered a week later that I was pregnant. This particular drug can cause miscarriage, apart from anything else. Many mothers in our group have declined to have their labours induced on the strength of their intuition, and all of these have had adequately functioning placentas and healthy babies. I myself almost always know without being told when one of the mothers in the group has gone into labour, unless I am particularly busy at the time or do not know the mother very well.

It would be folly to suggest that every mother's intuition is always going to be right, but only the most obtuse would suggest that machines are always accurate (and certainly few midwives working on hospital delivery floors could claim this!), or that doctors do not sometimes make a wrong judgement. What we need to arrive at is the best possible use of all available skills, but the least necessary use of procedures which carry undesirable side-effects. Obviously the best astmosphere for this is created by a good relationship between medical advisors and parents with respect on both sides and with no one trying to claim that they are infallible. Parents are experts just as much as doctors.

It goes without saying that no woman should be made to feel

she has to make decisions intuitively. Most of us however will have at least some feelings, however unobtrusive, during pregnancy: perhaps a desire to be by the seaside, or for peace and quiet, a dislike of long journeys, a need for company and laughter, a need to be with a particular person: these can be perfectly commonplace feelings but if heeded can bring great benefit to the baby. Some women may feel that a job is just what they need, others who never dreamt of giving up their job 'just for pregnancy' may suddenly realise that if the needs of the unborn child for peace, lack of competitiveness, aggression or tension perhaps, are to be fully met, then this may be what they have to do. Of course there may be financial or other considerations which prevent this option from being followed, but each mother or couple can only decide for themselves where their real priorities lie. (It would be sad if a 'feminist' perspective prevented due consideration being given to the needs of the emerging person — the baby — since a truly feminist society would of course make allowance for this without it entailing the long-term perpetuation of a particular role for particular women.) Some women may have very vivid or revealing dreams during pregnancy and these too should be heeded.[16]

When expecting our first child we were, like so many newly pregnant couples, renovating a house into which we had recently moved. When finally the room in which I was to give birth was nearly ready, we went there for the first time to undertake our meditation and prayer. During this time I was quite clearly told by one of my friends in the world of spirit that we should use this and subsequent times to prepare the room for the forthcoming birth. This entailed filling the room with vibrations of light and love, through visualisation and prayer, and when it came to the labour, psychic help was more easily given to the baby and myself by a spirit or discarnate healer, as a result of this preparation. Obviously this is more easily done when a home delivery is planned, but a woman going to hospital may still make preparation through absent visualisation, after a visit to the delivery floor, or even if she has never seen the room. Certainly she and her partner may 'prepare' the room as soon as they walk into it after labour begins. If you happen to be decorating a room at home, then don't forget to choose a colour which you feel will be helpful in labour or to surround a newborn baby.[17] Music too can enhance your baby's health during pregnancy or birth: find out what he or she likes by observing his or her movements in response to certain music, or decide for yourself intuitively.

During labour, the way to help a woman to be intuitive is to surround her with loving and constant support (preferably not with strangers), to listen carefully to what she says or asks for, and to eliminate as far as possible any outside interference, noise or obstruction. The single most important factor in ensuring the optimum health and safety, that is, spiritual, mental and emotional as well as physical safety, of a mother and her baby at birth, is her spiritual and emotional state and the quality of her surroundings. Her ability to act instinctively and intuitively, to encourage and welcome her baby, to use her own inner knowledge of what to do or to respond (even if unconsciously) to any spirit helpers she may have, is directly affected by who happens to be in the room at the time, and whether they are surrounding her with love or hostility or something in between. The use of visualisation during labour can not only help the mother to cope with contractions but also quite literally assist the physical progress of the baby towards birth. This could entail surrounding the baby with light and love, encouraging and reassuring him or her at the same time, and visualising in the first stage the dilatation of the cervix and in the second stage the gentle opening of the vagina, descent of the baby's head, and stretching of the perineal muscles.[18]

If we accept what has been written in the previous paragraph it is obvious that any intervention during labour should only be used if absolutely necessary. The unnecessary use of induction of labour can upset the planned astrological environment of the person being born, and can thus affect the pattern or absence of disease and types of events with which he or she is confronted in life and thus the opportunities to develop in spiritual terms. (This does not mean that there will be no opportunities, but that they may be different ones.) It can also provoke the infant to move into a disadvantageous position in order to try to resist being born when he or she is neither physically nor mentally ready. Denys Kelsey[19] describes a woman he regressed (through hypnotic regression) to a period immediately prior to birth. She exclaimed indignantly: 'But it is Me who should say when I want to be born!' At birth she was a brow presentation, in other words almost the greatest diameter of her head presented to get through the birth canal, instead of the smallest diameter, and through hypnosis she recalled deliberately moving her head into this position in order to resist the process. Kelsey does not say whether this was an induced birth or not, but it illustrates my point. Another case from a hypnotic regression is quoted by Helen Wambach:[20] 'My birth-canal experience started with a strong feeling that somehow "they" tricked me. They induced the labour and I wasn't ready yet.'

The adoption by the child of a position which impedes delivery is sometimes the result of his or her sensing the mother's reluctance to give birth. Such reluctance can also provoke the onset of uterine inertia, and although it can be due to fears on the part of the mother in the here and now, such as fear of pain or of having a child to look after, in a psychically aware mother it can be due to her reluctance to imprison yet another soul in matter, based on memories, conscious or unconscious, of previous incarnations.[21] There can also be a reluctance on the part of either mother or child to expedite the formation of an egocentric and in many ways isolated human personality from a soul, who comes from a whole or group soul. This latter is a difficult concept which I do not intend to elaborate upon here, but it is worth mentioning as an indication of the complexities of birth. If we understand that complications in labour are so often due to spiritual, psychic or emotional causes we can then allow our intuitions to direct us towards an appropriate solution even if we do not fully understand the cause. A medium or psychic healer can sometimes effect a cure which seems 'miraculous' only because it is appropriate to that real cause (and assists the self-healing abilities of the mother or baby concerned). None of this prevents the use of short-term physical interventions in a situation of crisis, but if the understanding is there, then such a situation is less likely to occur in the first place.

Another intervention in labour which is unfortunate from the psychic point of view is the fetal scalp monitor. The chakras or psychic centres are invisible to many people in our culture and are seven main ones in number. They are those centres in the body through which we receive spiritual force and indeed can radiate it outwards. When we know how to (and sometimes even when we don't), we can use them to see clairvoyantly and employ other psychic skills. They provide an essential link between our vitality (quite literally our 'life force') and the cells of our brains and our bodies. Any medium in training will learn how to use the chakras.[22] If it is realised that there is an important one, the crown chakra, on the top of the head it will be obvious that having an electrode attached to the fetal scalp could be something to avoid rather than rely upon when there is any sign of fetal distress. Many babies clearly do not like it and 'jump back' when an attempt is made to apply it. The careful use of intuition can be part of an intelligent and highly effective alternative.

Further interesting evidence as to the great sensitivity and awareness of the child during labour and birth comes again from hypnotic regression, and I quote here from Helen Wambach's research,[23] leaving each reader to make up his or her own mind about the admissibility of such evidence: 'I was aware that one nurse there scratched my face at birth and I was scared. My body actually jumped [i.e. in the hypnosis] at this impression of the scratched face.' '. . . the first breath was wonderful. I got feelings of great happiness and relief from others in the delivery room. I feel great loving hands and stroking and soft voices. This experience was very clear. I felt "love" [her inverted commas] in the room. I wonder if it was because my family was in the room. My grandfather delivered me.' 'As soon as I was born I felt intense cold and bright light. I was afraid of the prospects ahead of me. I felt that the doctors and nurses in attendance were impersonal and cold. They lacked compassion for my mother's fear and pain. I recall being very upset by this lack of feeling of those in attendance. I hovered over my mother throughout this ordeal.'

Many parents may have noticed that some newborns look remarkably 'old'. That is to say the experience and wisdom (or otherwise) of previous living is evident in their faces. This look usually leaves the face after no more than a few hours, but that does not mean that the baby does not continue to be very aware. Sadly, because babies cannot talk to us in our ordinary language, many of us assume that they cannot understand or communicate a great deal. We fail to realise that this very language, a wonderful tool in many ways, can also have been an instrument for the dulling of our own sensitivity. A baby is often more rather than less aware than we are, precisely because he or she does not yet rely on the spoken word, but uses telepathy. Another quote from a subject regressed to her birth experience: 'I felt cramped at first, then wondered, "How do I communicate with these people?" '[24] Joan Grant has a memory of various occasions (in this life) on which she was frustrated by being unable to communicate with her carers, though perfectly clear about what she needed. The earliest decision she remembers is her refusal of her mother's breast, because of the nauseating smell of the milk. This was probably because in it she could smell the drugs from which she had suffered during the fetal period, drugs which her mother had taken for asthma. 'I remember acute despair when I was offered a bottle only to find that it contained the same repugnant fluid . . .' On a later occasion she would accept only a spoon instead of the bottle associated with this fluid. 'As I became increasingly hungry . . . I beamed SPOON at everyone who came near me, and their failure to understand scared me, for it was very alarming to be at the mercy of bland giants who seemed so utterly stupid.'[25]

In his book *Magical Child*,[26] Joseph Chilton Pearce writes of a doctor's wife who watched women in Uganda who carried their babies on their fronts or backs in a queue to see her husband, sometimes for hours. None of the women used nappies and none of the babies were wet or dirty when their turn arrived, because they had been taken to the bushes at the right moment. When asked how they had achieved this feat the mothers were astonished and asked, 'How do you know when you have to go?' When living in Africa some years ago I too had observed this type of telepathy.

It is likely that many psychologists and neurophysiologists would protest that a human baby's brain soon after birth would not be sufficiently developed for the kind of awareness, thought process or memory that I have referred to above. But it is only those who are determined to allow nothing more than a material biological reality whose understandings must be confined in this way and the question is the same as we have already tackled with reference to intra-uterine life and Verny's 'neurological' and 'extraneurological' memory. Different levels of consciousness co-exist within the human state, and may interact in different ways at different stages of human development.

It will be evident that in this chapter I have not attempted to give any detailed 'prescription' for a psychic and spiritual birth, nor suggested any particular type of meditation or prayer or given any exercises for psychic development. At the end of this chapter will be found some addresses which may be helpful. There is also a bibliography, although it does not include books which describe in detail how to develop psychically. Although I have been at pains to emphasise that psychic abilities are available to all of us, and that their development is within our own control, nonetheless it is necessary to ensure that any actual communication with the world of spirit is undertaken with the right sort of help and protection, and in the service of love, and this is best found in apprenticeship with an experienced medium or teacher.

I have tried, with many gaps and much paucity of understanding, to emphasise the fact that birth is so much more than a physical or even emotional event and that human life is not merely an end in itself. In this connection I remember our daughter's 'christening': a beautiful service attended not only by those who welcomed her into this life, but also by those friends and helpers from the world of spirit who were 'seeing her off' on her latest venture into human existence. I hope that I have also managed to emphasise that the spirit is so much stronger than the flesh! If we have done all that we can to ensure for our child a healthy birth without unnecessary intervention and with due sensitivity, and nevertheless find that (for example) induction or caesarean section is required, or breast feeding is impossible, we can use that same sensitivity, love and spiritual awareness to heal any of the damage that may have been done and to help the child to cope with the results and become strong. Most of us cannot be sure of arranging absolutely everything exactly as we feel would be best for our babies, but we can help them to grow spiritually strong within themselves which of course is the only reliable approach to ensuring their well-being in the long term.

Implicit I hope in what I have written is the understanding that we do have choice in this life. While we may choose to come here to enter into certain experiences, it seems that there are many different conditions which can offer us the same or a similar experience and it is by no means certain at the outset which of these conditions we will enter into or indeed whether we will enter into any of the required conditions at all. This is why it is necessary and worthwhile to try to approach the intra-uterine lives and the births of our children with the most sensitive mental and spiritual outlook available to each one of us as parents. At each stage of a human being's development, especially at these delicate beginnings, we must try to ensure the best possible psychic and spiritual as well as physical conditions and opportunities. We need the best possible vehicles to advance that new and more comprehensive view of the world towards which psychical science and spiritual awareness are pointing.

REFERENCES

1 See Christopher Lewis, letter in *The School Science Review*, vol. 60, no. 213, p. 793, 1979.

2 Denis Kelsey and Joan Grant, *Many Lifetimes*, Doubleday & Co., New York, 1967; Pocket Book edition, 1968, p. 6. This particular quote from Joan Grant would come under the heading of 'far memory': in other words, she is one of those rare people who can remember previous incarnations. She has also written autobiography (specifically: in this book quoted) in the more usual sense of the word. While some of what she has written from far memory can certainly be corroborated by independent sources, some obviously cannot, and such work must therefore be evaluated in the spirit of 'proof', appropriate to the psychic or supra-mechanistic world-view, outlined below, pp. 79.

3 Examples are the work of Dr Gertrude Schmeidler, or Russel Targ and Harold Puthoff, but there are many others; see *Research in Parapsychology 1982*, ed. W. G. Roll *et al*, Scarecrow Press, 1984.

4 Lawrence LeShan, 'No graven images: psychical science *is* modern science', published in two parts in *Light* (Journal of the College of Psychic Studies), spring 1985, pp. 15–24 and summer 1985, pp. 51–6.

5 Lawrence, LeShan, *Clairvoyant Reality: Towards a General Theory of the Paranormal*, Turnstone Press, 1980, p. 13.

6 See also David Lorimer, *Survival? Body, Mind and Death in the Light of Psychic Experience*, Routledge & Kegan Paul, 1984.

7   Lawrence LeShan, *From Newton to ESP: Parapsychology and the Challenge of Modern Science*, Turnstone Press, 1984. Also Ken Wilber (ed.) *Quantum Questions: Mystical Writings of the World's Great Physicists*, Shambhala Publications, 1984. See Lawrence LeShan, *Clairvoyant Reality: Towards a General Theory of the Paranormal*, Turnstone Press, 1980, for a fruitful way forward, both for research and for the uses (specifically healing) to which the fruits of research may be put.

8   'No graven images', *op. cit.*, spring, pp. 22–4, 1985.

9   W. Penfield, *The Mystery of the Mind*, Princeton University Press, (USA), pp. 71–7, 85–90, 1975.

10 Thomas Verny with John Kelly, *The Secret Life of the Unborn Child*, Summit Books, 1981 and Sphere Books, 1982.

11 Verny, *op. cit.* pp. 30–9. See also Penny Simkin, 'Stress, pain and catecholamines in labour', unpublished typescript of talk at Active Birth Conference, Wembley, London, spring 1983 and Ashley Montagu, *Life Before Birth*, New American Library, 1977, especially chs. XI and XIII.

12 See, for example, Arthur Guirdham, *The Cathars and Reincarnation*, Neville Spearman, 1970, *We Are One Another*, Neville Spearman, 1974. *A Foot in Both Worlds*, Neville Spearman 1973, and others. Guirdham, a doctor (psychiatrist), has painstakingly checked the details of remembered lifetimes (his own and others') against historical facts to reach his conviction about reincarnation. Ian Wilson, *Reincarnation?*, Penguin Books, 1982 — this is a de-bunking exercise. Peter and Mary Harrison, *Life Before Birth, Reincarnation: True or False?*, Futura, 1983. Helen Wambach, *Reliving Past Lives*, Hutchinson 1979 and *Life Before Life*, Bantam Books, 1979: evidence from hypnotic regression. Gladys T. McGarey, *Born To Live: A Holistic Approach to Childbirth*, Gabriel Press (USA), 1980 — written by a doctor whose experiences have led her to understand reincarnation. Denys Kelsey and Joan Grant, *Many Lifetimes, op. cit.*, ch. 2 — Kelsey, physician and psychiatrist, arrived at his belief in reincarnation not through dogma or doctrine but through a series of experiences in dealing with his patients which were acceptable to his intellect. Some of the great religions of course also have traditions about reincarnation, but this is usually a somewhat different type of evidence and has to be assessed according to whether or not it helps the individual to make sense of things. See also W. zur Linden, *A Child is Born*, Rudolf Steiner Press, 1980, for the views of anthroposophists and Rudolf Steiner on reincarnation.

13 For a discussion of the evidence for and against survival of death by a person of integrity, see Paul Beard, *Survival of Death*, first published 1966, 3rd impression 1983, Pilgrims Book Services, Norwich. For near-death experiences, see Dr Raymond Moody, *Life After Life*, Mockingbird Books (USA), 1975 and *Reflections on Life After Life*, Corgi Books, 1978. For accounts from the spirit world see, for example, Helen Greaves, *Testimony of Light*, The Churches' Fellowship for Psychical and Spiritual Studies, 1969, or Cynthia Sandys and Rosamond Lehmann, *The Awakening Letters*, Neville Spearman, 1978.

14 W. Y. Evans-Wentz (ed.), *The Tibetan Book of the Dead*, Oxford University Press, 1927 (3rd edition, 1957).

15 See Gladys T. McGarey, *op. cit.*, for further light on this subject.

16 Gladys T. McGarey, *op. cit.*, ch. 7.

17 There are many books on the psychic uses of colour, and colour healing. One to try is Anne Wilson and Lilla Bek, *What Colour are You?*, Turnstone Press, 1981.

18 *Gently Born* (Matthew Manning Centre, 39 Abbeygate Street, Bury St Edmunds, Suffolk) is a tape by Gilly Neill which includes some visualisation exercises for pregnancy and one for labour. There are also guided breathing exercises for labour which I would not necessarily recommend for someone who wishes to act intuitively.

19 Kelsey and Grant, *op. cit.*, p. 186.

20 Helen Wambach, *Life Before Life*, Bantam Books, 1979, p. 125 — written by a psychologist who became interested in reincarnation and the birth experience and used hypnosis in her research.

21 See Arthur Guirdham, *The Psyche in Medicine*, Neville Spearman, 1978, ch. 2.

22 See C. W. Leadbeater, *The Chakras*, Quest Books, 1974. First published by the Theosophical Publishing House in 1927, this book remains a classic. Also Geoffrey Hodson, *The Miracle of Birth*, Quest Books, 1981, especially p. 87 ff, 'The mechanism of consciousness' for the chakras. This is a clairvoyant study of the development of a human embryo by a well-known psychic and theosophist and was first published in 1929. The best 'proof' to which many of us can subject his descriptions will be provided by our own inner resonance or note of judgement, i.e. does it make sense to us, does it 'feel' right, have we had similar experiences or seen similar things? But even without accepting every single word that is written, readers may nevertheless find it truly illuminating and salutary, partly because such information is so lacking in our culture.

23 Helen Wambach, *op. cit.*, ch. VII.
24 *Ibid*, p. 126.
25 Kelsey and Grant, *op. cit.*, pp. 152–4.
26 Joseph Chilton Pearce, *Magical Child: Rediscovering Nature's Plan for Our Children*, Paladin Books, 1979, p. 51.

RECOMMENDED READING

Apart from a few titles which I think are particularly useful, the following books are additional to those accompanying the text. I have particularly borne in mind those who may be interested in learning about the relevance of psychic research to the meaning of human experience, as opposed to its ability to prove itself by fitting into the restricted field of laboratory experiments.

Paul Beard, *Survival of Death*, Pilgrims Book Services, first published 1966, third impression 1983.

Fritjof Capra, *The Turning Point: Science, Society and the Rising Culture*, Wildwood House, 1982.

But see critique of Capra and other 'new-age' writers by Ken Wilber, in his book *Quantum Questions: Mystical Writings of the World's Great Physicists*, Shambhala Publications, 1984, Preface and Introduction. Here he points out the dangers of attempting to 'prove' a mystical world-view through modern physics: 'If today's physics supports mysticism, what happens when tomorrow's physics replace it?' (p. x).

Geoffrey Hodson, *The Miracle of Birth: A Clairvoyant Study of a Human Embryo*, The Theosophical Publishing House, First Edition 1929, Quest edition, 1981.

R. D. Laing, *The Voice of Experience: Experience, Science and Psychiatry*, Allen Lane, 1982.

Lawrence LeShan, *Clairvoyant Reality: Towards A General Theory of the Paranormal*, Turnstone Press Ltd, 1980. (First edition published as *The Medium, The Mystic and the Physicist*, 1974.)

From Newton to ESP: Parapsychology and the Challenge of Modern Science, Turnstone Press Ltd, 1984.

'No Graven Images: Psychical Science IS Modern Science', published in two parts in *Light* (Journal of the College of Psychic Studies), pp. 15–24, spring 1985 and pp. 51–6, summer 1985.

K. Ramakrishna Rao (ed.), *The Basic Experiments in Parapsychology*, McFarland, 1984.

G. N. M. Tyrrell, *The Personality of Man*, Penguin Books, 1947 — a classic on psychical research.

USEFUL ADDRESSES

The College of Psychic Studies, 16 Queensberry Place, London SW7 2EB.01-589-3292.
Membership, mediums, healing, meetings and courses, quarterly journal entitled *Light*, recommended booklist, sells books (will post books), library. Also available to non-members.
The Religious Experience Research Unit, Manchester College, Oxford OX1 3TD. 0865-243006.
This is in the process of making a systematic and objective study of people's descriptions of their moments of spiritual awareness, cutting across religious or cultural backgrounds, and considering the evolutionary significance of such awareness. They would be interested in hearing from anyone who has passed through such 'spiritual' events during the childbearing period, and they have already received some accounts from that time (for example, of out-of-the-body or near-death experiences). Publications list available.
White Eagle Lodge, New Lands, Brewells Lane, Rake, Liss, Hampshire GU33 7HY. 0730-893300. Also has a London address and local groups around the country. Help for people to realise the reality of the spirit within, and the reality of the spirit world. Healing, meditation, etc., according to guidance from White Eagle, including some insight into reincarnation. Library. Available to non-members.
The West London Birth Centre, 7 Waldemar Avenue, London W13 9PZ. 01-579-9584. Holds list of birth centres/groups/teachers around the country and might have information about those with a leaning towards matters intuitive, spiritual, etc. Also holds information about the Birth Centre Teachers' Course, which includes a session on psychic and spiritual aspects of birth.
The Psychic News Bookshop, 20 Earlham Street, London WC2H 9LW. 01-240-3032.
Watkins Books Ltd, 19–21 Cecil Court, Charing Cross Road, London WC2N 4EZ. 01-836-2182

PART TWO

The Alternatives

The wisdom and compassion a woman can intuitively experience in childbirth can make her a source of healing and understanding for other women.

Ina May Gaskin

Know your rights:
a parents' guide to birth

BEVERLEY BEECH

The majority of parents have very little idea of their rights with regard to childbirth. Many of them believe that the moment they set foot inside a hospital they have to do as they are told, no matter how much they disagree with the treatment proposed. The consumer groups have long been familiar with women's complaints about hospital treatment during labour and birth. These complaints include being forced to accept routine procedures against their will; fathers being sent out of the room whilst certain examinations are made (or even being excluded from the birth); babies being bottle fed by staff when the mother has expressed her desire to breast feed; babies taken away from their mothers against her wishes. In addition to all this, many women are unable to arrange to have their babies in the place of their choice, that is if they realise that they have any choice. As a result, parents began to question and investigate their rights in law.

Parents' rights in maternity care are not defined in any one official document. There is only one (lay) publication on the subject, *The Health Rights Handbook for Maternity Care*.[1] Until recently, it was widely believed that a woman admitted to hospital for maternity care had fewer rights than any other sane patient entering a British hospital. It was assumed that when a woman entered hospital for maternity care, she assented to whatever treatment was considered necessary BY THE SIMPLE ACT OF WALKING THROUGH THE DOOR. The reason behind this attitude lay with the Medical Defence Union. In their booklet 'Consent to Treatment',[2] published in 1974, they made the following statement:

The Union does not consider that a maternity patient need give her written consent to any operative or manipulative procedures that are normally associated with childbirth. When she enters hospital for her confinement it can be assumed that she assents to any necessary procedure, including the administration of local, general or other anaesthetic.

The Association for Improvements in the Maternity Services (AIMS) decided to question this assumption and sought legal advice on the matter. Their lawyers replied that they did not believe that the Medical Defence Union statement would stand up in a court of law. Since AIMS drew attention to this statement, the Medical Defence Union has revised its booklet and withdrawn the above paragraph. This attitude, however, still prevails and results in women being given treatment to which they do not consent. Many doctors will not receive the new edition and will remain in ignorance of the change. Furthermore, at the present time, a London teaching hospital actually incorporates the above statement in its maternity notes.

In order to make the position absolutely clear for all pregnant woman it is worth now stating the legal position: treatment cannot be given to any pregnant woman without her consent. *Any doctor or midwife giving treatment after the mother has refused leaves him/herself open to a charge of assault.* The only possible exception would be where a true emergency occurred, but even then the staff would have to show that there was insufficient time to explain their proposed actions to the mother. Furthermore, if the mother gives consent ahead of time and then changes her mind, her views must be respected. For example; a woman signs a consent form which states that she agrees to have an epidural. The anaesthetist arrives to insert it, by which time the mother realises that she can cope without it and states that she has changed her mind. The anaesthetist cannot then go ahead with the treatment, to do so would amount to assault. Giving consent ahead of time does not remove your right to change your mind.

The National Health Service was set up originally to provide a service for individuals who required health care. Unfortunately, as far as maternity care is concerned, it has developed in certain areas into an automated conveyor belt. Few parents are aware that they are able to exercise anything more than the very minimum of choice. The following is an explanation of the choices available to you and details of just what rights you have.

CONFIRMING THE PREGNANCY

It is possible to test urine 14 days after a missed period in order to confirm pregnancy. Some doctors insist that a woman has this test and may charge for it. If you do not want to have the test done then you can refuse.

CHOOSING A GP

A woman can choose a GP to look after her during her pregnancy and he/she may be a different doctor from the GP with whom she is usually registered. She can sign on for pregnancy, intra- and postnatal care only and receive all other care from her usual GP.

Note: some GPs object to women doing this and may threaten to or actually remove them from their list. However, in the case of a GP taking you on for maternity care only, once he has done so he cannot remove you without your permission or without having first applied to the Family Practitioner Committee for permission to do so. Should that happen then the FPC will have to find you another GP. You should contact AIMS immediately if this happens. If you find that the GP you have chosen to look after you during your pregnancy is not to your liking, then you can change him by writing to the FPC, informing them of your decision and asking them to find you another doctor.

CHOOSING A MIDWIFE

Women seeking a home birth have a limited amount of choice regarding the midwife. Usually, the midwives are attached to a GP's practice, but the system varies from area to area and, in some, the Director of Nursing Services (Midwifery) or the

Divisional Nursing Officer will assign a midwife to undertake a woman's care. If, however, the mother does not care for the midwife assigned to her, she has a right to refuse to be attended by her. She should apply to the Director of Nursing Services (Midwifery) for another midwife to be assigned. In hospital, women have less choice and are rarely able to choose the midwife ahead of delivery unless they are having a domino delivery. If, however, during the labour the mother is not happy with her midwife, then she can refuse to be attended by her and insist that another midwife be allocated.

CHOOSING AN OBSTETRICIAN

In order to make a decision about which obstetrician with whom to entrust your care, you will need to find out about his/her attitudes and policies. This is not an easy task and you will find more information about this in Ros Claxton's article 'Natural Birth in Hospital'. Although you do not have a right to insist upon seeing a particular obstetrician, you do have a right to refuse to see one. Early in your pregnancy your GP will refer you to an obstetrician (should you decide that you want consultant care). If he is a sympathetic GP he will take notice of your preferences and act accordingly. If he is reluctant to refer you to the obstetrician of your choice you can either refuse to see the said obstetrician until a change is made or else you can change your GP and then ask the new one to refer you to the obstetrician of your choice.

If during your pregnancy you discover that the obstetrician is not acceptable to you, then you can go back to your GP and ask him to refer you to another obstetrician. GPs are usually very reluctant to do this because you are, in effect, criticising the obstetrician. If your GP refuses to co-operate, then you should write to the Chairman of the District Health Authority and the Chairman of the Regional Health Authority telling them why you refuse to see the obstetrician in question. Changing obstetricians is not generally an easy procedure and you should contact AIMS for help and support.

Women returning to the same maternity unit in which they gave birth to a previous child are usually referred to the same consultant. If you do not wish to see him/her then you can ask to be referred to one of the other consultants. If this fails then follow the procedure outlined above.

WHERE TO GIVE BIRTH TO YOUR BABY

In theory, parents are supposed to have choice about where to give birth. In most areas, however, this choice has been severely restricted and you may have to argue very strongly to obtain the kind of booking you want. Under the NHS the choices are:

GP unit birth
Domino delivery
6—8-hour discharge from either a GP unit or a consultant unit
Obstetric unit birth
Home birth.

GP unit birth

Despite the statistics showing that GP unit births are far safer for 'low risk' women than any other hospital birth, the health authorities are still working furiously to close them down. Consultant obstetricians draw up criteria for admission to GP units and this usually ensures that few women are eligible. The procedure for booking into a GP unit is the same as for booking into an obstetric unit. If you do not fit the narrowly defined category of 'low risk' women who are allowed to give birth in a GP unit, then you will have to argue your case in order to be admitted. If you are considered to be 'high risk', your GP will be under considerable pressure to send you to the obstetric unit. If he goes against the consultant's policies, then he risks retaliatory action from the consultant, and it is because of this that many GPs acquiese to the consultant's dictats.

If you want to give birth in a GP unit but have been told that you cannot, then ask for the reasons to be put in writing. You should write to the Chairman of the Regional Health Authority, the Chairman of the District Health Authority and the Community Health Council. Again, do not battle on alone, contact AIMS. It is possible to change the professional's minds, although it must be recognised that parents do not always succeed in this kind of dispute.

Domino scheme

Under this option, you will be cared for by your local midwife, both in and out of hospital. She will look after you ante-natally, and once you go into labour she will visit you at home and decide when you should go to hospital. She will help you give birth in hospital and, usually after a couple of hours, will take you home again. She will then look after you for the statutory ten days following the birth. Many women like this scheme because it means that they have their care from a midwife they know. If you are told that this scheme is 'not available in your area', ask for this to be put in writing. After you have received their response, write back informing them that this is the kind of care you want and you would appreciate it if they now would take the opportunity of introducing it! (And be sure you send copies of the correspondence to AIMS for their records.)

6-hour or 48-hour discharge

In some areas, parents are offered the choice of booking a 6-hour or a 48-hour discharge. This means that, providing the birth has been straightforward and without complications for you or your baby, you will be able to leave soon after the birth. The community midwife must then visit you for at least ten days after the birth. Some areas encourage this system, particularly for women who are expecting a second or subsequent baby. If this kind of arrangement is not on offer in your area, then write to the Director of Nursing Services (Midwifery) or the Divisional Nursing Officer at your local maternity unit asking them to arrange this service for you.

Obstetric unit birth

The majority of mothers do not encounter problems getting into an obstetric unit, generally the staff are only too keen for you to be there! There is a minority of women, however, who do have problems, they are the ones who want to go to an obstetric unit outside their area. Hospitals draw up arbitrary boundaries and if you happen to live outside that boundary you are sometimes refused admittance. This system not only reduces the choice available to women, but it also ensures that the obstetricians have a guaranteed number of customers, and women are not able to voice their opinions by taking their custom elsewhere. Although, in theory, you have the right to choose any maternity unit in the country for the birth of your baby, in practice you are restricted by the distances you can travel and by the artificial restrictions imposed by the health authorities.

If you are determined to be delivered in a particular hospital, then you can resolutely refuse your GP's offer of any other unit. He is responsible for finding you a suitable place in which to give birth. You can also write directly to the consultant at the unit of your choice, explaining why you particularly want to attend his hospital. If this fails, then you should write to the Regional Health Authority. This kind of argument should not be conducted without help and support, so do contact AIMS.

Length of stay in hospital

The majority of British women giving birth in hospital are expected to stay in for anything up to eight days post-natally. The mean length of post-natal stay is gradually decreasing and by 1978 it was 5.5 days. If you wish to stay for a specific length of time, that can be arranged when you book in. Once you have had your baby, you can always ask to be discharged earlier than your original booking if you wish (or you can discharge yourself). The community midwife then has a legal obligation to visit you at home, for at least ten days after the birth. This is important, because she will be able to detect problems that sometimes develop post-natally. If you are worried about the baby you can request a paediatric home visit.

Now that hospital care is being increasingly centralised, some of the large maternity units are finding that they do not have enough beds to go round and are solving this problem by discharging mothers early. Some mothers have been reluctant to leave, but have been told that they have to go. When you book into a hospital for x days, you are entering into a contract with them. If, however, they decide that they want you to leave early, or transfer to another unit post-natally, they cannot insist that you do so unless you agree. It is, therefore, better for women to book in for the full period of time and then discharge themselves early, rather than book in for a short stay and later try to persuade the staff to extend that period. As the health authority has a 'duty of care' (and the midwifery profession is legally bound to provide care for you for at least ten days after the birth), they cannot force you to leave if you do not want to go.

Early discharge

No matter how long you have booked for your stay in hospital, you can discharge yourself at any time. It is worth noting that an early discharge is sometimes looked upon with disfavour by the hospital staff who may require the mother to sign a form stating that she has discharged herself against medical advice. You are under no obligation to sign this form if you do not want to. Croydon Area Health Authority took this one step further and required mothers to sign the following:

> I understand and acknowledge that as my discharge from hospital was not foreseen by them (sic) I do not hold the Community Midwifery Service of Croydon Area Health Authority responsible for providing their usual maternity follow-up facilities for me.

A health authority has a statutory obligation to provide the services of a midwife for up to at least ten days after the birth of a baby. Croydon AHA's action was illegal; they subsequently withdrew this form after pressure from AIMS.

At one London hospital, paediatricians recently decided that they would not allow babies to be discharged under 48 hours. They refused to say that they had such a policy or why it was being enforced, but it very successfully prevented women from having a domino delivery. Neither were the women aware that they could discharge themselves and their babies at any time, with or without the approval of the paediatricians. Only in very exceptional circumstances could a paediatrician insist on keeping a baby in hospital. To do so, he would have to obtain a court order to show that the baby's life would be at risk if he/she were to go home.

Home birth

Unfortunately, a woman who wants a home birth may well find that she receives little or no professional support and inaccurate information on this option.

1 Legal aspects

You are legally entitled to have your baby at home, irrespective of your circumstances. Even if it is your first baby, or you are an 'elderly' mother, or have had a previous breech or caesarean, the decision and choice are yours. The government reply to the Short Report[3] states:

> Where, however, a mother wishes to have a home confinement, despite the medical arguments against it, health authorities are expected to provide a domiciliary confinement service that is as safe as circumstances permit. Doctors and midwives can help ensure that she makes an informed choice, but they cannot make the choice for her.

The District Health Authority is legally obliged to provide a midwife to attend a woman wishing to give birth at home. In fact, according to her 'conditions of service' as required by the English National Board, a midwife called when a woman is in labour is obliged to attend. It is not necessary to obtain the services of a doctor in order to have a home birth. In some areas, women are told that the midwife is unable to attend them without a doctor. This is not an accurate statement of the legal situation.

It is not, however, illegal for a woman to be unattended or to deliver the baby herself. It is only illegal for anyone other than a medical professional to assist or attend her; 'attend' in this instance means 'to give professional attention to'. This definition is currently being debated and could come to mean 'being there in a supervisory capacity'. This aspect of the law was originally formulated to prevent unqualified midwives from attending women, and one of the reasons it is unclear at present is that it is being applied in a new way to harass home birth parents. In 1982, Brian Radley was prosecuted and fined for delivering his child; it is interesting to note that had his wife declared that she delivered the baby herself there would not have been a prosecution. It is a sad reflection of midwifery care in this country that any woman should feel that she prefers to have her baby without midwifery assistance. Ideally, no woman should be unattended in labour. If you are aware of your rights and have the support and advice of the birth groups, you should be able to ensure that you get the kind of care you want.

2   The 'Flying Squad' service

The 'Flying Squad' or Emergency Obstetric Unit was originally set up to provide emergency obstetric care for all pregnant and recently delivered women. Unfortunately there is no statutory obligation for the District Health Authority to provide a flying squad and the policy towards and quality of the service differs from area to area. It is argued that, since the majority of women now give birth in hospital, there is no longer a need for this service. However, examination of the activities of the flying squads reveals that very few calls are made to women with *booked* home births. The majority of calls are made to women who have ante-partum or post-partum haemorrhage, retained placenta, miscarriage, or else the baby was born before arrival in hospital. Thus, the withdrawal of the flying squad facility endangers the health and well-being of every pregnant woman and her baby. You should ask your local Community Health Council to check the provision of this service.

3   The 'high risk' category

In order to severely restrict the numbers of home births, consultant obstetricians have introduced 'guidelines' with which midwives and GPs are expected to comply. In some areas the following women would automatically be defined as 'high risk' and in need of a hospital delivery: all first-time mothers, women expecting their third or subsequent child, all women over the age of 30 and women who had 'complications' with a previous pregnancy (even if these 'complications' were caused by medical intervention). It is often difficult for a woman to determine whether she has been classified as 'high risk' because the authorities wish to prevent home births, or whether she truly has problems. If in doubt you should ask for the diagnosis to be put in writing and then immediately contact the Society to Support Home Confinements, AIMS or your local Birth Centre. Even if a woman is truly 'high risk' the decision about place of birth rests with her and the health authority still has to provide a midwife if she decides to stay at home. The midwife concerned should then take reasonable precautions so that if a crisis occurs she is in the best position to deal with it. A midwife cannot be sued for negligence merely because she attended a high-risk woman at home. It would have to be demonstrated that her procedure was negligent.

4 Responsibility for a home birth

Some health authorities seek to intimidate women by producing 'disclaimers of responsibility' which suggest that the responsibility for a home birth rests entirely with her and that, should anything go wrong, the professionals will not be liable. Women may be required to sign a form along the following lines:

> I have been advised by my general practitioner and midwife not to have a home confinement in view of the risk to myself and my baby. The principal risks in my case have been explained to me and I understand that this does not exclude other serious and dangerous hazards and that, as a result, my general practitioner is not prepared to provide medical cover. Nonetheless, I wish to have a home confinement and I accept the risks involved to both myself and my child.

This paper has no legal significance and no woman is under any obligation to sign it. (One woman put an asterisk by 'hazards' and added a footnote: 'the serious and dangerous hazards of hospital birth have not, however, been explained to me by my GP or midwife' and then signed the form!) These disclaimers are simply a form of harassment and neither the mother nor the midwife (provided she had acted in a fully professional manner) could be held responsible if something went wrong.

5   Obtaining medical assistance for home birth

If your own doctor is unsympathetic to home birth you can,
for the period of your pregnancy, register with another GP for
obstetric care only. Your local library has a list of GPs in the
area (those with GPO after their name give obstetric care). However, you do not legally need a GP in order to have a home birth
and since searching for one who will cover you can prove very
exhausting and frustrating, the Society to Support Home Confinements suggest that you book a local authority midwife instead.
This is done by writing to the Director of Nursing Services
(Midwifery) (see address in telephone book under 'Health'), using
the standard booking letter put together by the Society to Support
Home Confinements:

> Dear Sir/Madam,
> I expect a baby in . . . and intend to give birth at home. My
> GP (give name and address) feels unable to offer me medical
> care for a home confinement and I shall not attempt to find
> a GP who will take me on. Accordingly, I should be obliged
> if you would make the necessary arrangements for a midwife
> to undertake my pregnancy and delivery care in my own home.
>
>   I accept full responsibility for my decision to give birth at
> home and I know that you accept the responsibility of pro-
> viding me with a competent midwife, fully backed up by
> such facilities as are necessary to make home confinement as
> safe as possible.
>
> I look forward to your kind attention
> Yours faithfully
> . . . .
> Copies to:
> District Medical Officer
> Chairman District Health Council
> Secretary Community Health Council
> Local Member of Parliament

You should keep precisely to the above format, send all the copies
and keep one for yourself. There is no known instance where
service was refused after having been requested in this manner.

6 Examples of difficulties

Birth groups throughout the country receive numerous enquiries from women who experience difficulties in obtaining a home birth. The following examples are not uncommon:

a) A GP strikes a woman and her family off his/her list because she persists with the home birth option against advice. If this happens, write to the Family Practitioner Committee complaining about harassment and ask for another GP to be allocated to you (you can use any GP on an emergency basis in the meantime). If you have booked with a GP for maternity care he cannot strike you off without your permission — should he do so, then write immediately to the Family Practitioner Council complaining about breach of contract and contact AIMS.

b) The midwife shows very little enthusiasm for home birth and eventually finds some pretext for steering a woman towards hospital. If you are unhappy with the midwife you have been allocated, then you have a right to refuse to be attended by her and can apply to the Director of Nursing Services (Midwifery) for another midwife to be assigned. Request a fully competent midwife who is happy attending a woman at home.

c) A midwife will sometimes suggest that certain services will not be available to women booked for home birth. This is not true, all the facilities normally available to pregnant women booked for hospital are also available to home birth mothers via their assigned midwife who has direct access to the hospital for blood tests, oestriol tests, scans, etc. Clearly you cannot be expected to be provided with an epidural at home, but other drugs and equipment such as gas and air and oxygen for the baby should all be routinely available. Any suggestion that this might not be the case should be followed up by a letter to the Director of Nursing Services (Midwifery) asking for clarification.

d) One of the commonest ways in which a woman can be persuaded to give up her plans for home birth is the discovery of 'complications' in the ante-natal period. Examples include: the baby being 'too big' or 'too small' for dates; the baby is in the 'wrong' position; blood pressure is 'too high' or 'too low'. If medical problems do occur during your pregnancy you can always ask for a second opinion, plus contacting the birth groups. Often such problems fail to develop and if your pregnancy nutrition has been excellent you can have greater confidence in your health.

ANTE-NATAL CARE

Ante-natal care can take place in an obstetric unit, a GP unit, a GP's surgery or in your own home. The Midwives' Rules require that a woman is checked every 4 weeks until she is 28 weeks pregnant, every 2 weeks until she is 36 weeks pregnant and then every week until the baby is born. If you are fit and healthy, the midwife or doctor may decide that they do not wish to see you quite so often. If you have a problem, they may decide that they wish to see you more often. If you find that, in between appointments, you wish to see them, then you should telephone them and make another appointment.

In a good ante-natal clinic you will have plenty of time for discussion. If you do not know why you are being given a specific test or why you are being asked certain questions, then do ask for an explanation. Whilst the health authorities are obliged to provide ante-natal facilities there is no obligation for a woman to attend them. Obviously, it is recognised that good ante-natal care is of considerable benefit but one does question the usefulness of attending a bad ante-natal clinic, for example, where you never see the same person, or small group of people twice; where the woman has little more than a few minutes with the midwife or doctor; and where she has to wait very long periods of time before she is attended. If you are unhappy about the ante-natal clinic you are attending, then you can write to the Divisional Director of Nursing Services (Midwifery) at the hospital and inform them that unless changes are made you do not intend attending again and would appreciate it if they would arrange for you to receive your ante-natal care either in your own home or at the local GP's surgery.

The type of ante-natal care you receive is often dependent upon the kind of booking you have made. You may have 'shared care'; this describes care shared between your doctor or midwife and the hospital. If your own doctor does not offer this service, then you can, for the period of your pregnancy, change to another doctor who does. If you have booked for a home birth, then you are more likely to receive care from your local community midwife, although sometimes care is shared between the midwife and the GP. If you are having a hospital birth, you may receive total ante-natal care from the hospital. Many 'high risk' women are automatically referred for total hospital care. Some of these women would benefit greatly if they received the continuity of community care. If you are defined as high risk, you could ask for the reasons and request local ante-natal care. There has been increasing criticism of the overcrowded ante-natal clinics in hospitals, and some hospital doctors are now holding ante-natal clinics in local health clinics or in the surgery of a group practice.

Ante-natal tests

Some women have experienced problems when they have been referred by the midwife for tests without reference to the GP. The health authority is obliged to provide this service and any woman or midwife who has this problem should contact AIMS immediately. Many health authorities now have a policy of routine ultrasound examination during pregnancy in spite of the lack of evidence about its long-term safety. You have every right to refuse ultrasound scanning if you do not want it. Women having ultrasound examinations have sometimes found that their partners have been excluded from attending. Partners have no statutory right to be present, but you could point out to the staff that unless your partner is given permission to attend you refuse to have the examination done. The Maternity Services Advisory Committee Report[4] recommends that 'the reasons for procedures and tests and their results and meaning should be explained to each woman'. Unfortunately, it makes no mention of explaining the pregnant woman's need to have a companion with her during what, for some, can be a stressful experience.

Amniocentesis is another ante-natal test which can be carried out in pregnancy in order to establish whether or not the baby is suffering from Down's Syndrome. The risk of carrying a Down's baby does not begin to rise steeply until after the mother is 35 years old and it increases to only one in 200 born to mothers age 38. If you are a mature mother and have been offered this test, you will be offered a termination if you are found to be carrying a Down's baby. The decision whether or not to have the test carried out rests with the mother, as does the decision about termination.

Some women have found that when they particularly want a specific test to be carried out, it has been refused. One does not have a right to specific treatment but if a mother feels that she has particular circumstances that justify such a test then she can ask for it to be done. If she is refused she should either ask her GP if he can arrange for it to be done, or else write to the Chairman of the District Health Authority stating her reasons and asking them to act. If she still meets with refusal, she should write to the Chairman of the Regional Health Authority and also contact AIMS who will be able to advise her further.

Chorionic Villus Sampling

Chorionic Villus Sampling (CVS) is a new procedure which has been developed to detect some fetal abnormalities (such as Down's syndrome) early in pregnancy. It involves passing a thin tube through the cervix (neck of the womb) while an ultrasound scan guides it to the right place. A tiny fragment from the edge of the chorionic tissue is gently sucked into the tube and removed, and sent to a laboratory for testing (the chorionic tissue is what surrounds the embryo early in pregnancy and some of it will later develop to form the placenta).

The Medical Research Council is currently carrying out a randomised controlled trial of this procedure, and in order to have a CVS a woman would need to volunteer to take part in the trial. This means that she has a 50–50 chance of having CVS, or amniocentesis (depending upon the group to which she is randomly allocated).

As the test is carried out early in pregnancy (at about 8–10 weeks) women will be offered an early abortion if they are found to be carrying a damaged baby. Women who have previously had a damaged baby and mid-term abortion will be able to choose CVS if they wish.

The test will not be available outside the randomised controlled trial. It is hoped, therefore, that the value of CVS will be assessed in the shortest possible time. At the moment it is known that the miscarriage rate following CVS is higher than that following amniotomy.

The trial organisers, in conjunction with seven consumer groups, have produced an information leaflet which will be available to any woman considering taking part in the trial. Copies of the leaflet are available from the National Perinatal Epidemiology Unit, The Radcliffe Infirmary, Oxford.

THE BIRTH

Routine hospital procedures

In many hospitals certain procedures are carried out routinely during childbirth, regardless of whether a woman has a special need for such treatment. The routine use of procedures such as shaving the perineum, enemas, inductions, acceleration of labour, fetal monitoring, episiotomies, syntometrine injections, etc., have been widely criticised. You should inform the hospital or your birth attendants if you do not agree to a particular procedure being carried out. Remember, treatment given without consent can amount to assault.

Companion in labour

The Short Report[5] recommended that women should be able to choose up to two people to accompany them in labour. There is, however, no legal obligation for the hospital to agree to the Short Report's suggestion and indeed one father who wanted to stay with his wife at a Welsh hospital was ejected by the police in spite of the mother pleading for him to be allowed to stay. In another hospital a woman was better informed; as they hustled her husband out she screamed, 'If he goes, I go!' and threatened to get off the delivery bed. He was allowed to stay!

Sometimes, a partner will be asked to leave the room when a procedure or examination is required to take place. The Maternity Services Advisory Committee Report[6] now advises that, 'If the father is to be present during the labour and birth, the midwife should explain and advise on the role he might play. The father should not be asked to leave the room during examinations if he and the mother are content for him to stay.' This tactic is often used as a means of excluding the father and then staff 'forget' to ask him to come back in.

Positions in labour and delivery

The Maternity Services Advisory Committee Report[7] states: 'During early labour, the mother should be free to adopt the position in which she feels most comfortable, consistent with her safety and that of her baby. She should be free to walk about unless there are overriding medical reasons for her to be in bed.' (The staff should explain exactly what these reasons are.) The report goes on: 'During delivery, the mother should adopt the position which she feels is most comfortable and effective, provided this allows the safe birth of the baby. The midwife or doctor attending her should endeavour to adapt to the position the mother wishes to take.' In a letter to AIMS on the question of midwives' ability to deliver in alternative positions, Ruth Ashton, General Secretary of the Royal College of Midwives, has stated:[8]

Midwives have the necessary knowledge, understanding and skills to manage a labour in the squatting position. Sadly, and for a multitude of reasons, many midwives are either lacking in confidence or are too rigid to draw upon these when faced with an alternative way of assisting a delivery. Midwives do not need information about the management of any type of labour or delivery. They have all the knowledge and understanding they require. They need to be encouraged to be adaptable and they need the confidence to believe that their skills and knowledge are the basis of adaptability.

Stitching an episiotomy or tear

Following a home birth, it is sometimes necessary for a woman to be stitched after an episiotomy or tear. It is not necessary for her to be taken to hospital, the midwife or GP can do this at home unless the cut or tear is a large one, in which instance it is better carried out in hospital. In many hospitals, medical students are required to do the stitching. Stitching a woman's perineum is a skilled job and should not be undertaken by students who have no experience of stitching. If medical students need experience, let them obtain it in a casualty department stitching up arms and legs, rather than practising on the most sensitive part of a woman's body. If you need stitching, then insist on being stitched by a midwife qualified to do this or at least by a registrar. Women booked for private deliveries sometimes are given an episiotomy (or forceps delivery) not because it was needed, but because the consultant will then be able to collect an extra fee from the private insurance schemes. They do not pay out if the delivery is without intervention! Women having private treatment should bear this in mind.

PARENTS' RIGHTS OVER THE CHILD

A child in hospital is still in the custody of his/her parents, whose rights over the child supersede the hospital's rights. The hospital, therefore, should not do anything to the child without informing the parents first. For example, babies are often given routine vitamin K injections in hospital without the mother being informed. When children are being cared for by the hospital, this is being done 'by the authority and on behalf of the parents who remain in a position to exercise powers of control should they wish to do so'.[9] Many hospitals routinely separate babies from their mothers after birth or put them into a nursery at night. No hospital has the right to do this without first obtaining the mother's permission. Neither should they give bottles to breast-fed babies if this is against the expressed wishes of the parents. In fact, this kind of behaviour could be defined as an assault on the baby. The only area of argument would be in an emergency, life-threatening situation and even then the correct procedure would be for the hospital to obtain a court order if the parents were in disagreement with them.

MEDICAL AND MIDWIFERY STUDENTS

A mother who does not wish to be attended by a medical or midwifery student has a right to refuse and she can also refuse to admit students whilst she is in labour or giving birth. One woman reported that the consultant asked her if she minded 'a student' coming and watching the birth. When she next looked up she discovered that there were at least fifteen people in the room. She was very embarassed but said nothing. She had every right to point out that she had agreed to one and insist that the others withdrew.

MALE MIDWIVES

All midwifery training schools have now to accept male midwives if they apply for training. It should be made clear to you, before you go into hospital, that you may be attended by a male midwife. You have a right to refuse to be attended by a male midwife (or by a male doctor). If this is the case, you should inform the hospital before you go into labour. If they arrive unannounced during your labour, you can ask them to leave.

CONSENT TO RESEARCH

You have an absolute right to refuse to take part in any research project. The medical/midwifery staff are obliged to give a full explanation of the research programme, only when the research is considered to be of 'no benefit'. When the research is considered to be 'of benefit', the profession is not obliged to give a full explanation. Before you book into any hospital you should ask them to inform you of any research programmes they are currently undertaking or considering undertaking. The least we can expect if we are to be used as 'guinea pigs' is that we give our informed consent if we are to agree to being used in any research project.

AMENITY BEDS

If you would prefer to have a room of your own in hospital, you can ask for an amenity bed. Not all hospitals have them, but those that do will charge a small fee for each day you are in the room. Amenity beds are usually allocated on the understanding that if an emergency occurs and they require the room, they will move you out to an ordinary ward.

HOME HELPS

A newly delivered mother has the right to expect a home help for up to ten days post-natally. The social services department has a legal obligation to provide one and maternity cases take priority, according to the NHS Act.[10] Some local authorities means test applicants (the charge varies from area to area) and others make no charge at all for this service. Application should be made to the local social services department. Some mothers are told that they have to have special circumstances which justify the provision of a home help, but this is not true.

It will be clear from the above information that enforcing your rights under the NHS system of health care is not always easy an matter. It can involve you in stressful situations which ideally should be avoided during pregnancy. If you do find yourself with problems, it is most important not to struggle on alone. Contact AIMS or your local birth group who can often offer you invaluable support and help you to sort things out. If you are ever in doubt about the validity of any decision you should always ask for reasons to be put in writing. Sometimes that request alone can result in a sudden change of attitude! If it does not you should send copies of the letter, with details of the dispute, to AIMS and the secretary of your local community health council.

If you are unhappy about treatment received, you should again contact both AIMS and the community health council. They will advise you about taking your complaint further. The Maternity Defence Fund was set up in 1982 to aid women wishing to take legal action where this seemed appropriate and further information can be obtained from the address below.

REFERENCES

1   *The Health Rights Handbook for Maternity Care*, Beverley Beech and Ros Claxton, Health Rights Project, 1983, available from Association for Improvements in the Maternity Services (address given below).
2   'Consent to Treatment', Medical Defence Union, 1974.
3   The Government Reply to the Short Report, HMSO, 3 December, 1980.
4   *Maternity Care in Action*, Part 2, 'Care during childbirth', 2nd Report of the Maternity Services Advisory Committee, HMSO, 1984.
5   Social Services Committee, 'Perinatal and neo-natal mortality', 2nd Report (The Short Report), House of Commons Paper 1979–80, 663/1, HMSO, London 1980.
6   Report of the Maternity Services Advisory Committee, *op. cit.*
7   Report of the Maternity Services Advisory Committee, *op. cit.*
8   Personal letter to Beverley Beech, Chairwoman of AIMS, 27 May, 1982.
9   Justice Cantley, Roger v. Exeter and Mid-Devon Hospital Management Committee, 1974.
10 National Health Service Act, 1977, Schedule 8, para. 3(1).

RECOMMENDED READING

Beverley Beech and Ros Claxton, *The Health Rights Handbook for Maternity Care*, Health Rights Project, 1983, address given below.

USEFUL ADDRESSES

AIMS — Association for Improvements in the Maternity Services, 163 Liverpool Road, London N1 0RF.
Maternity Defence Fund, 33, Castle Close, Henley-in-Arden, Warwickshire.
Health Rights, 157 Waterloo Road, London SE1 8XF.

Becoming assertive: how it can help you work with the medical profession

CHRISTINE BEELS

Assertiveness is a skill that some people seem to have been born with; they are both confident with themselves and caring of others, they don't attack and bully, or manipulate and grovel; they can make requests, yet seem to cope pretty well if they don't always get their own way. Most of us can manage to be like that some of the time, situations which one woman can't handle at all are quite straightforward for someone else. However, most of us are not able to assert our wishes, needs or interests when we are flat on our backs looking up at a doctor, or standing awkwardly at the other side of his desk waiting for him to raise his head from important paperwork. If you are one of the many of us who had meant to say, 'I'd like to talk to you when I'm dressed and feel more comfortable', or if you stand and stand on the other side of the desk and wait and wait until he looks up, but you couldn't get the sentence out, or just stood and fumed silently, then you might like to read on. You might also like to read on if you have rushed from the clinic in tears feeling humiliated and angry, or if you have rushed out shouting, 'I'm never coming here again, you treat me like a child/idiot/number on a file'. Maybe you just crawl away wondering what's wrong with you — all these kindly people ostensibly with only your welfare in mind — how dare you feel so ungrateful? There must be something wrong with you.

I was a childbirth teacher (for the National Childbirth Trust) for many years and wish that I had discovered the skills of assertive behaviour earlier than I did. We did spend many hours discussing how parents might best ask for what they wanted, or ask for their rights, and I hope that various helpful techniques emerged from collective wisdom, but I am sure that parents often suffered more indignity, sometimes humiliation, with subsequent loss of self-esteem, than it is right for human beings to expect to tolerate, particularly during the emotionally heightened and charged and amazing times of pregnancy and giving birth.

I am going to describe for you in this brief chapter some of the things I would generally say and offer for discussion when I hold assertiveness training sessions — usually a day or two days' concentrated and thoughtful work with several women's experiences to draw upon. Of necessity, I can only offer some guidelines here. There are advantages in practising assertive behaviour in a group which would also happen on a workshop session, but it is quite possible to read this chapter, follow the suggestions in it, especially the practical ones, think them through as they relate to you and begin to make changes in how you approach people and situations. A mirror (full length) to practise in front of is an optional extra, but a genuinely useful one.

I mentioned self-esteem earlier; that needs expanding a little. Many of us can think with no difficulty at all of all the 'bad' or wasteful things we have done, said or been in our lives, our stupidity, and foolishness, but ask us to write down '5 things I do better than most other people', followed by '3 things I have done in my life that I am really proud of' and many creative, imaginative and lovable women cannot think of anything to write at all — in fact, are often reduced to tears after sitting in front of a blank piece of paper for 10 minutes. There are always other women in the room who can find lots of praiseworthy things about others, too, but nothing about themselves! Think about how you might complete such a list. Then give yourself a bit of 'self talk' about you as a person who is entitled to express opinions, hold beliefs and values and, most importantly in our context, who has the right to ask for what she wants. There is no way in which someone who undervalues herself and undermines her rights or abilities can easily learn the skills of assertive behaviour.

HAVE I THE RIGHT TO BE ASSERTIVE?

Yes. A definition of assertive behaviour always includes something about rights — our own and other people's. The usual definition, found in most books, is: the right to stand up for my basic human rights without violating the basic human rights of others. This list of rights which is reproduced here is for your consideration. You probably won't agree with all — or even many — of the items on the list. What's important is for you to think carefully about what the list is saying. They all have validity for someone at some point. You might like to go through them with a friend.

1   The right to ask for what we want (realising that the other person has the right to say No).
2   The right to have opinions, feelings and emotions and to express them appropriately.
3   The right to make statements which have no logical basis and which we do not have to justify.
4   The right to make our own decisions and to cope with the consequences.
5   The right to choose whether or not to get involved in a problem someone brings to us.
6   The right not to know about something or to understand.
7   The right to make mistakes.
8   The right to want to be successful.
9   The right to change our mind.
10   The right to privacy.
11   The right to be alone and independent.
12   The right to change ourselves and to be an assertive person.

Some of these (perhaps particularly number 5) arouse feelings of unease and disquiet in people who are bothered by the apparent lack of concern for others implied there. But I would like to emphasise that an assertive person does not violate the basic human rights of others and always encourages and promotes assertive behaviour in other people. Number 2 is one which has particular poignancy for pregnant women and so I think does number 6. In order to join battle (which is how it so often seems) with the medical profession we have felt the need to not show human emotions lest these be either used against us, or seized on as an example of female irrationality, and we have also felt the need to be as medically well-informed as it is possible for a lay person to be. I am not saying that those two factors should not or need not apply to the assertive person, only that it would be great if they could in this context! Number 4 is the 'grey area' in which many women do wish to exercise their right and medical personnel equally wish to exercise their rights.

WHAT IS ASSERTIVE BEHAVIOUR?

Being assertive involves telling someone else what you want or what you would prefer to do, or have happen in such a way that you are not hostile or threatening or punitive, nor do you try to 'put the other person down'. Being assertive is not about getting what you want if it means trampling over other people. It is about being open and straightfoward about feelings and needs, being aware of them as they occur and dealing with them *appropriately*. That may mean being aware of the emotion we feel, rather than denying it but not using it to deny the rights of others, by shouting or weeping, for example. The key word is that behaviour should be appropriate, which means for instance that anger is not ruled out for the assertive person — sometimes it's absolutely fine to be angry, but, for example, it may be that a hospital ward is not the appropriate place to express even quite justifiable anger. A strong letter written afterwards or a session in the sister's or doctor's office may be more appropriate.

Sometimes people who are generally under-assertive and passive, find that anger comes bubbling to the surface in some quite inappropriate situations and that their level of anger was higher than necessary. Aggressive people use anger, annoyance, bullying words and gestures quite often as part of their 'normal' repertoire. Appropriate behaviour may also mean that you choose not to make an assertive response to a situation; you know you could, but you don't have to!

Aggressive behaviour involves expressing feelings and opinions, too, but in such a way that other people often feel threatened and uncomfortable. Being sarcastic, manipulative, wheedling, gossipy, etc., is aggressive behaviour too. Racist and sexist remarks are aggressive. Aggressive words and phrases include threats (You'd better . . . If you don't watch out . . .), put downs (Come on . . . You must be joking . . .), and evaluative comments (should, bad, ought).

Passive people do not ask for what they want or need, and often keep their feelings and their tensions tightly locked away inside them, often thinking that their feelings are not as important as other people's anyway. As a result they sometimes feel guilty (often over trivial things), tired, depressed and anxious. I could write a great deal more about this because this is the permanent state of mind of many women in this country, particularly mothers of young children who are not very highly valued in our culture.

In my experience, most women interested in assertiveness training are coming up towards assertiveness from a position of passive behaviour. (I can recall only a couple of women in several years of this work who were seeking to 'come down' from aggressive behaviour.) Under-assertive words are qualifying ones (Maybe I . . . I wonder if you'd mind . . . I guess . . . Would you mind very much if . . .), and fillers (You know, um, er, ah, sorry), and negating or self-deprecatory remarks (It's not really important . . . Don't bother really . . . or even worse, the abject It's only me). Sometimes, we seem to be apologising for our very existence.

You'll have realised from reading those admittedly extremely brief descriptions of some of the behaviour characteristics of aggressive people that quite a large number of those who have the opportunity to exert power over us often behave in this kind of unnecessarily powerful way. Many members of the medical profession are no exception. Paternalistic behaviour isn't on that list, but I define it as broadly aggressive, because it makes assumptions about one person's right to make choices for another person or group of people, and to take those decisions for 'their own good'. Not only is it often genuinely shocking for such people to have decisions they have made questioned — by people with less knowledge, fewer qualifications, whatever yardstick is being used — but it is also of course very threatening and challenging. I think that very often the gains in dealing assertively with medical personnel may seem small; your gain may not be in actually achieving all that you hoped for, but in coming out of situations relatively unscarred. So many women leave the clinic or hospital feeling humiliated, angry with themselves, belittled, ill-informed, inarticulate and as though they've 'let down' the person for whom they are doing all this, either themselves or their baby. An assertive approach — stating what you would like to have happen, using the assertive strategies which are going to be described — can make us feel better about situations, in which actually we may still not have achieved all we hoped for. At least we didn't come away thinking 'I wish I'd said something'; we know we did the best we could.

ASSERTIVE SKILLS

I have been emphasising throughout that assertiveness is a skill which can be learnt and practised — like learning to cook or riding a bike. When people are being assertive, it's important that the overall impression they give is one of relaxed confidence (unless that's inappropriate of course!). So, a person generally establishes good eye contact with whoever they are speaking to, stands comfortably but firmly on two feet — no hopping from foot to foot — with their hands loosely at their sides, and talks in a strong, steady tone of voice. Many women need to raise their tone of voice very slightly. Assertive words include 'I' statements, which are often good starters to a sentence (I think, I feel, I would like), co-operative words (let's try, how can we) and empathic statements of interest (what do you think, what do you suppose).

Here is a summary of the most essential skills to acquire:

Knowing what you want to say and saying it!
Being specific.
Looking at the other person.
Not laughing nervously or giggling.
Not needing to whine or wheedle.
Talking in a clear and unambiguous way, using no sarcasm.

There are quite a few assertive strategies or techniques people can employ which, added to the skills listed above, can help with achieving objectives. There is one which I am going to concentrate on in this article, because it seems the one most relevant to working with the medical profession. It's called 'Broken Record' and is just what it sounds like. Before your appointment, meeting, etc., you decide on a few key points you want to make; whittle them down from the many things which have incensed or aggrieved you. Then you use the strategy of sticking to those few key points and repeating them. Of course, you acknowledge what the other person is saying — it would be a pretty irritating and pointless conversation otherwise — but you don't get sidetracked or diverted. People can be diverted down side paths with surprising ease, particularly people who are upset about a number of issues and I guess we have all been guilty of doing the sidetracking when it's been in our interests to do so! Here is an example:

You: Sister, I would really like my baby to sleep with me from the beginning while I am here. (Straight to the point, no hesitation, no apology.)

Sister: Hospital policy, Ms D., is to keep them in the nursery for the first two nights, you know that.

You: Yes, I know it's general hospital policy (acknowledging what Sister said, but not getting sidetracked into 'these stupid hospital rules'), but I really want my baby with me (broken record of original sentence).

Sister: We can't do that, Ms D., all the other mothers would be disturbed when your baby cries. (Don't interrupt to say your baby won't/doesn't cry!)

You: That might be a problem, but I really do want my baby with me, Sister. (No getting caught up in the crying baby problem — just leave it.)

Sister: Well, it is hospital rules, you know.

You: Yes, I do appreciate the hospital has to have rules, but I really want my baby with me. Could we try it for just one night and see how it goes? (Having firmly made your point, you offer a compromise — better than nothing.)

Sister: I'll think it over, Ms D., can't make any promises though.

You:　　Thank you, Sister. I'll ask you again later on then (not letting go of it, making it clear you will be back).

You may find that a little artificial — I can't reproduce the look and tone which add the realism to a dialogue like that. Do remember that if you are discussing something extremely serious and important to you there is no need to grin or smile at the time of talking. Most women smile too much. There is a place for smiles, and times when it's not *appropriate* — back to that key word again. What I hope that conversation showed was the repeated use of the one key sentence, the way in which 'Ms D.' didn't become angry or indignant, nor did Sister. The way in which she acknowledged what was being said but didn't get caught up in it. And offered a compromise suggestion when it began to appear that the straight request would not be granted.

Here is another example:

Doctor:　Home birth is really passé, you know, Ailsa. You can have just what you like in hospital now.

You:　　Yes, I know you can (does she call him by his first name — probably not!), but I would much rather be at home.

Doctor:　Active birth, water birth, there's a birthing chair for some women, did you know that?

You:　　Yes I did know . . .

Doctor (interrupting): Amazing thing that chair. Very expensive. Of course it's not suitable for all women, but if you wanted to try for it I'm sure we could fix that up.

You:　　Thanks very much, it sounds interesting. But I would much rather be at home.

Doctor:　In fact, we could probably arrange for you to have a look round the place beforehand — not usual — but as I said, times are changing. Then you can inspect the chair for yourself.

You:　　That's a nice suggestion, but as I said, I would much rather be at home.

Doctor:　Very old fashioned. Midwives don't like it.

You:　　I suppose it must seem that way, especially when hospitals have made so many changes, but I really want to be at home.

Doctor: We'd better think this over a bit. I'll have a think about it. . .

There was a real red herring there, where the doctor offered the diversion of the birth chair plus the other goodies and behaved as if he wasn't paying full attention to what Ailsa was saying. In this case, she basically knew that he was listening (in his fashion!) but there are some situations where the conversation and the points you are trying to make are interrupted and you feel as if you're banging your head on a brick wall. When that happens it's best to say how you feel. But there's no need to attack the other person: just repeat your sentence again, slightly louder and ask if the other person has heard you — it's very effective! The other thing which Ailsa did was acknowledge that her request might seem 'old fashioned', not that she agreed with that judgemental expression but that it 'might seem that way'. It's fine to do that, if your fundamental self-respect is not being challenged, in fact, it's often an honest and open admission, like admitting to fear or phobia.

Another difficulty many of us face is that of saying 'No' directly and of asking for more time, generally time to think something over, rather than making an immediate decision.

'We'll be giving you a scan this afternoon, Mrs Appiah — all right?'

'Yes' we answer weakly. You wanted to say, 'I wasn't expecting that at all; it's certainly something I need to think over carefully. I'd rather not have it today.' Or

'We've just given baby a drop of boiled water, Mrs Klein — she was so thirsty, poor thing.'

'Oh, yes, all right.' It's not all right, is it? You wanted the baby to have nothing in her system but breast milk, you thought you'd made that quite clear; but . . .

A short breathing space to think over something which is important to your welfare or your baby's is not a lot to ask for. It may be a surprise to those who have made an urgent, or hurried request, or one which presumes your immediate co-operation, but it is your *right* to ask for even ten minutes in which to think through your reaction and response.

PRACTISING ASSERTIVENESS

People who have been passive for a long time may feel that they are actually being loud and aggressive when they first begin to practise a different level of expression. They may feel selfish if they express a personal need or even guilty. (Even though other people have probably been doing this to them for many years!)

Generally, the response of other people, however, is positive. People like to be around assertive people; they know where they are with them which is in itself rewarding and often relaxing. They can feel confident in their company, sure of straightforward behaviour where no one is trying to score points or win something. This will apply to most areas of life, though in your relationship with the medical profession it may turn out to be less true. You may be regarded as a bit of a nuisance! However, in many of our relationships, particularly very close ones, it may also take some time for the changes in behaviour to be accepted and appreciated. People do slot us into little moulds and expect certain responses and ways of behaving. Breaking out of those moulds is challenging to others. It is usual though to hear comments like 'I really value the way you suggest things now. . . ', or 'I'm glad you decided that, I was fed up with always deciding which film we should go and see.'

Hopefully these guidelines will provide a starting point; the more thought you can give to some of the areas discussed, the deeper your response will be and the greater your chances of successfully asserting yourself in your relationships. For example, saying 'No'. There are many reasons why in our culture women have great difficulty in saying 'No'. We feel we will be rejecting the whole person who made the request or demand, whereas we are, of course, only refusing their request, not them as a person. Talking over these ideas with a friend may be helpful. Another idea is to practise in front of a full-length mirror. If you find the thought of learning assertive behaviour on your own too daunting, then contact your local women's group who may well run courses in this skill.

RECOMMENDED READING

Ann Dickson, *A Woman In Your Own Right*, Quartet, 1982.

Natural birth in hospital: how to avoid interference

ROS CLAXTON

The majority of women in this country give birth in hospital. It is assumed by all concerned that hospitals (and in particular the large obstetric units) are the safest places in which to give birth. Other articles in this book question such an assumption. In our view, the routine application of medical techniques that occurs in most hospitals creates more problems than it solves. Professor G. L. Kloosterman, the Dutch obstetrician, believes that 80–90 per cent of women are capable of normal deliveries without medical intervention.[1]

If women are given caring support and encouraged to give birth without unnecessary intervention (as they are for example in Pithiviers), hospitals could indeed become 'safe' places with labour and birth happier and healthier experiences for both mother and child. Since this is unlikely to happen in the foreseeable future, any woman desiring a natural birth in hospital usually faces a number of problems. For a start, she will be thought of as rather odd. If she questions routines and procedures she will be seen to be interfering in medical matters of which she, as a non-professional, has no right. She will probably be told that natural birth is dangerous, or that 'birth is only safe in retrospect'. Obstetricians are very sceptical about natural birth; it does not fit their medical model, they rarely see it and they might be out of a job if too many women achieved it! Midwives, traditionally the guardians of normal birth, are now being trained as obstetric nurses and are expected to follow obstetricians' rulings on interventions such as ultrasound, amniotomy, fetal monitoring, episiotomy and so on. In very few units are they allowed to work independently and to make decisions regarding normal birth. Obviously, the rate of medical interference differs from hospital to hospital and within hospitals from obstetric team to obstetric team, as does the rigidity or flexibility of the people working within these institutions. (*The New Good Birth Guide* by Sheila Kitzinger[2] gives an idea of the amount of variation.) It is even difficult to recommend particular hospitals as so much depends on who is on duty when you go into labour, how you react to being in hospital and how your labour proceeds. It may, therefore, seem like a monumental task for a woman desiring a natural birth in hospital to ward off attempts at interference and to judge when she should accept that such interference is really necessary. Our Birth Centre work is heartening in this respect. We found, over and over again, that if a woman knew what she wanted, had confidence in her beliefs, plus the support of a companion or companions in labour, she managed, not only to say 'no' when necessary, but to sense when it was right to say 'yes'. Local birth groups and some ante-natal teachers (not all are prepared to support a woman's desire for natural birth if it means too strong a challenge to hospital policies) offer invaluable information and support throughout this period.

In the early years at the Birth Centre, many people contacted us to ask how they could get a 'Leboyer birth' or for information about the 'Leboyer method'. They would request lists of doctors or midwives who worked in this way (now the requests are more for the 'Odent method'!). We had to tell them that we had no lists, that there was no such thing as the 'Leboyer method' and that it was up to them to define and request what they wanted. What Frederick Leboyer did in his remarkable book *Birth Without Violence*[3] and his film *A Child is Born*[4] was to focus attention on the baby's experience of birth. He emphasised the baby's sensitivity to light, sound and touch; that to breathe air for the first time is a major adaptation; that if the baby has immediate skin to skin contact with the mother and is held closely by her without the presence of glaring lights and harsh noise, this is a safe place from which to slowly adjust to the world, peacefully and without fear. What Leboyer advocated was not a new technique of giving birth, but a more sensitive approach to the baby. If the baby is treated with love and respect, all else follows from there, you let your own instincts and the baby's needs guide you. Now that the work of Michel Odent and the midwives at Pithiviers[5] has become well known, women are requesting not only a gentle approach to their babies, but more freedom of expression and movement for themselves. It is certainly true that more midwives and doctors have become aware of the importance of posture during labour, and may be prepared to dim the lights and 'allow' the mother time with her baby after birth, but one must beware of an approach which is still basically medical and which is waiting to intervene at the first opportunity. For women who are about to have their first child in hospital, it might be useful to outline what they may expect to happen to them. This will help to highlight the areas they wish to challenge. Obviously, not all hospitals are the same, so you might be pleasantly surprised if your hospital does not conform to the pattern described.

With regard to ante-natal care, if you are receiving all your care from the hospital you will probably have a long wait in the ante-natal clinic and are unlikely to be seen by the same midwife or doctor throughout this period (although you will be assigned to one particular obstetrician). The midwives you meet in the ante-natal clinic will not be the ones you will meet later in the labour ward. You will be weighed, your blood pressure and blood and urine samples taken. You will be given a routine prescription of iron tablets, even though there is no evidence that they are of benefit to all women. (Studies are beginning to provide evidence that iron supplements interfere with the uptake of zinc; zinc deficiency in pregnant women is strongly associated with low birth weight and difficult labour and may be implicated in spina bifida.) You will be expected to submit to examination by ultrasound scan even though there are no long-term studies that show this to be a safe procedure. You are unlikely to be encouraged to ask questions and the pathological nature of your condition will be emphasised. To quote Michel Odent: 'Each visit brings with it the risk of learning that the cervix is a little too soft, a little too short, a little too open; the uterus is a little too small or a little too large; that weight gain is too fast or too slow, blood pressure too high or too low, that the ultrasound machine could give a better diagnosis . . .'[6] If you go past your 'expected date of delivery', there will be talk about your being induced. Hospitals vary in the amount of time they are prepared to allow a woman to go past her dates; some will tolerate only a couple of days, others a week and some even two weeks.

When you are admitted to hospital, certain procedures are usually undertaken. You will probably be separated from your partner, given a vaginal examination, a perineal shave and an enema or suppositories will be administered. There is no physiological basis for removing pubic hair and research at Northwick Park Hospital shows that it does not prevent infection and is of no therapeutic or hygienic value.[7] Having an enema or suppositories is not a particularly pleasant procedure and most women will spontaneously want to empty their bowels without artificial assistance.[8] In most hospitals, amniotomy (breaking the bag of waters) is performed on admission in the belief that this will speed up labour. It also enables fetal monitoring to take place. Recent research questions this practice and Roberto Caldeyro-Barcia, the Uruguayan obstetrician, considers early rupture of the membranes (even when it happens spontaneously) to constitute a complication.[9] It also commits a woman to delivery within a certain period of time because of the risk of infection. (This often means that women are given a caesarean section because they have been in labour a long time.)

If labour slows down, a common occurrence when a woman is feeling uncomfortable or fearful in the hospital environment, it will be accelerated by the use of an oxytocin drip. Most hospitals will want to use either external or internal monitoring. (You can ask the staff to attach the monitor to your hand to give you an idea of what the babies must feel when it is attached to their head.) Unless your midwife or doctor understands the importance of movement and posture during labour, you will be confined to bed and will not be allowed to eat or drink. The rationale behind this practice of starving labouring women is that, should you need a general anaesthetic, there is less danger of inhaling vomit. This is a relatively new practice and in many cultures women are refreshed by herbal teas or light nourishing soups. At Birmingham Maternity Hospital easily absorbed foods are allowed during labour. These include tea, fruit juice, toast, honey, plain biscuits and stewed apple. Not all women wish to eat during labour but some may need an extra source of energy, especially if labour is long. The hospital alternative is to put you on a glucose drip.

If you show any sign that the contractions are hard or painful, you will be expected to need painkilling drugs or epidural anaesthesia. When you enter the second stage of labour, you will be moved from the labour room to a delivery room (not at all the best time to have to do this). You will be encouraged to follow the instructions of your attendants to 'push hard', rather than follow the messages coming from your own body. In many hospitals, episiotomies are given routinely. After the baby is born you will be given a routine injection of syntometrine to prevent post-partum haemorrhage and the baby's cord will be cut immediately. Some midwives have discontinued the routine use of syntometrine (it is only used in cases of emergency at Pithiviers); putting the baby to the breast soon after birth achieves the same result in a more natural way. Still, in some hospitals, the baby is held upside-down and smacked to stimulate breathing. The baby's nose and mouth will be routinely suctioned with a mucus catheter. Paediatrician Donald Garrow has said of this practice: 'Sticking a catheter down a baby's throat is bad. Pushing it into a baby's nose and mouth does nothing at all to help it breathe. Mucus catheters should be banned as dangerous instruments.'[10]

Your baby may be given to you for a short time after birth and you and your partner may, in more enlightened hospitals, be given some time alone together. The baby will certainly be taken away at some point (in some hospitals it is immediately after birth), to be checked, weighed, measured, cleaned and dressed. In many hospitals babies are removed to a nursery at night (and sometimes even bottle fed) so that the mother can supposedly 'get a good night's sleep'. The information given about breast feeding may be incorrect and you will probably be encouraged to limit the amount of time the baby is allowed to suck as well as feeding, not on demand, but according to a schedule. The staff may give the baby bottles of artificial milk if they think you have 'insufficient milk'. Your baby may also be given a routine injection of Vitamin K 'to prevent haemorrhage', even though there is no evidence of the necessity for this to be administered routinely.

It will be clear from the above information that a woman who hopes for a natural birth in hospital should try to find a hospital or obstetrician prepared to be flexible in their approach to intervention. It is not easy to find out about hospital policies and figures. Obstetricians are often reluctant to define their policies and hospitals do not like having to reveal their figures. One way to find out is to approach your local community health council who have a statutory right to statistical information. They will be able to find out the figures for induction, epidural anaesthesia, forceps/ventouse deliveries, caesarean section, episiotomy, and electronic fetal monitoring. If a hospital is difficult about divulging these statistics, it is probably a sign that it should be avoided if possible. Local birth groups and ante-natal teachers should also be able to supply you with information and may be able to guide you towards a more sympathetic hospital or obstetrician.

Unfortunately, the recent policy of closing down small maternity hospitals and GP units, thereby centralising care into large obstetric units, leaves women with very little choice. For those living in urban areas there may be a number of hospitals to choose from, in rural areas there may be no choice at all. The fact that there is more than one option to choose from is rarely made clear to you. GPs assume that you will go to the nearest hospital (they themselves are often under pressure to send you there). Hospitals often draw up catchment areas and refuse to admit anyone outside their area. If there is a GP unit available, you may find it difficult to book there unless you fit the particular 'low risk' categories set up. (Beverley Beech's article 'Know your rights: a parents' guide to birth' gives information on what to do if you have problems.)

Once you have made your choice of hospital (assuming that you have a choice), you now have to set about getting what you want. There are a number of ways you can approach this. You can request an interview to discuss your wishes; you can write a letter; you can tackle things as you go along. Choose whichever approach feels best to you. If you request an interview, it is important that you talk to someone with sufficient authority to sanction change if necessary, for example the senior nursing officer, supervising midwife or obstetrician in charge of a particular team. To help you cope with these potentially difficult situations, make sure you take your partner or a friend with you for support. Try not to get drawn into arguments about the pros and cons of the various interventions. Inform yourself beforehand so you are clear about what you do or do not want and practise your assertiveness training! It is not a good idea to go into hospital with the idea that you have to ask 'permission' for all that you want. In our experience at the Birth Centre we discovered that if parents assumed they had a right to their wishes and were firm and positive (without being aggressive) in their dealings with hospital staff, they usually managed to get what they wanted.

The following is a list of points you might wish to raise either at an interview or in a letter:

1 You do not agree to ultrasound being used routinely during pregnancy or labour. You would prefer to be examined by a skilled midwife instead.

2 You wish you partner and/or friend to be present throughout labour and birth.

3 You do not wish to have your waters routinely broken on admission.

4 You do not agree to being shaved or to having an enema.

5 You do not wish to have any form of medical intervention unless you are given full information as to its necessity.

6 You wish to be able to move around in labour and to give birth in a position which feels comfortable to you.

7 You do not wish to be given an episiotomy unless it is absolutely necessary.

8 You would prefer the baby not to be born under harsh lights, to be handled gently and given to you immediately. You do not wish to be given syntometrine after the birth (unless you show signs that you might haemorrhage) and you do not wish the baby's cord to be cut until it has stopped pulsating. You would prefer the baby's mucus to drain naturally if possible.

9 Your partner and yourself would like time alone together with the baby after the birth. If you have other children, you would like them to be able to visit you as soon as possible after the birth.

10 You wish to breast feed and do not agree to your baby being given a bottle. You do not wish your baby to be taken away from you at any time without your permission.

11 If, for any reason, your baby has to be taken into special care after the birth, you would like to have as much contact as possible with your child and to be able to express breast milk for him/her.

12 You would like these requests to be attached to your hospital notes.

If you find the thought of approaching anyone in the hospital with a list of questions and requests too intimidating, then you can compile a letter and send it to the Director of Nursing Services (Midwifery) at the hospital and ask for her comments. The letter could be along the following lines and could be signed by both you and your partner:

> Dear
> I am expecting a baby in . . . I would like to give birth to my baby in hospital and I would appreciate it if you would comment on your hospital's policy concerning the following:
>
> (You can then list the items you would like information about.)
>
> I would like it to be known that I do not consent to the following unless full information is given to me of the necessity in my particular case:
>
> (You can then list the items you do not want.)
>
> I have been careful to ensure that I am in good health and well-prepared for the birth.
>
> I would also like confirmation, should I book into your hospital for the birth of my child, that this letter will be attached to my notes.
>
> I look forward to your reply.

The only problem with making your requests known beforehand is that you may get labelled as 'difficult'. Some people prefer to work on what they want as the need arises (if you have already refused ultrasound that will give a clue as to your allegiances!). Sometimes hospital staff may appear sympathetic to your wishes beforehand but not so sympathetic when you arrive in labour;

do not be led into a false sense of security, your companion(s) especially should be aware of what you want and be prepared to speak on your behalf — you must be able to concentrate on your labour. Some Birth Centres can provide a 'birth support person' willing to be with women during labour. This can be of invaluable assistance and helps take the pressure off the woman's partner.

If all feels well, it is not always a good idea to rush into hospital at the first sign of a contraction (although this decision will obviously depend to some extent on how close you live to the hospital). The longer you spend in hospital, the more chance it provides for intervention. Women usually know when the time has come for them to seek professional help. Take flowers, plants, pictures, extra cushions and other personal possessions with you that help make the labour room your own. Be clear about what you want, make sure you have someone sympathetic with you at all times, keep a sense of humour and have faith in your own intuitive knowledge about giving birth.

REFERENCES

1   G. L. Kloosterman quoted in Suzanne Arms, *Immaculate Deception*, Houghton Mifflin, 1975.
2   Sheila Kitzinger, *The New Good Birth Guide*, Penguin, 1983.
3   Frederick Leboyer, *Birth Without Violence*, Fontana, 1977.
4   The film *A Child Is Born* on hire from Concord Films, 201 Felixstowe Road, Ipswich, Suffolk.
5   Michel Odent, *Birth Reborn*, Souvenir Press, 1984.
6   Michel Odent, *op. cit.*
7   Mona L. Romney, 'Pre-delivery shaving: an unjustified assault?', *Journal of Obstetrics and Gynaecology*, no. 1, pp. 33–5, 1980.
8   Mona L. Romney and H. Gordon, 'Is your enema really necessary?', *British Medical Journal*, vol. 282, 18 April, 1981.
9   R. Caldeyro-Barcia, Conference of the American Foundation for Maternal and Child Health, March 1974.
10 Donald Garrow quoted in Sheila Kitzinger, *Birth at Home*, Oxford University Press, 1979.

RECOMMENDED READING

Sally Inch, *Birth Rights; A Parents' Guide to Modern Childbirth*, Hutchinson, 1982.

Sheila Kitzinger, *The New Good Birth Guide*, Penguin, 1983.

Penny and Andrew Stanway, *Choices in Childbirth*, Pan, 1984.

Jill Rakusen and Nick Davidson, *What Technology Does To Childbirth*, Pan, 1982.

Michel Odent, *Birth Reborn*, Souvenir Press, 1984.

Christine Beels, *The Childbirth Book*, Mayflower, 1980.

Peter Huntingford, *Birth Right: The Parents' Choice*, BBC Publications, 1985.

Keeping the home birth option alive

ROS CLAXTON

The home birth issue has become one of the most controversial aspects of the birth debate. Fifty years ago, the majority of births took place at home. Since then, official policy has pursued the ideal of hospitalisation for all, and in 1984 less than 2 per cent of births took place at home. The desire for centralisation and standardisation of pregnancy and birth has eroded, almost completely, the home birth option. There was a time when Britain's domiciliary service and the high standard of midwifery was admired throughout the world; the emergency 'Flying Squad' back-up service was pioneered in this country. Over the last twenty years or so, the domiciliary service has been steadily dismantled. The official reason (based on disputed evidence) is that home is not a safe place in which to give birth; the issue of safety (as medically defined) has been used as a very persuasive lever to entice women into hospital. However, underlying this official reason is the more basic question of power — it is easier to manage and control the birth process if it takes place on professional rather than home territory.

Some women, however, do not feel safe in the medical environment of the hospital; only at home, on their own territory, can they feel relaxed, confident and secure; only at home do they feel that the physiological process of birth can proceed unhindered as, surrounded by family and friends, they create their own individual setting for birth and celebrate this unique event as a natural part of family life. Thus, born at home, the new child suffers no dislocation of the bonding process so important for future well-being and relationships within the family.

Home birth has been given such a bad press that there now exists the need to redress the balance and challenge the widespread myth that hospital is the only safe place in which to give birth. No one would deny that, as measured by mortality rates, women and their babies have a better chance of survival than they had fifty years ago when the majority of births took place at home. Improved standards of health, better nutrition and living conditions, smaller families and the fact that most women have finished childbearing by their mid-thirties, have all contributed to this amelioration. Undoubtedly, fifty years ago, many women in poor health were delivered at home who may have been better off in hospital (although one wonders whether the maternal and perinatal mortality rates would have been that much lower had the majority of births taken place in hospital). The horror stories doctors are so fond of telling us about home birth could be said to originate from this time. Today, we have the facilities for all those women who need to give birth in hospital. It should also be possible to provide an efficient domiciliary service, with adequate emergency back-up, for all who prefer to give birth at home. If hospital conditions were improved, the very small proportion of truly 'high risk' women who refuse to go there could also be reduced and if women were given a real choice, many more would probably decide to stay at home, thereby enabling the hospitals to provide better medical care for those who really need it. If the economic argument were to take priority, the case for home birth would, one suspects, be more easily won.

By virtually eliminating home birth, we may have lost more than we have gained. Within the animal world, all other females seek a quiet, familiar place in which to give birth; no farmer would ever dream of moving an animal in labour. In contrast, we interrupt the flow of life and take an intrinsically normal, non-medical event out of the woman's home, away from friends and community; she is then compelled to perform this personal and intimate act in an alien environment, in front of strangers. Is it any wonder that complications arise? Now she has to defer to the authority of others, their permission has to be sought at almost every stage of her 'confinement'; in order to have family or friends present, even, perhaps, to hold, feed or sleep with her baby when she wants to. When a birth takes place at home, goodwill reverberates through the community; friends and neighbours respond with warmth and generosity and the immediacy and closeness of the event forges strong links between people. To what extent, one wonders, may the hospitalisation of birth (and death) have contributed to the impoverishment of modern community life and the associated problems of isolation and alienation?

As birth moved out of the home, so too did the midwife lose her status as an independent practitioner. Formerly a familiar and respected figure in the community, she was able to give continuous care to the women she looked after and had the pleasure of watching the babies she delivered as they grew up around her. Her job, although fraught with difficulties when she delivered at home women who should really have been in hospital, must have been deeply satisfying and her skills highly developed. Few people today recognise a midwife, even in hospital, and her transformation into 'obstetric nurse' is almost complete.

There are many reasons why the home birth option should be kept alive. Apart from parental preference, it is important that an alternative exists with which to compare the hospital system. There has been much criticism by parents and birth groups of impersonal hospital routine and recent government reports, such as the Short Report, refer to the importance of 'humanising' the hospitals. In some places this has been interpreted merely as the need to improve the physical environment in which women give birth — pretty curtains and bedspreads appear, pictures are hung on the wall, dimmer switches installed and taped music provided. This is a beginning, perhaps, but more could be learnt about creating favourable conditions for childbirth by talking to parents who have had their children happily at home. This is not to say that women are incapable of having a good birth experience in hospital, obviously many women prefer to be there. Nor does being at home guarantee that the event will be trouble free. Wherever she is, a woman needs sensitive and skilled birth attendants preferably to give her continuous care throughout pregnancy and birth. An insensitive midwife or doctor can ruin a woman's experience of birth at home, just as caring attendants in hospital can enhance it.

When it does take place with sympathetic attendants, home birth has many special qualities that can never be duplicated in the hospital setting. The following remarks from parents and midwives illustrate the richness of the experience and show what we would lose if we let this option die. Today, midwives have few opportunities to experience either natural birth or home birth during their training. Not all midwives wish to deliver women at home, but there are those who find it both worth while and fulfilling. Some midwives are lucky enough still to be able to provide care continuously through the ante-natal period, birth and post-natally. The opportunity to do this differs from area to area but it is increasingly the case that midwives work in teams and that a woman may be looked after by more than one midwife. For those midwives still able to provide complete continuity of care, the contribution this gives to the safety of the woman and her baby is most important:

> 'I'm more likely to pick up problems. It is much safer when you are the one who always palpates, you really know how the baby is growing'.

> 'When you can provide total continuity of care this means it is much easier to detect any deviation from the norm.'

The fact that the midwife visits the woman in her own home to give ante-natal care, obviously provides the possibility for close relationships between her, the woman and the rest of the family:

> 'An atmosphere of trust is created right from the start.'

> 'After meeting the mother as a stranger for the first time, you often end up by gaining a friend.'

> 'The relationship is more intimate, there is mutual trust and respect. Friendship with the rest of the family is established naturally.'

> 'You feel that you have, for a time, become a member of that family and this is a great privilege.'

'The children get to know you and they accept the process of birth as a completely natural event.'

Attending a woman in labour at home can be a very different experience for a midwife, for often a woman feels more relaxed and confident in her own surroundings:

'There is more opportunity for women to maintain confidence in their ability to give birth and do what comes naturally.'

'Women who are planning a home birth are usually more confident and it is much easier to get out of them what they would really like. Women booked for hospital often have inhibitions about being really honest with me and are much more likely to tell me what they think I want to hear.'

'It is calmer and more relaxed. The attitude and relationship that have been built up during the ante-natal period makes for happier conditions.'

'Being more relaxed, women tend to find it easier to regress, moan, rock and be generally unhibited.'

This is not to belittle the importance and significance of parental choice, as one midwife points out:

'In the past I have cared for women who would have preferred to be in hospital but couldn't get a bed and they resented me. I have cared for women in hospital who would rather have been at home and they resented me. The best relationship, and it is lovely, is when you give total care to a couple who are having their baby, where, they have made an informed choice, is the right place for them.'

Some midwives feel nervous about working outside the hospital environment and this can create difficulties both for them and the mothers they attend. Other midwives prefer and feel happier working at home:

'I do not feel relaxed in a hospital setting, always looking over my shoulder and at the clock. I feel much safer at home and much more confident in a natural setting.'

'When I go into hospital I find myself falling back into the trap of presuming that disaster will happen. One's fantasies run riot in that environment and it's much harder to sit back and have faith in the process and the woman's ability to *give* birth.'

'Birth at home is more like something we are meant to do rather than a catastrophe which must be dealt with by experts.'

'There are no rude interruptions, no noisy staff bustling in and out, filling up shelves! The woman can get into her own momentum without being the subject of a "peep show" for doctors, other midwives and auxiliary staff. She is the star and everyone answers *her* needs rather than the staff's needs.'

Domiciliary work provides midwives with the nowadays rare opportunity to practise as independent practitioners, an opportunity welcomed by some:

'Home is the place where I am able to feel that I am the practising midwife that I was trained to be. I trained in the mid-fifties and when midwives transferred to hospitals in the late sixties, early seventies, we did *not* transfer as independent practitioners. We joined the hospital team and there are no prizes for guessing who assumed leadership of that team.'

'At home I am truly a practitioner in my own right with responsibility I welcome towards the woman and her family. In hospital, I'm plugged into a hierarchy, bound by hospital, consultant and regional policies which must determine the way I practise.'

'The midwife comes into her own in home births. She is practising as she was trained and so feels better about herself. A woman who delivers at home usually feels good about herself and they can reinforce this feeling in each other. I don't think hospitals make women feel good about themselves either as "patients" or midwives.'

For parents, the decision to give birth at home may be taken for a number of reasons and often involves careful thought and discussion:

> 'This, I felt, was the most "grown-up", responsible decision I had ever made. It certainly was not taken lightly. I had a strong feeling that this was the right place for me and my baby to be — but I did a lot of reading and talked to a lot of people before I felt 100 per cent confident that home rather than hospital was where I should give birth.'

For some women, it is the obvious place to give birth:

> 'All my life I had never thought of birth taking place anywhere but at home. It wasn't till I was actually pregnant that I realised most people thought the opposite.'

> 'Giving birth isn't an illness, so why should I be in hospital?'

> 'Home is best for such a sacred and holy event.'

The possibility of feeling more relaxed and confident in their own home is for some women a major factor to be taken into account when making the decision:

> 'The more I learned about birth, the more I realised that I needed to be completely relaxed and thought that this would be a hopeless struggle in the alien, starched hospital environment.'

> 'I knew I would feel confident and relaxed at home, that I was capable of giving birth naturally if I was in a conducive environment.'

For women seeking a natural birth, it is important to minimise the possibility of unnecessary medical intervention:

> 'During my first birth, the process was interfered with from the word go. I wanted to avoid that happening again.'

> 'I didn't want to spend my labour fighting off hospital routines.'

At home, the father and the rest of the family can be more involved and there is less disruption to normal life:

> 'We wanted birth to be a family occasion, both during the birth and in the subsequent hours and days.'

> 'Although our first birth in hospital had been satisfactory, with the minimum of intervention, we wanted the continuity and the minimum of disruption which home birth gives.'

> 'I couldn't bear the thought of having to be separated from my first child, we had never been apart for any length of time before and it seemed to me to be asking for trouble to suddenly disappear and then next be seen holding a new baby.'

> 'I got so homesick and lonely during my hospital stay with my first baby.'

Ante-natal care provided by hospitals is frequently criticised by mothers attending the clinics — long waiting periods, impersonal attention by varying numbers of doctors and midwives often make it an unsatisfactory experience. Home birth mothers, on the other hand, are frequently happier with the ante-natal care they receive and describe it as 'very good and caring', 'excellent, no waiting, questions answered willingly and everything discussed fully', 'nice friendly GP, community midwife lovely, very keen on home births, quietly confident and open-minded', 'everything was on a one to one, personal basis, I wasn't just a number on a hospital list'. Where there is continuity of care, the possibility of developing a close relationship with the midwife during pregnancy is especially appreciated:

> 'My midwife became a very special friend. She was eager to learn about everything I was interested in.'

> 'We trusted and had confidence in each other. I felt confident because I knew the midwives who were going to attend me during labour.'

> 'I don't know how to describe the deep feeling of love and respect I have for the Senior Midwife and her assistants.'

Because ante-natal care takes place at home, other children are often present and mothers appreciate the way midwives may include them:

'She was very good to my 2 year old and always included him in her examinations.'

'My daughter loved listening for the baby's heartbeat and trying to feel which way the baby was lying. I'm sure it made the baby much more of a reality for her and helped her to "bond" with her sister.'

The environment in which a woman gives birth is important — the physical appearance of the room, lighting, plants, pictures and music, for example, can all play a part in providing a sympathetic atmosphere in which she is able to work harmoniously with her body during labour. Being at home makes it easier for parents to prepare for birth in their own individual ways:

'We made the room very cosy, flowers and paintings above the bed which we were particularly fond of. A roaring coal fire in the fireplace, low lights, the baby's basket, blanket and clothes all set out. We had prepared music in case we wanted to hear some, as it turned out we forgot all about it!'

'Having something else living and growing in the room seemed very important to me. My 5 year old made a special picture to hang on the wall with a collage of coloured yarns to show the baby "since it won't be used to bright colours, and can only feel water and the bag, and I want to show it and let it feel this".'

For others, being in their own home is enough in itself and they do not feel the need to prepare a birth room in a special way:

'We did nothing special — we just took the births into our own continuing lives at home.'

'I didn't feel the need to make any "welcoming" touches — I just felt the baby would come as, when and how he liked.'

When birth takes place at home, the decision about when to move to hospital is removed; neither does the labouring woman have to undergo a journey, which, for many, is an uncomfortable and difficult experience:

'The pressure over when to go to hospital was removed.'

'I didn't have to endure a bumpy ambulance drive in the middle of strong contractions which is what happened in my first labour.'

'I have very quick labours and feel that the journey to hospital would have been a very uncomfortable, rushed and disturbing affair.'

'I would hate to have to go somewhere else, change scene and particularly ride in a car during labour. I even felt impatient with the disruption of changing sheets, ringing the midwife and so on and wanted everything to settle down and leave me in peace.'

Bearing in mind the close connection between one's emotional state and the progress of labour, it is essential that a woman be in an environment where she is able to relax and feel confident. A woman who is only able to feel this way in hospital should obviously give birth there; for her, hospital is the 'safe' place. Other women can only feel this way at home, which makes home a 'safe' place for them:

'I feel being at home made all the difference — it made me feel calm and in control. In my own surroundings I was able to do what I wanted and ask for any help without having to fit in with a hospital routine. It was *my* labour and not simply the nth in any given week in hospital.'

'It was the safe feeling that I could devote all my energy to giving birth without having to be alert for interventions.'

'I could be myself, knowing I had all the space I needed.'

'It made giving birth a normal, natural, straightforward event. As I laboured, our bedroom was a peaceful place, quiet and relaxed. There was nothing intrusive or hostile, unlike hospital, which is both of these things.'

The early stages of labour may pass quickly when one is at home and can find other things to do:

> 'I put my eldest child to bed, cooked and ate supper and got on with a number of other things I had to do. When I eventually felt the need to call the midwife, I could hardly believe that I was already 7 cms dilated as I hardly felt I'd been in labour.'

> 'It seemed much easier. I could do what I felt like and all attention was not focused on my labour and contractions — in hospital you have little to do except think about them. At home, with my first child to play with, there are other things to do and it's easier to relax and forget about time and progress.'

After the birth, many parents appreciate the special feeling of closeness that exists with no forced separation between mother, baby and the rest of the family. The woman is free to move in her own time at her own pace:

> 'It was such a joy to just be with our new daughter, all together. To have her in bed with us, to put her to the breast whenever she wanted, to just go along with the flow of joy and wonder without having to ask permission or feel that you were breaking hospital rules.'

> 'He was ours the minute he was born. I would have hated being in hospital and having nurses say, "We're taking baby to nursery now." I couldn't bear to be parted from him.'

> 'She was ours and belonged in our home from the start. We did everything at our own pace, as we wanted.'

Professionals, however well-meaning, can sometimes be over-whelming and confusing in the advice they give, especially to first-time mothers, about how to handle their babies. For some, coping alone at home can have its advantages:

'I suspect I would have felt less confident about handling and feeding my first baby if I hadn't been at home with little advice, so I just had to get on with it. There is an enormous confidence that comes from having your baby at home. If you can have your baby on your own responsibility, you feel you're ready for anything being a parent requires.'

'Having the birth that we both hoped for, I think we always felt very calm with Inti and never had any doubts that we could cope. Inti settled into his own routine in his own time and the three of us allowed ourselves the time to get to know each other without any outside interference.'

Few hospitals allow older brothers and sisters to attend a birth. At home this possibility exists and has a special meaning for those parents and children who choose it:

'It was wonderful for the children, to have the baby come so simply into our lives. When our third baby was born, her two brothers were there — I think sharing in the excitement and awe of birth meant a lot to them. They seemed to accept so easily that she and I were connected, and that she had special needs that must take priority. They were exquisitely aware of her awareness, of the transition she was making into our world and watched her opening growth with keen excitement.'

'It was a marvellous experience for my son who stayed for the birth of his brother. They now have a special bond.'

Even if they are not actually present at the birth, older children can still share the experience and family life proceeds with less disruption than when the event takes place in hospital:

'It seemed a calm and tranquil way to bring a child into the family. My older son suffered no disruption and after the event we were able to continue with family life.'

'It made a perfectly natural event for our 2 year old who slept through the birth and found a baby brother next morning, pink and rosy in his basket.'

'Hannah's two sisters came bouncing in about half an hour after she was born and proceeded to help their father "bath" their new sister.'

'Our little boy was not frightened or distanced by the experience.'

The desire for natural birth in hospital often puts pressure on partners to ward off attempts at intervention; liaising between the woman and her medical attendants can be a stressful and difficult role. At home, it is possible to be more relaxed:

'Although our first child's birth in hospital was great, I felt a considerable amount of pressure on me to "front" the thing, in other words to manage all the medical and ancillary staff, to make life calm and easy. Being at home gave me two immediate advantages — my own territory and less of them.'

When a birth takes place at home, fathers play an intrinsic part in events; it is not possible, for example, to ask them to leave during examinations or soon after the birth as so often happens in hospital:

'At home I was more naturally a part of the process as of natural assumption and right. As it happened, I felt that the birth (and those which followed later) was a major life event, which being shared intimately, gave an even greater depth to the relationship of love between my wife and myself, and between the triad of relationships formed by the birth of our son.'

'I enjoyed not having to be rushed away from my wife and baby so soon after such a very deep emotional experience.'

'I enjoyed the whole event. It was satisfying to be much more employed in the process. The family as a whole were more involved and the celebrations spontaneous and a lot of fun.'

Other fathers have commented:

'Having a baby at home is more civilised, less formal, more involving for your other children and less time consuming.

In our experience the whole process is over quicker and the food's better.'

'Home birth is a magical experience. It's often called an emotional experience but I'm not sure this is quite right. Looking back, the overriding memory I get from the birth of our two children is of a complete lack of confusion. I don't really recall any emotion, I just recall being part of something so totally logical, so inevitable. Being part of something so timeless, so deeply rooted in nature and instinct, something that *has* to happen and *has* to be done the way you're doing it, you feel very small. You just play your part and a rule-book that's a billion years old tells you how. The time for emotion is a couple of hours later when you're downstairs filling the kettle and it suddenly hits you that you've got a child upstairs. That's the time to burst into tears.'

Part of the 'mythology' of birth in this country is that even if a woman is feeling happy after the birth of her child, she is bound to suffer 'baby blues' a few days later. Large numbers of women suffer more seriously from post-natal depression, a condition rare, if not unknown in non-industrial societies; nor do the women who give birth naturally at Pithiviers seem to suffer from it. That is not to say that it never happens to mothers who give birth at home, obviously personal circumstances will affect a woman's emotional state, but it certainly appears to happen less frequently:

'I felt depressed for a year after the birth of our first child in hospital [there had been much medical intervention]. After the subsequent natural births of our next two children at home, I was filled with joy for weeks afterwards and this joy seemed to carry us through for a long time after, even when the broken nights were beginning to get to us.'

'About three days after the birth, the midwife asked me how I was feeling. I replied, "I feel really high." She looked at me in disbelief and then said, "We can give you pills for that if you like." '

The sense of continuity experienced when a child is born at home can be very satisfying:

'The continuity is very important to me. It's deeply satisfying to reflect that a child is conceived, carried, born and nursed all within the same loving space. I feel it has consecrated our home. A home that has never had a child born in it, now seems empty to me.'

'I have always felt a satisfying sense of continuity with Matthew — very organic — conceived, born and raised under the same roof.'

Unless there are complications, few women would choose to go to hospital after having had the experience of a home birth, as one woman comments:

'I think experiencing it is believing it — it is difficult to put into words. My last doctor, an older country doctor, said, "Once a woman's had one at home, she never wants to go to hospital again." If only more women had that "once". I think the experience reverberates through the rest of your and your child's relationship and lives.'

The special qualities of birth are often lost in hospital, buried beneath the demands of the institution. At home it is easier to experience the event in a wholistic way:

'When my first baby was being born, when just her head had been delivered, her eyes were wide open, and she slowly looked right round the room at every person who was there. I felt she was taking in, in full measure, the atmosphere we had created for her birth — the glow of the fire, the colours of the flowers in vases around the bed, the nice colours of the room. We had been in that room for months, pregnant, waiting for the birth and it felt as if the baby was coming out into what was, admittedly, a harsher atmosphere than she had enjoyed in the womb, but also, in some way, a familiar one. The other lovely thing about home birth is the special energy that attends each birth — an almost tangible golden bubble that stays around for days afterwards — people come into it and go out of it and it almost seems to cushion and protect the new baby and the family in the first week or so after the birth. I would have hated to have left that bubble behind in some hospital delivery room!'

'I see birth, not as a procedure separate from everyday living, but as proceeding from the very roots of it. Being at home highlights the naturalness of birth, the everyday simplicity of it, as well as the transcendent quality of the experience. When I was in the early stages of labour and feeling full of joy and energy, I was mostly in our sitting room. For about a week after the birth, whenever I went into that room, there was still a tangible aura there left from that experience, that re-kindled the joy. In hospital, the experience of birth is easily fragmented and "de-spiritualised". At the same time, its natural, everyday quality is lost or obscured. I would have thought that this fact alone must be responsible for many complications in labour.'

The birth of a child allows a glimpse into the gateway of creation; it is truly a magical time, a time when ordinary life becomes charged with a special power, its transcendent nature bringing with it possibilities for new insights and personal growth. To have birth happen, quite naturally, in your own home, creates a shared experience of a very precious kind that can only enrich our lives. It is up to those who care about this issue to make sure that the choice of birth at home remains open for all who desire it.

RECOMMENDED READING

Vicki Junor and Marianne Monaco, *The Home Birth Handbook*, Souvenir Press, 1984.

Sheila Kitzinger, *Birth At Home*, Oxford University Press, 1979.

Sheila Kitzinger and John Davis (eds), *The Place of Birth*, Oxford University Press, 1978.

Ina May Gaskin, *Spiritual Midwifery*, The Book Publishing Company, 1980.

VIDEO FILM

Home Truths, produced by Yvonne Baginsky and Jack Shea, available from Circles, 113 Roman Road, London E2 0HU or Concord Films, 201 Felixstowe Road, Ipswich, Suffolk.

Nutrition — towards better beginnings

NANCY STEWART

Enduring a long wait in an international air terminal when I was seven months pregnant, I noticed an Iranian family also waiting for their flight to be called. The generations present ranged from the elderly patriarch to the toddling youngest. Suddenly from a bag someone produced several large, ripe melons, cutlery, and napkins — and I found myself wishing the waiting lounge fare ran to something other than chocolate bars, and that the in-flight meal weren't so far away. Then I notice the patriarch walking straight towards me. 'Please,' he said, 'my daughter-in-law wants to ask you this, but she is too shy. In our country we have a custom. If you are eating something, and there is a woman expecting a child, she must be offered first. Will you do us the honour to eat some melon?' When I gratefully assented, the young woman brought me a tray laid out with fork, knife and napkin, and the most wonderful wedge of melon I'd ever tasted.

I have since learned that other countries have similar customs, all reflecting a basic folk wisdom that more sophisticated approaches to pregnancy often ignore: that to build a healthy baby, there must be plenty of the right materials — and that these building blocks must come from the food the pregnant woman eats. The absence of such a central awareness in medical ante-natal care leaves many women and their babies subject to avoidable difficulties in pregnancy and birth.

For most women, ante-natal care today involves a series of repetitive visits to see a doctor, either in the GP surgery or hospital clinic. At these visits a pregnant woman may be weighed, her blood, urine, and blood pressure may be checked, her ankles examined for swelling; her baby may be palpated, scanned, and auscultated. In some cases amniocentesis, fetoscopy, oestriol and oxytocin challenge tests may be employed. All these procedures represent obstetrics' increasingly sophisticated attempts to chart the progress of a pregnancy, and to signal any difficulties which may have developed. Not one of these, however, can prevent the difficulties developing in the first place. An ultrasound scan may show that a baby is under-sized, but it cannot boost that baby's growth. Oestriol tests may indicate a placenta is failing, but cannot improve its functioning. Why, then, does modern obstetrics ignore the fundamental importance for the health of both mother and child of what a pregnant woman eats?

Most simply, perhaps, the answer is that obstetrics does not deal in health, but rather in disease. Doctors are trained to diagnose and, with varying degrees of success, to treat pathologies, but their training does not normally include the study of human nutrition, nor the role of nutrition in promoting health. There is also, I think, the underlying attitude that nutrition is a boring topic which is best confined to home economics classes or buried away behind the door marked 'dietician'. What someone ate for breakfast certainly lacks the glamorous appeal of the latest real-time scanner, or micro-surgery techniques. And there are two other possible explanations for medical disinterest in pregnancy nutrition that reflect the too-common status imbalance between an obstetrician and a pregnant woman. First, doctors may see the subject of food as carrying low status — it is traditionally a woman's role to feed people, and as such may be seen as beneath the gaze of men of science. One lecturer in obstetrics, responding to a self-help group that publicised a body of evidence linking poor nutrition with pre-eclampsia, complained about the emphasis given to diet: 'This reflects, I think, more the 'kitchen' role that is forced upon housewives and mothers rather than an insight into the causes of pre-eclampsia.' Secondly, if nutrition is granted its proper importance in pregnancy health, the skills the doctor has on offer are diminished in value by the degree to which the pregnant woman assumes responsibility for her own health. He can no longer promise her the safest pregnancy possible by attending a clinic for his ante-natal 'care', when she is providing the real care in her daily life. And much of his specialist birth and newborn technology becomes irrelevant, when she removes herself from a 'high risk' category by ensuring that she has fully nourished her body and her baby.

Perhaps midwives, in partnership with women, could give nutrition its proper place in ante-natal care. Earlier this century, a midwife's duties sometimes included baking egg custards for undernourished pregnant women. It is to be hoped that along with a reappraisal of traditional midwifery and women's own abilities in giving birth will come a new recognition of the traditional wisdom about nutrition in pregnancy, and women's abilities to promote their own pregnancy health.

Many different kinds of studies provide convincing evidence for the protective effects of good nutrition. One study compared outcomes for two groups of 750 women, many of whom were malnourished before pregnancy. The group who received careful nutrition counselling and vitamin and mineral supplements had *no* cases of pre-eclampsia or eclampsia (64 cases in the controls); *no* prematurity (37 in controls); and three cases of infant mortality (41 in the control group).[1] Another researcher studied pregnant women's diets, and then obtained independent paediatric assessments of the babies at birth: of the babies born to women on good or excellent diets, 94 per cent were in superior or good condition at birth, while only 3 per cent were in poor condition. But among those whose mothers' diets were poor, only 8 per cent were in superior or good condition, and 67 per cent were in poor condition (stillborn, under 2.3 kg/ 5 lb, or in poor health).[2]

There are indications that excellent nutrition protects against anaemias, infection, placental abruption, pre-eclampsia, and low birth-weight.[3, 4] Birth itself is straightforward in well-nourished mothers: one study found that well-nourished mothers had labours on average five hours shorter than those of poorly nourished mothers, and they had fewer complications requiring caesarean section, and faster post-natal recovery.[5]

The central role of maternal nutrition in childbearing health can be understood in terms of the basic physiology of pregnancy. During pregnancy, there is an integral connection between mother and child; they must be considered together as one system, so that the only way to promote the health of the child is to promote the health of the mother. And the pregnant mother's health depends on her meeting the increased nutritional demands of pregnancy. Beyond building the baby itself, she requires extra nutrients for the growth of a strong, co-ordinated uterus, which by full term will be up to 30 times its pre-pregnancy size. She must provide for the placenta, both enabling it to grow sufficiently large to serve as the transfer point to the baby, and maintaining it as a healthy organ in its own right so that it can function efficiently. She must provide for the expansion of her own blood volume to 40–60 per cent above her pre-pregnancy level. She must provide for the nutritional stress on her liver of coping with the enormous metabolic task that pregnancy entails; as well as its role as the 'master gland' regulating the body's use of food, the liver both produces the protein molecule (albumin) necessary for maintaining the expanded blood volume, and breaks down pregnancy hormones equivalent to about 100 birth control pills a day.

When the mother's nutrition is excellent, she maintains a good blood flow through a healthy placenta. Contrary to the common belief that a developing baby is like a parasite that can somehow obtain everything it needs directly from the mother's tissues, the baby's only link with the mother is through the placenta and umbilical cord. As the placenta begins to develop in the early weeks of pregnancy, it secretes an enzyme which dissolves the mother's fine uterine blood vessels at the site of attachment. Her circulation at the placenta then involves a pool of blood, fed by her arteries and drained away through her veins, which depends on the expanded blood volume to maintain its supply.[6] A thin membrane separates the mother's blood from the baby's circulation on its side of the placenta, and it is through this membrane that oxygen, nutrients, and other substances in the mother's bloodstream pass into the baby's circulation, through the umbilical cord to the baby, while waste products are passed back to the mother's bloodstream for disposal. It is only in this way, through nutrients in current circulation in the mother's bloodstream, that the baby receives its nourishment. When this is understood, there is no room for nonchalance about a pregnant woman's need for plentiful, high-quality foods every day throughout her pregnancy.

A pregnant woman's need for more good foods than when she is not pregnant is enshrined in the old maxim about 'eating for two'. In a traditional culture with sufficient available food, a pregnant woman could probably rely on her appetite to signal her increased nutritional needs — just as pets and livestock can be relied on to eat more during pregnancy. But for most women in industrialised socieities, the instinctive guidance of our appetites cannot be taken for granted. For one thing, we may be choosing processed, refined foods in which vital nutrients have been destroyed in the refining process. Processed foods can even rob our bodies of the nutrients other foods have provided, by not bringing even the nutrients necessary for their own digestion and use. The B vitamin pyridoxine, for example, is required for the body to metabolise protein, but is limited in many refined foods, so that eating a food which does not carry with it the amount of pyridoxine necessary for its own metabolism will actually deplete the body's supply of the vitamin. White bread, for example, has only 0.50 mg of pyridoxine per 100 g protein, while wholewheat bread has 1.60 mg. Luncheon meat has 0.16 mg and pork sausage 0.66 mg, while eggs bring 1.95 mg and lentils 2.50 mg. At the same time, some foods laden with chemical preservatives may satisfy our appetites without really feeding us, as the preservatives continue to preserve the foods against our own efforts to digest them! As Dr Barbara Pickard has said, 'Any food which is so processed and modified and loaded with preservatives that even the bacteria and moulds do not want to attack it is hardly likely to be of great nutritional value to you either.'[7]

Other factors stand in the way of heeding our instincts regarding pregnancy nutrition. High on the list is the ever-present image of the long-and-leggy fashionable woman, to whose shape her more sturdily built sisters often aspire. A history of strict, and often unbalanced, dieting leaves a woman in poor condition to begin a pregnancy. Low pre-pregnancy weight is in fact associated with a higher risk of many pregnancy complications. Even for non-pregnant people, there is no evidence that the 'recommended weights' often cited by health agencies hold any special advantages for health, excluding extremes at either end of the spectrum. But in pregnancy, efforts to avoid gaining much weight in deference to the fashionable image can actually be dangerous for both a woman and her baby. A woman worried about excess weight after the birth can be reassured that the extra pounds in a healthy weight gain consist partly of retained fluid, which is shed immediately after the birth, and that breast-feeding over the following weeks helps to burn up any extra fat stored for this brief but important period.

Sometimes the effort to control weight gain in pregnancy results from a medically advised limit. Over the years, changing medical fashion has led doctors to advise limits varying from 4.5 kg (10 lb) to the more currently popular 12.5 kg (2 stones), but there is no evidence supporting any such arbitrary bounds. And any arbitrary limit can lead a woman to curtail her food intake as she approaches the 'magic number' late in pregnancy — just when the stress is greatest on her system, when the baby is having a rapid growth spurt, and when the baby's brain is in its phase of most rapid development. Supplying sufficient nutrients at this time is vital. It does not work to adopt a diet of high-protein foods and fresh salads, cutting out starchy bread and potatoes to limit calories and avoid gaining weight. If a woman does not consume enough calories to meet her energy needs, her body burns up the protein for energy, so it is not available to build her baby and sustain her pregnancy health: instead of a high-protein, low-calorie diet, she is in effect on a *low*-protein, low-calorie diet.[8]

The evidence on weight gain indicates that babies whose mothers gain the most weight during pregnancy are at least risk of problems. Birth-weight is more closely linked with the mother's weight gain than with any other factor, and birth-weight is highly associated with the child's future mental and physical development. One analysis of over 10,000 births found that babies whose mothers gained over 16 kg (36 lb) had the lowest levels of brain damage and mental and motor abnormalities, while the incidence of abnormalities steadily increased as the mothers' weight gains dropped.[9]

This doesn't necessarily mean that a woman should strive to gain a lot — weight gain may give a clue about the mother's nutrition, but by itself is not an adequate measure. Gaining 16 kg (36 lb) from crisps and desserts won't do either mother or baby any good. Another study of 746 Scottish women with normal pregnancies, who *ate to appetite* in pregnancy and all gave birth to big, healthy babies, found that their weight gains didn't follow any pattern from week to week, and the weight gains over the last half of the pregnancies ranged from virtually nothing to over 18 kg (40 lb).[10] Every pregnant woman is different — activity levels, food choices, metabolism rates, and life stresses provide infinite variations in how her body uses food. She need not try to match some 'ideal' weight gain that is probably not ideal *for her*. The important thing is to ensure excellent nutrition for her own pregnancy, eating to appetite from a range of wholesome foods, and she can then let her weight gain take care of itself.

If we are to begin to change the ante-natal question from 'how much weight am I putting on?' to 'what exactly am I eating?', we need a description of a good pregnancy diet to check the answer against. The exact components of a healthy diet in pregnancy are as varied as are pregnant women, since each woman has her own individual eating preferences and habits, exercise routines, metabolism, and life stresses. It is unnecessary for a woman to work out each day a precise diet to meet her needs; and it is almost an impossiblity, considering that there are over fifty nutrients known to be essential to human life, all present in foods in differing amounts according to how the foods were grown, how fresh they are, how they are prepared — and with a multitude of interactions between nutrients affecting how the body uses them. And eating by calories and milligrams is enough to take anyone's appetite away! But numerous research studies and years of clinical experience, such as the work of Tom Brewer in California and Agnes Higgins at the Montreal Diet Dispensary, have combined to outline the basic features of a good pregnancy diet.[11] With a few guiding principles based on this knowledge, it is relatively simple to check one's daily nutrition status.

PROTEIN

Protein is the basic building block of all body tissues, and so is vital in pregnancy to produce the baby, placenta, uterine growth, and extra blood supply. *Animal proteins* (meat, fish, poultry, eggs, milk, cheese) are 'complete' proteins, which means they contain all the necessary amino acids for the body to use them to produce human protein. *Vegetable proteins* are 'incomplete' —

they contain only some of the essential amino acids, and need to be eaten together with other foods that supply the missing ones. Pulses (dried beans, lentils, split peas, peanuts) are good sources of vegetable protein, but must be eaten together with seeds or grains, like rice, bread, or pasta. The protein in grains is also complemented by dairy foods, so a dish like wholewheat macaroni and cheese provides good, usable protein.[12]

Milk and eggs are good, relatively inexpensive sources of protein, and can often be added to boost the value of cooked dishes. Both of these foods have been criticised from time to time, eggs for their cholesterol content and milk for its 'indigestibility'. But cholesterol in the bloodstream does not come directly from the food eaten, but is produced by the body — and eggs have a very high ratio of lecithin, which keeps fats in suspension and helps prevent clogged arteries. So eggs, which contain everything necessary for a chick to grow, are a valuable food to help build babies. Some people have been led to believe that milk should be avoided because adults may lack an enzyme necessary to digest milk sugar. But this milk sugar intolerance affects only about 1 out of 20 northern Europeans, and 1 out of 5 Africans. Unless a woman experiences stomach cramps and diarrhoea after having milk or cheese, she can take advantage of milk's excellent food value.

Eating a good proportion of vegetable proteins rather than meat makes a high-protein diet less costly, provides good bulk and fibre, and helps avoid many of the chemical and hormonal residues that become concentrated in intensely reared meat animals.

It's often said that we in the western world consume more protein than we need. That may be true, on average, for the non-pregnant population. But a pregnant woman is an individual, and she needs extra protein in pregnancy — so it should never be taken for granted that she is obtaining enough high-quality protein in her diet. Studies have shown that the least chance of problems in pregnancy and the healthiest babies results when a woman has at least 75 grams of protein per day, and many workers in this field recommend a minimum 80–100 grams[13].

CALORIES

Extra calories are needed in pregnancy for energy, and to spare the protein for tissue-building. A minimum calorie level of 2,600 per day is recommended. All foods have calories, but particularly carbohydrates like grains and starchy fruits and vegetables; and fats. While there is no need to fear calories in pregnancy, it is preferable that they come from wholesome foods rather than from sugar-laden or highly processed snack foods that satisfy the appetite without providing other important nutrients.

WHOLE GRAINS

Whole grains are a rich source of B vitamins, as well as providing minerals, protein, and carbohydrate for energy. Whole grains are much better food value than white or refined grains, and are more satisfying. Choices include wholewheat bread (not just 'brown' breads, which are often poor-quality loaves with only a portion of wholemeal flour), and whole grain crispbreads and biscuits (such as Ryvita, digestives, oatcakes). Breakfast cereals needn't be the empty foil for milk that most processed cereals represent: muesli, porridge, and some ready-to-eat cereals like Weetabix and Shredded Wheat are all valuable foods. Home-baking provides the opportunity to replace at least part of the plain flour in recipes with wholemeal flour, as well as avoiding the additives in many prepared foods. A change from a diet of refined grains is best made gradually, to allow the digestion to adjust to the new, healthy fibre content.

FRUITS AND VEGETABLES

Fresh fruits and vegetables are excellent sources of many vitamins and minerals. This crucial element of a healthy diet is neglected in too many British households — as a nation, we consume per person per day less than half the French figure, and just over a quarter of the Italian equivalent.

Freshness is particularly important for vitamin C foods, as this vitamin is easily destroyed by heat, by light, and by contact with the air, and can be washed out in water. So vitamin C foods are best eaten fresh and raw, cut just before serving. Vitamin C is needed for growth and development of most body tissues (it is a primary nutrient necessary for healthy growth of the uterus during pregnancy), while increasing resistance to infection and promoting healing. A constantly replenished supply is necessary, since the body does not store vitamin C, so a pregnant woman should have each day two servings of a vitamin C food such as: orange, grapefruit, lemon, tomato, green pepper, parsley, rose hips, potatoes baked whole in their skins.

Green leafy vegetables are important for contributing iron and other minerals, folic acid, and vitamins A and C. A good guide is two daily servings from: cabbage, brussels sprouts, spinach, lettuce, broccoli, kale, cress, watercress. Sprouted seeds such as mung bean, alfalfa, or fenugreek seeds are also rich sources of nutrients.

Yellow or orange-coloured vegetables and fruits should also appear in the diet at least five times a week. These foods — such as carrots, swedes, parsnips, peaches, apricots, pumpkin — contain vitamin A which helps guard against infections.

The preparation of fruits and vegetables has a big impact on their food value. Faded, limp, overcooked vegetables offer as little in the way of nutrients as they do to the palate. Fresh foods are first choice, with a good portion eaten raw. When fresh produce is not available, frozen vegetables are more valuable than tinned. Vegetables should be cooked in as little water as possible (steamed or pressure-cooked) to avoid throwing the goodness out in the cooking water — which should ideally be saved to make a nutritious stock for adding to soups, stews, cooking rice, etc.

FATS

While an excessive fat consumption is a danger to health, a moderate amount of fat is an essential part of a healthy diet. Good-quality fats provide important nutrients which are involved in development of a baby's nervous system, and they are also required for the absorption of vitamins like A and E. Butter and unrefined natural oils such as corn oil, safflower oil, soya oil, and olive oil are preferable to processed, hydrogenated fats or lard. Good-quality fats are also contained in other foods, like whole milk, cheese, meat, oily fish, nuts and seeds.

SALT

Salt is an essential nutrient and, contrary to common advice, should not be limited in pregnancy (except in rare cases of underlying disease like kidney or congestive heart failure). While dietary salt in the general population is controversial, extra salt is needed in pregnancy to maintain the expanded blood volume for placental perfusion, and to guard against dehydration and shock from blood loss at birth. A study conducted at a London hospital in 1958 revealed the dangerous consequences of salt restriction: 1,000 women were told to decrease their salt intake, while 1,019 were instructed to increase salt. The women on low-salt diets had much higher rates of miscarriage, perinatal death, pre-eclampsia and eclampsia, caesareans, and other complications.[14] The normal swelling of ankles, fingers, and face experienced by about 80 per cent of healthy pregnant women is *not* a cause for concern in a well-nourished woman, and should not be confused with the pathological swelling of pre-eclampsia — and in neither case should salt restriction or diuretic drugs be used to deplete the body of essential sodium and fluids. In pregnancy the body's salt-regulating mechanism is very efficient, so a woman can simply salt her food to taste.

WATER

Water is needed by all body tissues. A pregnant woman can satisfy her thirst with water, fruit juices, mild herbal teas, grain 'coffees'. Coffee and tea, which contain caffeine, should be avoided or limited in pregnancy, a precaution often supported by a natural aversion to caffeine drinks in pregnancy.

SUPPLEMENTS

The best source of vitamins and minerals is a healthy diet. Pills can never substitute for the range of essential substances, sometimes present only as a trace, that foods contain. It should never be assumed that taking vitamin and mineral supplements can replace the need to eat well.

Natural supplements like Brewer's yeast (rich in iron and B vitamins), wheatgerm, or codliver oil can be useful additions to the diet. In special situations when a prepared pill might be considered, a balanced composite of nutrients is preferable to single vitamin or single mineral preparations, or unbalanced combinations, since an excess of one nutrient can cause a deficiency of another. Some nutrients, like vitamins A and D, can be toxic in large doses. There are indications that large doses of iron — commonly prescribed during pregnancy — may be both unnecessary and possibly harmful.[15] A woman who is really well nourished is unlikely to need such supplements.

THINGS TO AVOID

Food additives, alcohol, and *any* drug which is not absolutely necessary are best avoided in pregnancy, as the effects on a developing baby are not fully known. In our polluted world, where we are surrounded by unavoidable toxins in our air, water and food, however, it is worth noting that excellent nutrition offers a degree of protection against the effects of many toxins.

In considering optimal nutrition for each pregnant woman, it is essential that each woman's individual needs be considered. Since various life stresses can increase nutritional demands, pregnancy health may require food intakes above the minimum standards in many cases. Agnes Higgins of the Montreal Diet Dispensary recommends supplements of an extra 20 grams of protein and 500 calories daily to compensate for each condition of nutritional stress, including serious emotional problems, underweight before pregnancy, pregnancies less than a year apart, previous poor obstetric history, full-time work during pregnancy, breast-feeding while pregnant, failure to gain 4.5 kg (10 lb) by the twentieth week, persistent vomiting. For twin pregnancy, an additional 50 grams of protein and 1,000 calories are required beyond the recommendations for singleton pregnancy.

Making changes in the way we eat is not always simple. It can involve basic changes in lifestyle, since our eating habits are tied up in our social existence, and connected with such things as how and where we shop, how we cook, our emotional reactions to food, and our family and cultural background. But the requirements of good nutrition can be met in many ways to suit each individual. And what better time to make changes for the better than around the pivotal time of pregnancy, when the shifting to accommodate new relationships and new responsibilities provides a powerful opportunity for growth and change. A new awareness of the importance of nutrition will reap benefits far beyond the birth of a healthy baby, as it overflows into breast feeding and feeding a growing family, and enables each individual to take more responsibility for promoting her own health.

REFERENCES

1 W. T. Tompkins, 'The significance of nutritional deficiency in pregnancy: A preliminary report', *Journal of International College of Surgeons*, 4:147–54, 1941.

2 B. S. Burke *et al*, 'The influence of nutrition during pregnancy upon the condition of the infant at birth', *Journal of Nutrition*, vol. 26, pp. 569–83, 1943.

3 D. Shanklin and J. Hodin, *Maternal Nutrition and Child Health*, Charles C. Thomas, Springfield, Ill., 1979.

4 Gail Sforza Brewer, *What Every Pregnant Woman Should Know: The Truth about Diet and Drugs in Pregnancy*, Penguin, 1979. (This book explains the nutritional cause and prevention of pre-eclamptic toxaemia, while giving support to the well-nourished pregnant woman whose physiological swelling or blood pressure rise is misdiagnosed as pre-eclampsia.)

5 J. H. Ebbs *et al*, 'Nutrition in Pregnancy', *Canadian Medical Association Journal*, vol. 46, pp. 1–6, 1942.

6 As demonstrated by Margaret Ramsey, Carnegie Institute, Washington DC, 1963.

7   Barbara Pickard, 'Are you fit enough to become pregnant', published by the author, 1981.

8   B. S. Platt and R. J. C. Stewart, 'Reversible and irreversible effects of protein-calorie deficiency on the central nervous system of animals and man', *World Review of Nutrition and Diet*, 13:43–85, 1971.

9   J. E. Singer, *et al*, 'Relationship of weight gain during pregnancy to birth weight and infant growth and development in the first year of life', *Obstetrics and Gynaecology*, 31:417, 1968.

10 F. E. Hytten and A. M. Thompson, 'Maternal physiological adjustments', in *Maternal Nutrition and the Course of Pregnancy*, Washington DC, Committee on Maternal Nutrition, Food and Nutrition Board, National Research Council, National Academy of Sciences, 1970.

11 Gail Sforze Brewer with Tom Brewer, *The Brewer Medical Diet for Normal and High-Risk Pregnancy*, Simon & Schuster, NY, 1983.

12 Frances Moore Lappe, *Diet for a Small Planet*, Ballantine Books, 1975.

13 Worthington-Roberts *et al*, *Nutrition in Pregnancy and Lactation*, 2nd ed., C. V. Mosby Co., St Louis, 1981.

14 Margaret Robinson, 'Salt in pregnancy', *Lancet*, no. 1, p. 178, 1958.

15 D. J. Taylor and T. Lind, 'Haematological changes during normal pregnancy: iron-induced macrocytosis', *British Journal of Obstetrics and Gynaecology*, vol. 83, pp. 760–9, 1976.

RECOMMENDED READING

Gail Sforze Brewer with Tom Brewer, *The Brewer Medical Diet for Normal and High-Risk Pregnancy*, Simon & Schuster, NY, 1983.

Barbara Pickard, *Eating Well For A Healthy Pregnancy*, Sheldon Press, 1984.

Catherine Lewis, *Good Food Before Birth*, Unwin Paperbacks, 1984.

Yoga for pregnancy and birth

SOPHY HOARE

THE NEED FOR PREPARATION

Every healthy woman has the potential ability to give birth naturally, and to feed her baby with her own milk for the first months of its life. For the birth process to take place naturally and safely, every woman has to realise this potential, has to discover and understand her own innate ability so that she has the confidence to trust in her body and the creative life force that works through her.

In the past it has been the role of the midwife and other birth attendants to provide the kind of physical, emotional and spiritual support that will help the labouring woman to discover her own power. Nearly all women need this support, especially when approaching labour for the first time, for birth is after all a momentous experience in which life is at stake and is every time a journey into the unknown. Apart from the support she receives at the time of birth, a woman's confidence in her body will be conditioned to a large extent by the prevalent attitudes to birth in the society in which she lives. Unfortunately for natural birth, our society fosters attitudes which are quite negative in this respect. Within the existing health care system, a woman's confidence is gradually and steadily undermined from before the time she conceives, throughout the pregnancy to birth and beyond. From the time a woman is first aware of her pregnancy, she starts to hand over responsibility for herself and her baby to the medical profession. A pregnancy is not generally 'officially' accepted until it has been confirmed by a doctor. Ante-natal care is often conducted in such a way that it instils more anxiety and stress in the pregnant woman than confidence or joy. As the birth approaches, if her pregnancy is not conforming to the required pattern, a woman may be told that she will have to be hospitalised, will have to be induced, will have to be electronically monitored, will 'need' an epidural, an episiotomy or a caesarean, and so on. Most women meekly accept what the medical 'experts' are telling them about their own bodies and go into labour with their chances of discovering their natural ability to give birth hopelessly reduced.

Given the non-supportive nature of our present system, the woman who wants a natural birth clearly needs a special kind of preparation to develop her confidence and independence and to withstand the pressures that may be put on her by those who believe they know her body better than she does. She needs to be not only well informed intellectually, but, even more important, to increase her self-knowledge through a practice such as yoga so that she can perceive and trust her own instincts, discriminate between the conflicting opinions surrounding her, and literally have confidence in her own body.

The practice of yoga has strong affinities with the discovery of our physical and instinctive self during the process of pregnancy and birth. Both involve self-realisation. Realising (in both senses of the word) our ability to give birth is not something learned or imposed but is literally dis-covered. In a similar way, when we work on ourselves in yoga we release physical and emotional blocks which stand in the way of complete freedom of action and obscure our essential selves; we become more and more ourselves, less conditioned by what others tell us or expect of us. The actual process of yoga practice — the here and now experience of placing our body in the asanas or postures — takes us directly into ourselves, brings us face to face with our limitations, our weakness, our stiffness, our lack of balance and symmetry, our mental resistance, and so on. The practice teaches us where to be firm and where to let go; it increases our capacity for acceptance as we release into difficult stretches and at the same time develops our sense of inner strength and potential. This breeds a confidence in the body which is perhaps the most valuable asset for a pregnant woman to have. We learn that the body has its own intelligence and that it knows what to do if we will only trust in it and let it function without the hindrance of the mind; the mind must learn to listen to the body. When this becomes possible, the extraordinarily powerful physical sensations of childbirth can be more easily accepted and surrendered to; there is no fear; there is an instinctive knowledge that the sensations are right and positive, if painful — a manifestation of the natural process.

For childbirth is an intensely physical experience, for most of us probably the most primitive and powerful physical experience we go through between our own birth and death. Even the most cerebral woman cannot escape this fact. In our society most people's lives are physically undemanding. The average Western woman's body is not robust, but weak, stiff, hesitant and rarely if ever pushed to its limits. For many women, pregnancy may be the first time since childhood that they have become really aware of their body. With the majority of people out of touch with their own bodies, it is little wonder that we live in a society in which the individual has surrendered her sense of personal power to the professionals, the 'experts', and that they in turn have an attitude of little faith in the individual's potential, further undermining rather than boosting a woman's self-confidence.

ATTITUDES

The conventional attitude to pregnancy is negative to the point of regarding it almost as a disease, an attitude that is reinforced by the fact that most births now take place in hospital. At best, pregnancy is seen as a time when one is not one's 'normal' self; we talk of 'getting back to normal' after the birth. Pregnant women are advised to take care of themselves in what is usually a rather negative way. They are told to rest, not to over-exert themselves, to be extremely cautious about physical activity, especially in the first three months and the last month or two (which amounts to well over half the pregnancy), not to put on too much weight, and so on. When you practise yoga, you start to take care of yourself in a very positive way. According to yoga, the body is the temple of the soul and as such should be neither neglected nor pampered. While careful attention is paid to keeping healthy, the care bestowed on the body is not self-indulgent; it is both loving and tinged with the austerity that is a part of any discipline. In this way a healthy balance is achieved, a fine 'tuning-in' to the body. Yoga comes to be regarded as a precious means of living in a skilful and balanced way, invaluable during pregnancy for safeguarding the health of yourself and your child. The conventional, medically approved attitude is that, by not exercising during pregnancy you are playing safe and avoiding risks. Yoga shows us that such an attitude can be harmful. Neglecting the body can and does lead to problems of pregnancy, from varicose veins and piles to high blood pressure and associated serious diseases. Practising the appropriate yoga postures keeps the body strong and resilient and regulates the hormone balance, essential for a safe pregnancy and birth. Perhaps most importantly, not working the body encourages a timid and fearful attitude which can disturb the whole process of pregnancy and labour and cause complications, such is the close relationship between body and mind. The more pregnancy is regarded as a disease or abnormal state, the more it becomes one. The positive approach to your own health that yoga develops not only helps to ensure a healthy pregnancy but is an invaluable psychological asset during the whole childbearing period.

YOGA AND NATURAL BIRTH

During labour, the value of yoga lies in helping us not to disturb the natural working of the body through fear or tension; it helps us to undo the blocks that may stand in the way of a natural, normal, safe birth. All medical intervention disturbs this process. By intervention is meant any obtrusive procedure which attempts to transfer control of the birth from the mother's own body and instincts to those 'managing' the delivery: typical examples being induction or acceleration of labour, foetal monitoring by machines attached to mother or baby and restricting movement, pain-killing drugs, forceps, episiotomy and so on. Because an attitude of non-intervention (except in the rare cases where a serious complication arises), of trusting primarily in the body's own intelligence, is not in line with the prevailing attitudes in our society of wishing always to control and dominate the natural process, to be uncompromisingly in favour of natural birth is what Michel Odent refers to as a 'counter-cultural act'. Yoga has traditionally been a counter-cultural practice; since its earliest days its function has been to cut through cultural dependence and bring the individual in touch with his or her own powers, to have faith in the truth that is found within. In this sense yoga is a revolutionary practice, and for this reason it is a valuable tool for those wishing to give birth naturally in a highly technological society.

Yoga is not a method for ensuring an easy birth; there is no such magic formula. Yoga is a life practice, a way of working on ourselves to be able to retain our equanimity in the face of any circumstances. But, of course, working on yourself will influence what happens to you. Being fit and healthy optimises your chances of a happy pregnancy and birth; a positive attitude communicates itself to other people, influencing their actions, however subtly. The repercussions of our own behaviour are far-reaching, if largely unknowable. So, by practising yoga, you are assuming responsibility for yourself and reducing your dependence on others and your vulnerability to external conditions. Paradoxically, the more in-dependent you become, the more you experience the inter-dependence of all things and are able to trust in the natural process and in other people, including your professional care-givers. And a relationship of trust with those people is essential for an undisturbed natural birth. Yoga is a way of preparing the ground from within. It is an ideal preparation for birth, a way of equipping yourself to deal with the unexpected, for every birth experience is different and, for all your careful planning, cannot be predicted; one has to be ready to venture into the unknown.

THE BENEFITS

The physical benefits of practising yoga during pregnancy are almost too numerous to list. The postures help to develop strong, supple feet, essential if you are to carry your baby with ease as well as building strength in the legs and back. At the same time they create an awareness of correct posture, bringing the whole body into alignment. This combination of strength and balance is particularly important in pregnancy, when the change in body shape often distorts posture, causing permanent tension which may not even be noticed until it results in pain and excessive fatigue. Common problems associated with poor posture and inactivity can persist for long after the baby is born, a typical example being back pain. It is not unusual to hear women complain that they have not been in good physical shape since the birth of their first child. The yoga postures stretch and strengthen the spine thoroughly and evenly. Improving circulation to the spine affects the entire body since the nerves have their origin in the spinal column. Improved muscle tone protects the joints, whose ligaments become looser than usual (sometimes dramatically so) under the influence of the pregnancy hormones. The advantage of yoga here is that it strengthens without tightening. Strength and mobility are both improved, so while yoga increases the suppleness that is necessary for birth, it protects against over-stretching, as long as it is practised as it should be, without forcing the body. As the joints become more mobile, positions that are useful during pregnancy and labour (for example, squatting, kneeling, sitting cross-legged) can be assumed with ease. The postures also expand and open the chest, freeing the lungs and heart from pressure due to hunched posture and facilitating deep breathing, thus ensuring a good supply of oxygen to the baby. Circulation is improved, together with any associated problems such as cramp or varicose veins. As well as the more apparent benefits, yoga regulates the functioning of the internal organs, glands and nerves. In fact, most of the ailments that our society considers a normal hazard of pregnancy are quite unnecessary!

When you have explored your body through yoga practice, you are likely to feel freer throughout your pregnancy and labour to follow the dictates of your body rather than those of convention, finding the appropriate posture for every situation. In this way you grow steadily more in touch with your body and instincts, handling yourself with a grace and ease which are far removed from the awkward, cumbersome figures that many women become in the later stages of pregnancy. Your body does not become a stranger to you, you are confortable with the way you are, so that carrying the baby may be less of a burden and more a joy and a privilege.

These physical benefits of yoga have important psychological effects. Having confidence in the way your body works is an outstanding advantage in labour, when you have to let your body take over completely, to trust that it 'knows what it is doing' in the face of powerful and often painful and overwhelming sensations. The process of yoga stretching provides a good preparation for accepting the experience of birth. Yoga teaches how to discriminate between the 'positive' pain of stretching and the 'negative' pain of injury. Facing and responding appropriately to pain occurs all the time in yoga; injury happens only when you stop listening carefully to the body, so you really do learn to tune in to your body. This requires concentration, letting the mind become still and receptive, just the frame of mind which appears to be necessary for a safe and natural birth, and which Michel Odent tries to encourage at his hospital in Pithiviers by adjusting the environment in which women give birth. The physical environment (reducing sensory stimulation), certain postures, immersion in warm water, and affectionate bodily contact with a caring birth attendant with a minimum of verbal communication, all help a woman to shift from her everyday mind with its busy rational brain to an inwardly turned, meditative state of consciousness which facilitates the birth process. Since most women today are going into labour in conditions rather different from those at Pithiviers, it is clearly a great advantage to be used to turning your attention inwards, through yoga practice, and to find a place within yourself where you are distracted as little as possible by obtrusive external stimuli. Moreover, while in labour you need to be in a state of mind in which you are unconcerned about what sort of behaviour is expected of you. You must be free to do whatever your instincts tell you, whether this means shouting or moaning or rocking your body to and fro. In other words, essential to the altered state of consciousness is a kind of social de-conditioning. This probably comes more easily to those who practise yoga because they have become accustomed to listening to their body and relying on their own inner voice rather than on what other people tell them. Yoga helps to undo, or at least loosen, a certain amount of our cultural conditioning, which, in our society, tends to take us away from the physical and the primitive.

WHAT IS YOGA?

In its broadest sense, yoga is a path of self-development which leads to an identification with something greater than one's personal self, a source of energy and support which can be reached when we are able to let go of the fears, ambitions and desires which belong to the ego-self. Yoga is about taking responsibility for our own lives and at the same time surrendering to life. The Sanskrit word 'yoga' means yoke or union and conveys both the experience of union of the self with the greater life force and the idea of harnessing yourself to a fairly exact discipline.

This discipline, the classical practice of yoga, consists of the observation of fundamental ethical precepts; the regular practice of physical postures, or asanas; breathing exercises; relaxation; concentration and meditation. Moral conduct is the foundation of all yoga practice, and a healthy robust body with firm and balanced posture is a prerequisite for effective breathing and meditation practice. In fact, these various aspects of yoga (or limbs, as they are traditionally known) are all interdependent. Thus yoga is a discipline not only of the body nor of the mind, but of the whole person; it encompasses physical, emotional, mental and spiritual health. When the body is regarded as the temple of the soul, exercising it takes on a completely new dimension compared with other forms of exercise and sport, a dimension that seems especially appropriate when it is the vehicle for creating a new life.

The word for yoga posture, 'Asana', means literally seat, implying that, with practice, you should be able to stay in the postures long enough to relax into them and achieve a state of balance and steadiness. Firmness and suppleness are equally important in this respect. A pliant, weak body will benefit from asana practice by becoming stronger and more centred; a strong, stiff body will become more open and flexible. Physical attitudes are related to mental attitudes. At first, due to each individual's particular weaknesses and tensions, many of the postures are difficult to practise and involve considerable challenge and effort, both mental and physical. However, although there is effort, there should never be strain; the body should not be forced but taken by degrees to its limit of stretching and allowed to stay at that point and accept and assimilate the experience before proceeding further. Practised in this spirit, the asanas are appropriate for pregnancy, when the body can work hard but strain must be avoided. As the asanas become easier to adopt and hold, your attention turns to finer and finer points in the way your body works, so that you never exhaust the possibilities of any pose — further refinement is always possible. Thus there is no fixed goal and there is never stagnation. Though the postures are held in stillness there is always movement and something at work (even when progress is not very apparent!); gradually your powers of discernment increase so that you become more able to listen to and take heed of the body's messages. These developments have obvious advantages during pregnancy and labour, helping you to flow with the process of growth, change and birth, to have confidence in the body and to dissolve fear.

There are literally hundreds of asanas, and each has a particular effect on the body and mind. Yet they are all variations of certain fundamental principles of posture which are most simply expressed in the relatively small groups of basic asanas. It is postures from this group which are most useful during pregnancy, especially the second half of pregnancy when the enlarging abdomen rules out most of the more complicated poses. The postures most suitable for pregnancy are thus the standing postures and the basic sitting and inverted poses.

The standing postures, often neglected in books recommending exercises for pregnancy, are very important for developing strength in the feet, legs and back so that the physical load of the baby and extra body-weight can be carried with ease. They teach correct posture, reducing strain and fatigue and improving breathing and circulation. Practising the standing poses throughout pregnancy helps to develop a sense of positive energy, personal power, self-confidence and joy. By teaching you always to stretch up and make space in the body, rather than being pulled passively downwards by gravity, they cultivate a feeling of lightness and space both for your own limbs and joints to move and for the baby within. The standing poses make you aware of the importance of the feet and their contact with the ground, and of the energy that can be obtained from the earth when this contact is realised. They help to bring your awareness to your physical centre, associated in yoga and other Eastern disciplines with psychological stability.

In the first half of pregnancy most of the standing postures can be practised, with few limitations apart from possible fatigue in the first three months. When there is extreme tiredness or nausea, they should be practised at an appropriate time of day and not held for too long. In the second half of pregnancy some of the standing postures have to be discontinued or modified in order to keep the front of the body free and avoid any squashing or downward dragging pressure on the baby.

The sitting postures become more and more important as pregnancy progresses. They stretch the legs and spine, strengthen the back and teach how to sit well at all times in everyday life. They increase flexibility in the ankle, knee and hip joints, enabling you to adopt positions that are beneficial for you and the baby during pregnancy, labour and after. For example, sitting or kneeling on a firm surface with a straight back is better for your spine, and makes more space for the baby, than leaning back in a soft armchair. Although the armchair may seem more inviting at first, in the long run it is far less comfortable than the physiologically correct yogic sitting positions. Many women in the later stages of pregnancy complain that they 'can't get comfortable'. This is their body telling them that they are sitting or standing badly. Sitting, or kneeling, on the floor with a straight back and the body in balance helps to bring the mind to rest at a steady point of equilibrium. Sitting still for only a few minutes a day will give your mind a chance to become still and receptive, alert and clear. It is for good reason that the classic yoga sitting and kneeling poses have been used for meditation and prayer in many different traditions from time immemorial. This daily session of sitting quietly is not only invaluable in helping you to put things in perspective in your daily life, but also familiarises you with the inwardly turned frame of mind which will help you to ride your labour and birth.

The sitting postures have another useful function towards the end of pregnancy. Some of them work particularly on the hips and pelvic area, helping your body to function well during the birth and making you more aware of the muscles around the pelvis and in the pelvic floor so that you can release them consciously during labour. Many people are tight in the hips and inner thighs and feel vulnerable in this area, the tightness being a form of self-protection, and it requires a great deal of concentration and awareness of the breath to be able to let go. For this reason, practising these particular postures can be a valuable preparation for breathing through and releasing into the contractions of labour.

The inverted postures, such as Headstand and Shoulderstand, have their own particular benefits during pregnancy. They have a direct effect on the glands, regulating hormone production and helping to protect against miscarriage. They can be very helpful in the early months in relieving nausea, and throughout pregnancy the reversed pull of gravity is very beneficial, improving circulation, relieving heaviness and keeping the internal organs healthy, thus preventing many ailments that are regarded as typical of pregnancy. The inverted poses are stimulating, energy-restoring asanas which improve your sense of balance and give you both literally and figuratively a new perspective on life.

One of the most important yoga postures is Savasana, the Corpse pose, in which body and mind are deeply relaxed. Savasana is practised lying flat on the floor with the spine lengthened and the limbs spread out in such a way that every part of the body can relax completely. It is practised at the end of every yoga session to restore energy to the body, to centre yourself and to detach yourself from the fruits of your labours at the same time as allowing the body to assimilate the work that has gone on, so that a lasting impression is made on it and the unconscious mind. This kind of deep relaxation is of obvious benefit during pregnancy and after, helping to undo tensions and reveal the unchanging centre of the self, as well as enabling us to surrender to life in a way that is often difficult for people in our world which places so much value on being rational and 'in control', but which is helpful, necessary even, when confronting an experience such as birth.

The valuable parallels between our yoga practice and opening ourselves to the birth experience can be seen in the following remarks, which apply equally well to both. They may be helpful in colouring your attitude to your labour especially if your environment is less than relaxing:

Take your attention away from your head to the centre of your body to feel grounded and stable.

Release tension on the exhalation.

When a sensation is painful, go towards it, listen to it. Do not try to interpret before listening.

Do not try to *do* anything, only to undo what is stopping you from accepting what is happening in your body.

Be attentive to the moment, not to a future goal.

Your body knows how to do this. Have faith in your body and the way it works.

AFTER THE BIRTH

After the birth you will benefit both from having practised yoga throughout pregnancy and from continuing to practise. Apart from the many and obvious physical advantages, there are two important qualities that the yoga practice will have helped to develop: the confidence in your own instinctive knowledge that is necessary for breast feeding and generally caring for your baby in a straightforward and relaxed way; and the continuing ability to flow with the changes that take place through the whole childbearing period. The post-natal period brings with it as many changes as the pregnancy and birth; it is a period as unique as the pregnancy and a continuation of it. It is perhaps a mistake to think in terms of returning to normal as soon as possible after the birth, and indeed an illusion to think that there is such a thing as a static 'normal' condition. The condition of life is one of flow and change, with a kind of dynamic balance maintained in the midst of change. To try to hold on to a fixed image of yourself leads to suffering when the image can no longer hold its own against reality; at the same time, behind ideas and images can be found the unchanging centre of the self when we are able to let go of our fixed attitudes and expectations. Yoga brings us in touch with the flow of life and with the enduring centre; in this way changes in our circumstances can be accepted without fear of losing our personal identity. As we observe the changes in ourselves through pregnancy and after we can give ourselves wholeheartedly to the process and be the richer and healthier for it.

Birth can be seen now not as a procedure separate from the living of each day, but rather as a *proceeding* from the very roots of it. The greatest preparation that can be made for the birth of a child is to allow for the constant arising of birth in one's self. And this arising can take place only in a space that is clear and free of expectation.

Maria Rosenstone

RECOMMENDED READING

B. K. S. Iyengar, *Light On Yoga*, Allen & Unwin, 1982.
Sophy Hoare, *Yoga and Pregnancy*, Allen & Unwin, 1985.
Frederick Leboyer, *Inner Beauty, Inner Light*, Collins, 1979.

Preparing yourself with confidence

CAROLE ELLIOTT

To know that you know could well be a sub-title for this chapter because every woman has the information about having babies stored inside her. Having babies is instinctive, they are grown instinctively and can be given birth to instinctively. Every woman can, during her pregnancy and birth, tap into a kind of universal or collective unconscious of womankind giving birth to human beings through the ages, a tremendous reservoir of strength and energy. A guideline to women is: act on your instinct, your power as woman, derive wisdom from your intuition, recognise an indwelling knowledge that cannot be denied and may be itself requesting freedom for expression.

Pregnancy is a process that is both truly creative and utterly receptive, unifying and integrating mind, body and spirit. A woman must acknowledge, appreciate and approve of herself in order to extend herself, for she plays a magnificent role in giving a being of value to the Universe which has called it to life. The adventure of discovering yourself through pregnancy is a journey and the actual birth, in which the child is so unknown and yet in one sense very known, is a joyous expression of Nature coursing her energies literally through intercourse and manifesting in the form of a new life given as a gift through these two.

Pregnancy and birth provide us with an opportunity as at no other time for healing ourselves. Arthur Koestler said, 'There is a fine dividing line between self-repair and self-realisation.' In particular, the birth process can be an experience of growth for the mother and those around her because such incredible channels of energy are open to everyone at that time.

Survival of the species is, of course, a primary concern of nature and our birth patterns tend to reflect the society we live in. Perhaps primitive woman was alone giving birth while her mate kept away marauding animals or hunted for food. Later, childbearing women were supported by other women and men were very separate; now in Western society birth patterns are again in a state of change as technological births appear to reinforce the individual's feelings of alienation. With sex roles changing there is an increasing tendency for men to become more aware of the gentle, 'feminine' side of their nature and for women to be in touch with the more outgoing, 'masculine' side of their nature. Thus, both parents may be sensitive to the development of their unborn child, becoming active participants in the birth and sharing parenting. Of course, fathers sometimes make decisions not to be involved or women want to do it on their own and in these cases loving and caring support from other women and friends is essential.

Preparation for birth can take place physically, mentally and spiritually. Some women, or couples, prepare themselves before pregnancy in order to be in optimum health and fully conscious at the time of conception. The idea of preparing before conception is wonderful, but many women do not plan their pregnancies in this way. One friend, told by medical experts that she was sterile, did not become aware of her pregnancy until she was nearly five months pregnant and had not been taking care of herself. However, close to term, she threw herself wholeheartedly into preparing herself on all levels and gave birth at home, joyously and naturally. There are no rules, each pregnancy is individual and unique. In my observation, people give birth according to the way in which they live, sometimes there has to be a willingness to change making a transformation on all levels. You cannot just change one isolated part of yourself, for change means a continuum of growth, needing flexibility and constant reassessment.

In talking about natural birth, I am not referring to the sort of birth often experienced in Third World countries, births without real joy, where there is a high rate of infant mortality and where fathers are not actively involved. In order to facilitate a natural birth, it should ideally take place in a familiar environment with a caring, supportive midwife and sympathetic friends around you if you wish; an environment where you, your partner and the baby can feel in touch with the process, working together towards an outcome that is fulfilling for all.

We have now reached a situation where we have to read books and go to classes to find out about the experience of pregnancy, the process of birth and how to be a parent. In the Asian countries where I have travelled, they are very amused by this. There, within the extended family, they have experience of small babies and children throughout their lives and they just know how to have babies and care for them — they know this like they know their own name, without questioning. In our society, few women or men have much experience of small babies and child-rearing can be a very isolated process.

Through books and classes you may become more informed, but the best way to be in touch with what is going on is to know yourself, to know your own body and to listen to the messages that come from using your intuition and the right hemisphere of the brain's mode of working, your female and receptive side. In this way, you can work towards the total integration of mind, body and spirit.

Choosing the right pre-natal class is, however, still important, and wherever there are choices you should shop around to find one that suits your needs. Classes should include preparation of mind and body and should provide information about stages of pregnancy, labour and life after birth. Opportunities should be provided to share fears and hopes, to exchange information, to ask questions, see films and slides and observe and hold new babies. Some classes now offer tuition in massage for the newborn which is an added pleasure and interaction to share with your baby. Birth teachers could helpfully include some classes early in pregnancy about the options that are available so that parents can make informed choices.

Finding a hospital where you can experience the sort of birth you would like is not always easy and it may be that, if you can afford it, an independent midwife or sympathetic private doctor would be worth considering if they are willing to support women having the births they want. This is particularly the case where women are regarded as 'high risk', as it is even more important that these women receive the right sort of support.

More could be done for fathers during the pre-natal period. 'Couples' classes' should have some evenings for men only, led by a father, where they can discuss their fears and questions with each other whilst the women, similarly, meet separately, later coming together to exchange questions and ideas. A lot is expected of fathers to be, the woman at least has the child growing within her and can feel very connected. The father can of course keep in touch through massage, talking and singing to the baby and being closely involved with the mother. Often, in this society, men are absorbed in their work and do not share much intimate time with the mother. Thrust into the role of support person in the birth situation many men feel quite out of their depth. They see their women experiencing what may seem at times to be intense pain, and they have to be there, fighting for the kind of birth they have decided they want; they must become the 'champion' or 'knight' fighting the 'dragons' of the institution! At the same time as trying to give emotional support to the woman, they find that they are only just tolerated by hospital staff, often given an uncomfortable stool to sit on and no food.

It is very important that the birth attendants are sensitive to the father and the relationship between them should be very clear. Ideally, the father should have met the birth attendants several times to talk about the birth. Fathers often go through their own kind of pregnancy; there are so many issues involved in the changing relationship of a couple, they have to move from being lovers, maybe from a relationship where each plays parent to the other; the husband may have fears of losing his lover and his 'mother' to a new being who will take up the woman's time and nourishment. Also, there are financial responsibilities and the concern of caring for and educating a child for anything from fifteen to twenty years ahead.

If you decide to have other people attend your birth, it is important to choose the right 'guest-list'. Choose people with whom you have a real rapport and with whom you feel comfortable and relaxed; people should not be invited out of a sense of duty because they want or expect to be there. You may need to say no for your own ease and well being.

It would help pregnant women feel more confident if ante-natal care could be 'de-mystified'. In Australia and as part of the Active

Birth Movement in London, we offered 'self-help' ante-natal care. The women learned to take each other's blood pressure, feel the positions in the uterus of each other's babies, listen to the baby's heart-beat, check their own urine and keep their own weight and record charts. This helped counter-act the problem of lack of continuity of care which often means that women hear differing opinions about their condition from week to week, an experience which often undermines their confidence.

Another way a pregnant woman can help herself to give birth with confidence is to enquire about her own birth. Talking to women students on a Birth Teachers' course about their own births and then about their first experience of birth, I found a remarkable tendency for the two to be similar. Often, it had been the initial, difficult first birth that drove the women to find out more about birth and to assist other women to have better births. Their subsequent births were much more natural and joyous. I have also re-birthed pregnant women, many of whom found the insights they gained through the experience very helpful in both healing their own birth trauma and enabling them to approach their labour more positively. A woman could talk to her parents, if she can, about the way in which she was born, how her mother felt when she was pregnant and about what was happening to the family at that time. It is my belief that we make decisions about ourselves and the world around us when we are in the uterus, whilst we are being born and after the birth. These decisions are very much a product of the experience we have, whether it is one of fear and terror, one of warmth and reassurance after the struggle, one of separation or being on one's own. Some early decisions that keep repeating themselves as patterns in our lives, in our relationships with other people, and our relationship with work, sex and money, may be exemplified in the following statements: 'Life is a struggle', 'I'm not wanted', 'I'm not meant to be here', 'there's not enough out there for me', 'I can't get what I want'. All these feelings I believe to be very much linked with one's birth, whether one was breast fed or bottle fed, whether one was fed on demand or on schedule and so on.

It is important to prepare the body physically, not only for pregnancy and birth but also to be fit for breast feeding and carrying your baby in a sling afterwards if you should want.

Yoga, stretching, swimming, walking and dance are all good ways to exercise and many women have also benefited from using therapies such as massage, the Alexander Technique, metamorphic massage and so on. It is important to feel good about your body and to trust it. Many women, influenced by modern ideals of feminine beauty, feel themselves to be ugly and clumsy during pregnancy and this thought is often reinforced by their partners. For me personally, a pregnant woman is magnificent in her abundance of round and blossoming shapes, a marvellous symbol of Nature growing to fruition. Why not look in a mirror daily and acknowledge your beauty by saying, 'I am strong and beautiful.' This and other positive thoughts can help raise your self-esteem and enable you to feel more confident during your pregnancy.

In the early stages of pregnancy, women often experience nausea and emotional turmoil. Apart from the hormonal and other physiological changes taking place, there are many unresolved fears and tensions surfacing. Even in a planned pregnancy, doubts about one's ability to give birth, about being a responsible parent, about changes in one's primary relationship, surface. This seems fairly normal and it is useful to be aware of what is going on in your body and the actual stage of development of the baby. One friend, for example, found herself unusually anxious up till the third month of her pregnancy, then a feeling of calmness and inner stability came over her. This coincided with the changeover from maternal to placental hormones and she felt this as a release from total responsibility for the baby, who at this time begins to have a life support system of its own, operating through the placenta inside its 'bag' and its own blood supply interactive with the mother's.

It is valuable to learn about the development of the child within the uterus by reading, for example, such books as *A Child Is Born* by Nilsson[1] and *The Secret Life of the Unborn Child* by Verny.[2] Be in touch with the baby growing at each stage, the excitement of the first movement, the awareness of your own baby's characteristics. Many mothers are so in touch with their babies they know what different movements mean, they know the environment the baby enjoys, how he or she feels when they are walking, swimming, resting, making love or even when they are agitated. There can be an exquisite psychic connection between the mother and the baby, a bonding that takes place before birth.

Keeping a journal of your pregnancy and birth can be interesting, recording the richness of your experience, your feelings, your movement and also the times when you feel jangled, out of time, out of rhythm. Record your dreams. Pregnant women have such powerful dreams, sometimes blissful, sometimes frightening. Dreams serve a useful purpose in bringing material from the unconscious mind into consciousness; they may be divinatory (pregnant women have experienced pre-cognitive dreams of their baby and birth which have been amazingly accurate), or problem solving (revealing solutions to problems), or repairing (bringing fears and doubts into conscious awareness for consideration and clarity). Record your impressions of the being growing within; your communications with your partner, your closeness or separateness. Drawing pictures of your baby can be exciting and revealing. Talk to your baby, sing to your baby, play music to your baby. Just as plants have been discovered to flourish and turn towards harmonious music, or to wilt and shrink away from harsh, loud music, so some mothers report having had to leave noisy pop concerts because of protest from the baby. Perhaps we could stage concerts for the unborn!

Visualise your baby in her or his watery environment, curled up, stretching, kicking or resting, attached by a pulsing cord to the placenta, all contained in the 'bag' inside your uterus. Ponder on the miraculous placenta, a tree of Life continuously and unconditionally nurturing your baby; they are 'twins', both formed by the divisions of cells from the original fertilised egg. Imagine the sounds your baby hears, two heart beats with different frequencies, the baby's and yours, the swish of the placenta, the extraordinary symphony of your own digestive processes, your voice, laughter, tears and further away, the father's voice. Visualise the birth, the transition from a world of water to a world of gravity and lung breathing and a myriad other sensations.

Be aware of the community of pregnant women around you. One sensitive woman describes getting up regularly at 4.00 every morning to empty her bladder and sensing all the other pregnant women up in the quietness of their homes compelled by the same urge. This could be a comforting thought when feeling tired and alone sometimes in the dark of night, breast feeding the little being who isn't always a bundle of joy for you at that time! Be in touch with your senses, as a wise woman friend says: have a sense of wonder, a sense of beauty, a sense of joy and a sense of humour. The latter can be particularly useful when things seem grim, so try to see the humour in situations. Be adaptable and flexible, letting go of expectations.

Good birth experiences affect society as a whole. The way birth is conducted in a society tells you a lot about that society. This society is not child orientated and does not make it easy to be parents. There are many places where your baby is not welcome and women can be made to feel very self-conscious when breast feeding. There is a lot of contradictory advice on how you should or should not discipline your child, children being regarded as a problem and a burden rather than joyous, spontaneous creatures. In Bali, an island which I have frequently visited, babies are not permitted to be put down on the floor until after a special ceremony at six months of age: up till that time they are always held by someone who regards it as a privilege to do so. How wonderful! So, we must persevere in restoring birth to women and babies because the future of the planet lies in the hands of its children.

Until recently, birth preparation classes have taught breathing techniques which focus on complicated levels and rhythms of breathing. I am not in favour of teaching breathing patterns to pregnant women because these are intended as distraction from the powerful energies of birth and help keep a woman in her head rather than allowing her to be in her body. The key to coping with labour is to open yourself up to the experience through relaxation, not controlled breathing, for if you breathe naturally you will also relax. Your breath is always with you, so let it be natural and unmeasured, allow your natural rhythms. If you can surrender and be receptive you will breathe in your own rhythm. Trust your body to know how to breathe. Be aware of breath as movement, as spirit, every breath is a reminder of a connection to the source reflecting Nature's rhythms — pulse/impulse/contraction/expansion. Consider the in-breath as inspiration, inspiration in every moment, and use the out-breath to let go completely, to release all tension. Notice how tense you feel if you hold your breath and how centred you feel when you breathe again. The breath is constantly renewing, reconnecting you to the source and has been used for centuries upon centuries by mystics as a means for reaching enlightenment. It is truly wonderful, present at birth and absent at death. Once, several years ago in Australia, I was preparing to deliver a baby when I noticed that I was holding my breath, as indeed were all the other people present, anxiously awaiting the first breath. Instructing the others to do the same, I took some deep breaths, the baby was born into a breathing world and, naturally, breathed. How simple and how obvious!

One of the things I would like to see is a new vocabulary for birth. Words have such power that perhaps it is time for an appraisal of their use and meaning. 'Labour' seems appropriate because giving birth can be considered as an expenditure of energy to achieve a task. But the word 'contraction' seems to me to have a very restrictive, closing-down, one-sided feel about it. Certainly the uterus contracts and squeezes the baby, pushing it down on to the cervix in order to stretch and open it; but since it is a double message, why not emphasise the opening, expansive nature of this process. Expansion rather than contraction, for me it is a liberating thought: 'My expansions are coming every two minutes now . . .', or waves or rushes, as Ina May Gaskin from The Farm in Tennessee, so aptly describes them. Consider your own words of power. Make your own vocabulary for birth.

And sounds. A labouring woman has very powerful forces coursing through her — like a river flowing — she should go with, or into them. It is wonderful to make sounds. Sounds vibrating through every cell, resonating and releasing tension. Many women feel inhibited about making sounds so it may be valuable to think about the possibility before starting labour. Give yourself permission. Try: I can growl, I can moan, I can groan, I can cry, I can yell, I can bite and so on. Become accustomed to making sounds, to the idea that you might want to. These are options, try them out, don't be afraid to feel the animal in you, being animal is not unlovely, especially when you need to be. Your baby will recognise and appreciate your animal sounds as well as your singing and chanting. At one birth I was invited to recently, the baby's head was visible at the height of the pushing urge, but there was little progress. I said to the mother, 'Make your sounds; tell the world what you're feeling' and the sounds she then made were strong, animal, female, primitive sounds and the baby's head was born.

Fear is one of the main obstacles to giving birth naturally and we should try to look at what we are afraid of. For many women, particularly first-time mothers, it is fear of pain and the unknown. It would be foolish to say there is no pain, but the pain experienced as part of the natural process is entirely different from that which results from disease and sickness. It can help to perceive pain as a statement of change in the body, of stress which is natural, and of stress leading sometimes to distress, but always receding, always changing; powerful energies pulsing through you, constant regeneration and renewal. To cope with pain in labour, stay in each moment letting go of past and future, taking each 'expansion' one at a time, each instant leading to another, then another. Recognise your own instinctive, co-operative nature, feel your own pace, feel yourself as part of the Universe, perceive the divisions of night and day, the tides of the sea, the cycles of the seasons, cycles of regenerated life, cycles that give you rest, then action, then rest again, expansion and contraction. Remember that welcoming your baby is the end result of this intense experience.

The fear of being out of control in labour is a very real one for many women and I often shock them when I say, 'It's safe to be out of control, you should be out of control.' By this, I do not mean being in a state of panic; I mean moving out of the rational, logical mind and entering a deep, intuitive, safe space which allows primal forces to do their work. This is really diving in at the deep end, into the deep waters of feelings, intuitions and instincts, a new but really so old way of reacting and inter-acting, listening to your body, paying attention to its signals, being totally in touch with your body and your baby. Letting yourself go with freedom into that dark, wonderful, primeval, wise space known to women giving birth from generation to generation. Abandon yourself to Nature and her works.

Birth is a journey into the unknown and it's also an adventure — an adventure of self-discovery as the possibility of transforming oneself becomes available at that time. Birth is transforming for parents and for birth attendants because it is very much a time of being in the present. There is no time for lingering in the past, or worrying about the future, one is totally in the moment, going from one 'expansion' to the next. It is like the journey of a thousand steps that starts with the first step; sense the magic of this. Know that the unknown factor you can count on is that Nature's forces are magic for you at this moment, magic is the contribution of Nature that you can ride on. The head appears — a crystal clear moment of welcome — an enriching moment. An instant change in being, as the personality of the new-born forces itself into Life outside the womb. The infant is now a single individual, which translated means 'undivided' — an undivided part of the whole.

Wonder at the cycle of completion, the baby conceived, grown and born out of the woman's body, to be immediately returned to her arms and breasts in a loving instant of welcome. The completion of a cycle that expands to include the father and the family. So a new cycle begins, a new beginning.

REFERENCES

1 L. Nilsson, *A Child Is Born*, Faber, 1977
2 T. Verny, *The Secret Life of the Unborn Child*, Sphere, 1981.

RECOMMENDED READING

Arthur and Janet Balaskas, *New Life*, Sidgewick & Jackson, 1979.
Janet Balaskas, *Active Birth*, Allen & Unwin, 1983.
Barbara Dale and Joanna Roeber, *Exercises for Childbirth*, Century, 1982.
Elizabeth Noble, *Childbirth With Insight*, Houghton Mifflin, 1983.

How to avoid an unnecessary episiotomy

SOPHY HOARE

It has been said that one cannot improve on a natural birth. One of the remarkable things about the pain of childbirth is its fleeting quality. However much a woman experiences pain in her labour, or however overwhelming the sensations, once each contraction is finished the pain disappears without trace. Even at the most hectic part of a natural labour, there is total relaxation between contractions; after the birth there is little or no sense of injury to testify to what the body has been through. Indeed it would be strange if nature did not intend the mother to be whole and healthy after delivery, since she must immediately take charge of a new dependent person.

However, for between 50 and 90 per cent of women in England today, this natural process is not allowed to take place. These women experience varying degrees of pain for days, often weeks, sometimes months after the birth, as a result of the 'only surgical intervention which takes place on the body of a healthy woman without her consent and often without informing her':[1] episiotomy.

Episiotomy — a cut in the perineum to enlarge the opening in order to speed delivery — is the most commonly performed obstetric operation. In some hospitals it is performed routinely on all women having their first baby and on many of the others. Yet it is a procedure that has been inadequately tested, with almost no research done on its effects. In 1981, the National Childbirth Trust published the results of an inquiry made by Sheila Kitzinger into women's experiences of episiotomy.[2] Of the women who took part in the survey, those who had episiotomies (with a spontaneous vaginal delivery) experienced more pain at the end of the first week after the birth than those who had tears. They had problems with breast feeding (too painful to sit down or change position easily) and were more likely to suffer from dyspareunia (painful intercourse), and for longer. Women were either told at the last minute that they would have an episiotomy, without discussion, or were not even informed. The stitching was often painful, sometimes done with no anaesthetic offered, and sometimes badly done and later re-done. Sometimes there were problems with a badly performed incision or stitching a whole year after the birth. Some women found episiotomy and stitching of the perineum more painful than any part of labour and what they dreaded most about having another baby. All in all, it emerged that episiotomy causes a great deal of unnecessary pain, it does not avoid tears or improve the condition of the perineum after childbirth and it may disturb the mother's relationship with her baby, the start of breast feeding and the sexual relationship.

What can you do to avoid episiotomy? Here is a '4-point plan' to help.

1   INFORMATION − get informed

First of all, know that episiotomy is rarely justified − only in cases where rapid emergency delivery is indicated or when the perineum is persistently thick and resistant. These cases are exceptional.

Become acquainted with the arguments often given to justify episiotomy and know how to counter them:

Done to prevent a serious tear.
There is nothing to indicate this. Most serious tears occur with, rather than in the absence of, an episiotomy.

Done to prevent prolapse.
No proof at all; no research has been carried out on this.

Done to speed delivery to avoid brain damage to the baby from a prolonged second stage of labour.
There is no proof that episiotomy prevents brain damage, or that

a long second stage causes it. In fact, Dr Caldeyro-Barcia has demonstrated that it is prolonged breath holding and strenuous pushing by the mother which may deprive the baby of oxygen, not the length of time in second stage.[3]

Done for 'neatness', to avoid an ugly tear and to improve healing.

A tear heals better than a cut (unless it is a very severe tear). A cut across natural skin folds and muscle is more painful and takes longer to heal than a tear, which will have a better blood supply to its edges. Also, with an episiotomy, it is vital to the healing process how well repaired it is. A badly done episiotomy and stitching (not uncommon) can cause great pain and result in lumpy scar tissue, much less 'neat' than a naturally healed tear. In addition, the volume of blood loss at episiotomy tends to be underestimated.

Here are some actual reasons why episiotomies are done:

They are often done because a midwife lacks skill in handling the second stage of labour. Midwives today are often trained to rely more on episiotomy than on care, skill and sensitivity, and they often lack confidence that they can deliver a baby without one. They are especially conditioned to think that a woman having her first baby cannot give birth without an episiotomy.

Midwives often feel hurried into performing an episiotomy because doctors do not allow the second stage to go on for more than a set time before intervening with a forceps extraction. Thus episiotomies are often given not long after the start of second stage when it is still too early to judge whether it is really necessary.

Occasionally, an episiotomy is done for no other reason than to give a student a chance to practise.

Finally, if you are having your baby in hospital, do some research into hospital policy. Find out about the hospital's attitude to episiotomy and its statistics. If this looks ominous, try elsewhere.

2   COMMUNICATION — talk to your midwife

Leading on from the above, it is obviously essential to discuss the whole question of episiotomy with your midwife and doctor as early in pregnancy as possible. If you know who your birth attendants will be and you talk things over with them in good time, you may persuade them to co-operate with you to avoid episiotomy, and if you are lucky, they may not need persuading. If you are having a hospital delivery and do not know who will be present at the birth, make sure that it is written in your notes that you do not want an episiotomy. Bear in mind that in Sheila Kitzinger's survey, in which only 15 per cent of women involved had no injury to the perineum, 66 per cent did not even discuss episiotomy with their doctor or midwife during pregnancy. It is worth showing that you are aware, informed and prepared to take steps to help yourself. At the same time, let them feel that, if they respect your wishes, you respect their professional judgement. Sometimes midwives may feel threatened that a lay person (in their view) is encroaching on their territory. When dealing with somebody 'difficult', if you remain positive and relaxed, this will communicate itself to the other person.

If you are really worried about not being able to communicate with the right people (women often find that they see a different midwife and doctor at every ante-natal visit), then the only way to ensure any continuity of care is to have a home birth or domino delivery. Even if the midwives are not immediately sympathetic to your approach, at least you have time to try to build up a trusting and fruitful relationship with them.

3   PREPARATION — make yourself fit

This section describes the steps you can take to help ensure that you will not *need* an episiotomy. The most important thing you can do is to make yourself fit, in other words to have a healthy, strong body which functions well in every respect, free of ailments, having firm muscle tone, a healthy pulse rate and the ability to relax.

The first step is to eat well. An awareness of diet should start as early as possible, ideally before conception. Make sure your diet is varied and balanced, with no obvious excesses or deficiencies. Be especially careful to take adequate vitamin C and vitamin E. The healthier you are, the more you are able to listen to your own instincts with regard to eating. A healthy body will often reject the substances which are harmful during pregnancy, such as alcohol and stimulants like coffee or tea, and may crave foods it needs. So, as well as informing yourself on the basics of nutrition, listen to your own body and let your natural appetite be your guide.

Secondly, take plenty of exercise. Try to take some exercise every day which makes your heart beat faster and makes you puff. Swimming, bicycling and fast walking are excellent, or any sport you already practise. If you do already take regular exercise, continue with it for as long as your body is happy. Do not give it up because your head tells you that you should stop because you are pregnant! The only exceptions here are sports that are dangerous or contain a high risk of falling, such as horse-riding or judo. In addition to your more vigorous exercise, practise some yoga postures. Yoga is an ideal preparation for birth since it stretches and strengthens all the muscles of the body. The standing postures will give you general strength and suppleness so that you can go through the whole of pregnancy and labour feeling light and agile, and the sitting and squatting poses stretch and stimulate circulation around the pelvic area. These poses also prepare you for natural birth positions such as squatting, semi-squatting or kneeling, positions which decrease the chances of tearing the perineum but which require some flexibility of the joints. If you do nothing else, at least practise squatting every day (with a book under the heels if you are stiff), and sit on the floor in preference to chairs. Sit cross legged or with legs spread wide apart, or with soles of the feet together in front of the groins, and if you like support your back by sitting against a wall. Make sure you are sitting well forward on the front of the buttock bones, not tilting back at the base of the spine. A folded blanket placed under the buttocks helps to achieve this. An aspect of yoga which is very valuable for birth is its emphasis on relaxing unnecessary tension. Relaxation is obviously a crucial factor in facilitating an efficient, natural birth and avoiding damage to the perineum. To *give* birth, a woman must be able to release the pelvic floor muscles, even when she feels great pressure on them. Yoga teaches how to become aware of unwanted tension and how to relax and release muscles which are being stretched to their extreme limit.

A third very important step is to pay attention to the pelvic floor muscles themselves. These should be exercised regularly, frequently every day. Exercise makes them stronger and more supple, so that they will stretch more easily during birth and spring back like good elastic afterwards. It also makes you more aware of the muscles so that you can release them *consciously* during the second stage of labour. Unfortunately, these muscles are often neglected because they are invisible and because people are unaware of the importance of their role in supporting the internal organs. There is an excellent book, entitled *Essential Exercises for the Childbearing Year* by Elizabeth Noble,[4] which describes in full the structure and function of the pelvic floor muscles and a range of pelvic floor exercises. The author comments that problems with the pelvic floor are so common that society takes them for granted and that 'doctors tend to think of the firm, efficient perineum as the exception', and consequently feel justified in performing episiotomy in the belief that it will prevent tearing.

A simple and effective exercise is the repeated contraction and release of the pelvic floor muscles. This can be done at any time in any position, but if you are not familiar with it, practise it at first lying down (the bath is a good place). Place one hand on the pubic bone and draw up the pelvic floor muscles so as to tighten all the internal passages, thinking of tightening the vagina as high as the level of your hand. Hold for a few seconds, then relax completely. Do this up to five times in succession as often as you can, at least ten times a day. Make sure that you do not tense the muscles of the abdomen, buttocks or thighs instead of the pelvic floor muscles, and that you do not hold your breath while contracting the muscles; keep your breathing relaxed. As well as practising this exercise, become aware of the pelvic floor muscles at other times, especially after any bearing down movement, such as a bowel movement, coughing, sneezing, laughing, lifting, etc. Always follow such a movement with a strong up-lifting pelvic floor contraction.

The other step you can take to avoid tearing and episiotomy is perineal massage during pregnancy. This, like exercising the muscles, increases circulation in the area, making the tissues more supple and able to stretch easily. In the last few weeks before the birth, you or your partner can massage the labia, vaginal area and the perineum, using a nut oil such as almond oil. This is how one mother described the technique used successfully to prevent tearing at birth; with the previous baby a large episiotomy had been done and the non-elastic scar tissue was especially noticeable:

My husband massaged the area until the cream [in this case, cocoa butter] was completely worked in which typically took four or five minutes. He then used more cream as a lubricant and inserted several fingers shallowly into the vagina and gently stretched the opening, until I felt a slight burning sensation. At that point he maintained the stretch for several minutes, or until the burning sensation stopped. After only one week, there was a noticeable increase in flexibility and stretchiness. After two weeks he could insert the tips of five fingers (about 4 centimetres) before the burning sensation warned me of excessive stretching. After four weeks we worked up to about 7 centimetres which is approximately ⅔rds the diameter of an average baby's head at birth. At this point we dropped to massaging every other day.

One of the advantages of using massage in this way is that you can check how effectively you are practising your pelvic floor exercises — how firmly you can contract the vaginal muscles and how completely you can relax the whole perineal area. There may be some tension spots that you are unaware of.

4   CO-OPERATION — what to do during labour

Avoid intervention

To begin with, avoid any intervention from the doctors unless there is a sound medical reason for it. Try not to let the natural process of birth be disturbed in any way. It helps if you can discuss this with your doctor and midwife during pregnancy. While in labour, question any procedure that is carried out on your body, even if it appears to be a routine matter, and ask to have the reason and effects fully explained to you. One small act of intervention can impede the natural birth process to the extent that further intervention is needed. Remember that epidurals and other forms of regional block greatly reduce the chances of a spontaneous delivery without episiotomy, and that when labour is induced or artificially accelerated women tend to experience more pain and anxiety and are therefore more likely to have a rigid perineum, and to ask for anaesthesia. Juliet Wilmott, midwife, writes:

> The fear, tension, pain syndrome is . . . more likely to occur where a labouring woman is immobilised in bed, attached to drips and monitoring equipment, attended by many different strangers, or left on her own, then bundled on to a trolley to be rushed from the first stage room to the delivery room when birth is imminent.

Try to have someone with you (husband, friend or trusted midwife) who will stay with you all the time and will ensure that you do not have a crowd of people coming and going and watching you during the latter part of labour. A peaceful atmosphere is very important if the birth process is not to be disturbed.

Posture

Injury to the perineum is less likely if you are in an upright position for the second stage. Some variation of the squatting position seems to be the most common natural birth posture. In this position the birth canal opens to its widest, making more room for the baby's head, and the mother is not having to push against gravity. The supported squatting position (being held under the armpits by one or two helpers) is especially good, since you do not have to support yourself and your thighs and entire pelvic area, including the perineum, can be completely relaxed.

Lying on the back is the worst position to give birth in — the most dangerous position for mother and baby. In fact, the supine posture is in itself a form of intervention, since it is rarely if ever used by women who give birth instinctively. The most important thing is to allow your body to find its preferred posture, and not to be persuaded by someone else to lie down on your back.

Relaxed breathing

During the second stage, with the strong pushing contractions, *as soon as you feel a burning or tearing sensation*, relax your breathing to a very light panting. Do not push at this point — this is very important. Not only must you not push, but it is essential that you do not tighten up. If the burning sensation is very strong and painful, so that you feel as though you are tearing, it can be reassuring to feel with your own hand where the baby's head is, so that you realise that you are not splitting apart, simply stretching to a normal degree. At this stage it is important to keep in close touch with the midwife and to co-operate with her when she asks you to stop pushing, to pant and to release the pelvic floor muscles. Remember that your uterus will do the pushing for you and that it is up to you to *let* it happen and to let the vagina open to allow the baby through. Unfortunately, too much emphasis has been placed on strong deliberate pushing with prolonged breath holding. As a result, in Sheila Kitzinger's words: 'Many women are engaged in a battle between their own expulsive powers and rigid pelvic floor musculature and a tight perineum. When the stress is put on pushing rather than opening up, such a struggle is almost inevitable.'[5]

Never, never push if you feel no urge to do so, even if you are being encouraged to. Your body will tell you when it is ready.

Other things that can be helpful in relaxing the perineum are a long hot bath during labour (stay in the water as long as you find it comfortable and relaxing), hot compresses applied by the midwife and also perineal massage.

REFERENCES

1 Sheila Kitzinger (ed.), *Episiotomy: Physical and Emotional Aspects*, The National Childbirth Trust, 1981.

2 Sheila Kitzinger with Rhiannon Walters, *Some Women's Experiences of Episiotomy*, The National Childbirth Trust, 1981.

3 R. Caldeyro-Barcia, *Birth and the Family Journal*, vol. 6, no. 1, 1979.

4 Elizabeth Noble, *Essential Exercises for the Childbearing Year*, John Murray, 1978.

5 Sheila Kitzinger, *The Rhythmic Second Stage*, leaflet published by the Birth Centre, London, 1979.

'How to avoid an unnecessary episiotomy' was originally published by the Birth Centre London together with 'Notes for midwives and post-natal care of the perineum' by Melody Weig.

Natural healing — a wholistic approach to health

ROS CLAXTON AND CAROL RUDD

Throughout history, women all over the world have sought and discovered ways of healing appropriate to their needs during pregnancy and birth. Different cultures developed a variety of healing techniques utilising the natural resources available to them: in Britain, for example, the traditional midwife would have known exactly which plants she could safely use to assist a woman through pregnancy, labour and breast feeding. The Western medical approach is a relative newcomer in the history of healing; as the scientific model came to dominate our way of thinking, all other systems were deemed 'backward' or 'primitive'. Although many natural healing techniques and remedies have never been subjected to scientific scrutiny, they have an accumulated wisdom which stands the test of time. There has been a recent resurgence of interest in natural healing methods as the limitations of orthodox medicine become more apparent. Particularly during pregnancy, women are more conscious of the dangerous side-effects of chemical drugs; the thalidomide tragedy is a potent reminder of this and of the shortcomings of drug trials. If used sensitively and carefully, natural healing methods can provide a safe alternative for the pregnant woman.

The word 'healing' is derived from the Anglo-Saxon root 'hele' which means 'to make whole'. This allows 'healing' to be seen in its wider perspective as a continuous movement towards 'wholeness'. Pregnancy is not an illness, but we may during this time discover physical, emotional and spiritual blockages which impede us from growing with and learning from the experience. It is a time of heightened awareness and sensitivity when, as part of the creative process, the 'life force' acts to cleanse and harmonise the system on all levels. Natural healing methods can both facilitate and encourage that process and help a woman 'tune in' to that part of herself which knows what to do without being told. Since there is a special affinity towards healing during pregnancy, a woman has a perfect opportunity for personal exploration, purification and growth.

In the wholistic approach to health, mind, body, emotions and spirit form one integrated and inter-related system. Thus, disturbance in one area creates disturbance or imbalance in another. Underlying the many methods of natural healing is the recognition that all living things are animated by a 'life force' given different names in different cultures, for example, 'chi', 'tao' and 'prana'. When this life force is disturbed, the whole system it supports is thrown off balance and illness occurs. The symptoms of disease are seen as manifestations of this imbalance and represent the body's attempt to heal itself; the body should be allowed to work through its symptoms wherever possible, for to continually suppress them causes, in the long run, further damage to the organism. It is the task of the healer to identify the areas of imbalance and provide a stimulus to encourage the life force — be it herbs, homeopathic remedies or acupuncture needles; these and other possibilities may be the appropriate catalyst to release the body's self-healing powers.

Many of us neglect or abuse our bodies through smoking, poor nutrition, lack of exercise, stress and so on. We ignore our emotional and spiritual needs. All of this can create imbalance in our system and will have a bearing on our health in pregnancy. Ideally, we should try to improve our health (in the widest sense of the word) before conception. This way we could avoid a number of major and minor ailments and at the same time improve the health of our babies. However, it is not too late to start healing oneself when pregnant and many women have found natural healing methods to be very beneficial during this time.

The wholistic approach to healing outlined above contrasts radically with the conventional medical view of pregnancy and birth. The medicalisation of birth has created many problems for the pregnant woman. The mechanistic view of the human body, upon which modern medicine is based, emphasises the physical aspects of pregnancy and birth; mind and body are seen as separate entities and interactions between the two are given little credence. There is no faith in the natural process, indeed the desire is rather to improve upon and control nature. The symptoms of disease are viewed as disturbances to be suppressed and the role of the doctor is to intervene and treat, either chemically, through the use of drugs, or physically, through surgery. This system of thinking rarely encompasses the whole individual and leads to the classification and labelling of pregnant women according to what is seen to be their particular problem — for example, 'elderly primagravida', 'placenta praevia', 'breech'; such labels serve to limit perception of the individual and her particular needs. A picture is formed of how normal labour should progress, specific lengths are prescribed for each stage thereby constricting the variety and spontaneity of birth. Pain in labour is seen as a separate phenomenon to be treated pharmacologically and the routine use of medical interventions creates more iatrogenic complications.

Underlying this medical approach to pregnancy and birth is the notion that the doctor is the professional expert or authority treating the passive patient who accepts little or no responsibility for what is taking place. This attitude of dependency has to change if one is to become involved in a wholistic approach to health. The first step is to learn to accept responsibility for one's own state of being, seeking causes within as well as without. Having accepted responsibility, one needs to be prepared to take an active part in the healing process working together with the practitioner to identify those aspects of life which enhance the natural process and those aspects which oppose it.

It is essential that we become aware of our need for an external 'authority'. It is just as possible to replace the obstetrician as expert with the homeopath or acupuncturist as expert and to take natural remedies as one takes drugs. 'Alternative' medicine too can be used as a crutch to escape self-responsibility, in the same way as orthodox medicine. Indeed, one's greatest asset during pregnancy may well be the sympathetic NHS midwife or doctor if they encourage your self-awareness and inner confidence. Hopefully, allopathic medicine will begin to heed current criticisms of its shortcomings and eventually move towards a more wholistic and humanistic approach.

It is not suggested that you use natural healing methods to completely replace conventional ante-natal care, but as an adjunct. The particular method or methods you choose will depend on a number of factors: your individual needs, your own ideas about natural healing, the therapies you feel most attracted to and the availability of practitioners in your area. Unless you live near a NHS doctor who practises homeopathy, you will have to pay for treatment although some practitioners will reduce their fee if you are unemployed or a single mother. If you are suffering from a minor ailment there are a number of self-help remedies available too, some of which are described below, but you should seek professional help if you have a chronic or serious problem. All the major therapies are linked to a professional body which gives thorough training and holds lists of qualified practitioners and your local Birth Centre or Natural Health Centre may also be able to help.

Described below are some examples of natural healing methods with emphasis on their particular relevance to pregnancy and birth. Unfortunately it is impossible here to be fully comprehensive and we are aware that many valuable therapies have had to be excluded because of shortage of space, but the reading list or individual practitioners will be able to provide you with more information.

HERBAL MEDICINE

Herbal medicine, the use of therapeutic plants in the treatment of disease, has been traditionally practised in many cultures for centuries. Women, in particular, practised this art as healers, midwives or 'witches' and the World Health Organisation has recently been supporting efforts in the Third World to extend this traditional use of plants as medicine. The type of plants used varies according to area; Chinese herbal medicine utilises different plants from those used by the American Indians or in Britain. Nowadays, there is cross communication between herbalists and many foreign herbs are imported. Whilst modern drug manufacturers are able to isolate the pharmacologically active substance in the plant, refine it and market it, herbalists believe that the whole plant, not just the supposed active ingredient, is beneficial; herbalist Michael McIntyre says 'the whole plant is like a symphony.'

Herbal remedies are made up as infusions, decoctions, tinctures and tablets. Ideally, fresh, organically grown plants should be used. On a self-help basis, infusions, such as herbal teas, are easy to use. It is a good idea to avoid taking anything during the first three months of pregnancy and care must always be taken that herbs used are not dangerous, for example, pennyroyal can induce miscarriage. The art and skill of herbal medicine is to match the plants with the individual and one should consult a professional herbalist for any serious problems.

One of the best-known herbs, used in many cultures during pregnancy, is raspberry leaves which help tone the uterus. This can be taken as a tea during the last trimester (three heaped teaspoons to a pot, drink the equivalent of a wine-glass two to three times a day). Raspberry leaves should not be taken by very athletic women, otherwise there is a danger that the uterine muscles may become overtoned. Squaw vine (*mitchella repens*) is another well-known female tonic. A number of herbs can be used when miscarriage is threatened, false unicorn root (*helonias*) and cramp bark (*viburnum opulus*) are two. For morning sickness (when the vomit is clear and watery and thought to reveal an underlying weakness of the digestive system), you can drink lemon balm, chamomile, mint or raspberry leaf tea. Crystallised ginger can help or you can try cinnamon water (two cinnamon sticks boiled in a pint of water and sweetened with honey). When there is fullness in the chest and the vomit is sour and bitter, the sickness is thought to be due to a liver imbalance. For this you can try small sips of gentian, wild yam, rosemary or dandelion root.

The aroma released by certain plants can be very strengthening during labour. You can hold, and squeeze in your hand, southernwood, mugwort, wormwood, lemon geranium, rosemary, coriander leaves or sweet basil. Rosemary oil or lavender oil rubbed on to your forehead, wrists or neck, can be very soothing during labour, as can chamomile oil and lavender oil (diluted in another oil) gently massaged on to the stomach and back. Calendula, witch-hazel or salt water can help heal a tear or episiotomy and calendula can be used to heal the baby's cord. Honey, almond oil, comfrey or calendula ointment can all be used for sore nipples and chicory, marrow, dill, coriander, nettles or raspberry leaf tea will help increase the milk supply. Caraway, dill, aniseed or fennel tea will help a baby suffering from colic (either drunk by the mother or else a very weak infusion can be given directly to the baby).

HOMEOPATHY

The system of medicine known as homeopathy was developed in the eighteenth century by a German physician, Samuel Hahnemann. The fundamental principle upon which it is based is the 'law of similars' or 'like cures like'. Hahnemann discovered that a drug which produces certain symptoms in a healthy person is the very drug with which to treat those same symptoms which appear when a person is ill. He found that when a remedy is diluted in distilled water (potentised) and then shaken (succussed), it becomes more effective. Homeopathic remedies are made from animal, vegetable and mineral substances, many of which are poisonous in a non-homeopathic state; the process of distilling and shaking not only makes the remedy less toxic but more powerful and effective. This overcomes the problem of drug side-effects and renders a system that can be used safely during pregnancy. Clinical evidence on the efficacy and safety of homeopathic remedies has been accumulated for over 150 years.

It is thought that homeopathic remedies work by stimulating the 'vital' or 'life' force, thereby strengthening the body's immune system. Homeopaths believe that during pregnancy, the 'vital force' is particularly strong which makes it an ideal time for healing; pregnant women, like children, present clear symptoms that can be easy to match homeopathically. According to the homeopathic view, it is also possible during pregnancy to treat the constitutional background of the mother, so that her baby may be born 'clean', that is to say, free from the constitutional weaknesses of its predecessors.

Homeopathic remedies can be used to treat a wide range of problems and ailments that occur during pregnancy and birth:

sickness, high and low blood pressure, tendency to miscarry, pre-eclampsia, toxaemia, post-partum haemorrhage, retained placenta, are all examples. They can help turn a breech or posterior baby and can encourage labour when a baby is overdue. Homeopathic remedies can be used during labour, if contractions slow down or when a woman is tense or afraid. After the birth, homeopathy can be used to assist a baby with breathing problems and can help heal a tear or episiotomy.

For every known problem there is always a choice of remedies depending on the particular symptoms shown by the individual. Although homeopathy can be used successfully on a self-help basis, the skill lies in matching the remedy with the individual. The homeopath looks at the whole person, their mental, psychological and physiological state before prescribing. This can often be a difficult thing to do for oneself and you should seek professional help for any serious problem. The following remedies are just a few of the ones that can be used to treat sickness in pregnancy and indicate the complexity and subtlety of prescribing:

Ipecachuana — you feel irritable; there is resentment about the pregnancy.

Sepia — you feel indifferent towards loved ones; there is depression and intolerance of noise and smells.

Phosphorus — you feel indifference, but crave sympathy. You feel anxious for others and fear being alone. There is desire for fresh air and cold drinks, but you may be sick after them.

Pulsatilla — you weep easily, moods are changeable and you crave sympathy.

Ignatia — you do unaccountable and unexpected things.

Aurum — deepest depression is the keynote here.

Two of the best-known remedies for use during pregnancy and birth are caulophyllum and arnica. Caulophyllum (derived from squaw root) can be used to tone the uterus. One dose weekly of the thirtieth potency can be taken for three weeks at the end of pregnancy (homeopathic remedies come in a number of different potencies according to how many times they have been diluted and succussed; these potencies range from 6 upwards. It is suggested that on a self-help basis you use remedies no higher than the thirtieth potency). Arnica is the remedy for bruising and can be given after birth. (Note: only one remedy should be given at a time and in a limited number of doses. As soon as there is improvement, the remedy should be stopped and only repeated if the condition starts to deteriorate. The remedies should not be touched by hand, but should be measured out into the lid of the bottle or put onto a clean piece of paper and tipped into the mouth where they should be held under the tongue until they dissolve).

BIO-CHEMIC TISSUE SALTS

The bio-chemic system of tissue salts was devised by a German homeopathic physician, Dr Schussler, in the 1870s. It is based on the idea that certain mineral (tissue) salts are necessary to the healthy functioning of the body (modern bio-chemical research has since confirmed and amplified many of his findings). In Schussler's view, twelve basic salts provide vital nutrition to the cells. Apart from the twelve individual salts, there are various combinations that can be used to treat different ailments. The salts are produced homeopathically and are safe for use on a self-help basis.

John Damonte, a homeopath, devised the following programme of tissue salts for use during pregnancy to help ensure that the baby gets what it needs for healthy development and that the mother assimilates her food well so that vital minerals are not drawn from her body. Each combination should be taken three times a day and can be used as a nutritional supplement. You can start the programme in the appropriate month according to the stage of your pregnancy.

The Pregnancy Programme

(6x refers to the potency)

2nd and 6th month	Calcium Fluoride 6x	One of each 3 times
	Magnesium Phosphate 6x	a day
	Ferrum Phosphate 6x	

3rd and 7th month	Calcium Fluoride 6x	One of each 3 times
	Magnesium Phosphate 6x	a day
	Natrum Muriaticum 6x	
4th and 8th month	Calcium Fluoride 6x	One of each 3 times
	Natrum Muriaticum 6x	a day
	Silica 6x	
5th and 9th month	Calcium Fluoride 6x	One of each 3 times
	Ferrum Phosphate 6x	a day
	Silica 6x	

Calcium Fluoride aids the development of bones and helps keep the connective tissue elastic (it should help avoid stretch marks).

Magnesium Phosphate aids the development of nerves and should help avoid any cramping pains as the uterus grows.

Ferrum Phosphate aids the assimilation of iron which helps prevent anaemia (homeopaths, like other natural therapists, are opposed to the routine administration of iron pills).

Silica is concerned with strength, fibre and backbone and can aid scar tissue.

Natrum Muriaticum helps control salt and fluid balance and prevents too much amniotic fluid being formed.

BACH FLOWER REMEDIES

Edward Bach was a homeopathic doctor who died in 1936. He believed that emotions are at the root of all illness and that the mind can control disease. He used the distilled essences of wild flowers which he found had positive healing qualities and could help transform negative states of mind. His experiments led him to isolate thirty-eight flowers which cover the following areas: fear, uncertainty, lack of interest in the present, despondency and despair, over-care for the welfare of others, loneliness and over-sensitivity. Bach intended them for simple home use and they can be safely used during pregnancy to help bring about a positive state of mind. For example, rescue remedy, a mixture of five flowers, can be used as emergency first-aid in cases of emotional upset or shock; holly is the remedy for jealousy and can be used to help siblings deal with emotions aroused by the arrival of a new baby.

ACUPUNCTURE

The origins of acupuncture, a system of healing developed by the Chinese, can be traced back at least 5000 years. The technique involves the insertion of needles into the body at certain defined points; heat, pressure and massage may also be used. The system is based on traditional Chinese philosophy which believes that the life force 'chi' runs through the body along a system of invisible channels or meridians. The activating force behind 'chi' is the constant movement of energy between 'yin' and 'yang', polar opposites which manifest themselves as positive and negative/male and female. Chinese medicine sees the body as a delicate balance between 'yin' and 'yang', health being determined by how these forces interact. The balance constantly fluctuates and if permanently upset will lead to ill-health. The art of the acupuncturist is to diagnose the imbalance and to create a harmonious flow of energy within the body.

The network of meridians corresponds to the twelve organs of the body which are known as 'officials'. The use of needles or moxa (dried mugwort which is heated) at the points which lie along the meridians is said to facilitate the 'officials' to promote health. Thus the needle or the moxa is seen to act as a catalyst for the body's own self-healing process. In China, acupuncture is used in conjunction with herbal medicine, but few acupuncturists in this country combine the two approaches.

Ideally, it is believed that acupuncture should be used pre-conceptually to improve a woman's health and prepare her body for pregnancy. Used ante-natally, acupuncture can be effective in relieving nausea, urinary problems, high and low blood pressure, fibroids, oedema and fatigue, for example. It can be used to turn a baby in the wrong position, when there is a retained placenta or post-partum haemorrhage. In China it is used as anaesthesia during a caesarean birth. Acupuncturists believe that stimulating a specific point in the third and sixth months of pregnancy (known as 'building guest') can promote the baby's health.

Used during labour, acupuncture can help promote the free flow of energy encouraging, for example, better circulation, smoother muscle tone and easier contractions. Since acupuncture affects the mind as well as the body, harmonising the energy in this way can help a woman feel stronger and better able to cope with labour. By using different acupuncture points, the natural process is encouraged, especially if contractions have slowed down or stopped. When used during labour, acupuncture can offer pain relief in that it increases the endorphins, the body's own pain killers. Not all acupuncturists are prepared to provide acupuncture as a method of pain relief during labour for they feel it is too much of an intervention and prefer women to find other, more natural methods of pain relief. Even a woman who has been used to having acupuncture during pregnancy may dislike the insertion of needles during labour especially if it restricts her mobility.

If you are having your baby in hospital, you must obtain the consultant's consent to your having an acupuncturist in attendance (some hospitals agree to this readily). It is not a good idea to try acupuncture if you are also receiving homeopathic treatment as they tend to counteract each other.

OSTEOPATHY

The founder of osteopathy, Andrew Taylor Still, was a doctor working in America at the time of the Civil War. He became convinced that good health is dependent upon the integrity of the spinal column. Central to the osteopathic approach is the idea that the body's healthy functioning is dependent on the balance of its structure and its bodily fluids. Still said that 'the rule of the artery is supreme' meaning that if there is good arterial blood supply to every organ and tissue giving nourishment and oxygen, plus good venous and fluid drainage to carry away waste products, one then has a very potent field of health to resist disease and degeneration. The body fluids are regulated by the nervous system which is why the osteopath pays so much attention to the spine and the spinal nerves. Malalignments in the vertebrae can cause spinal and muscle tension and irritation through the whole pathway of the nerve exiting from that segment.

Osteopaths work with their hands aiming to release the body's force to health, its immune system and its homeostatic equilibrium. By realigning the important pivot points of the spine, the osteopath aids harmonious posture. A branch of osteopathy has become known as 'cranial osteopathy'; here, the rhythmical pulse of the cerebro-spinal fluid which massages the nervous system, the spine and the cranium, is used as an aid to diagnosis and treatment. (The name is misleading because these osteopaths work to encourage this internal irrigation system throughout the whole body and not just on the skull.)

In common with other therapies, osteopathy is particularly useful if used pre-conceptually in that it can help normalise and harmonise the body. Women are found to be particularly responsive to treatment during the ante-natal period. Pregnancy can create problems for some women, for example, the changing weight load can lead to lower back ache. Sometimes, the posture becomes S-shaped which creates stress between the shoulder blades or in the neck and is very weakening for the soft tissues, the spine and the pelvis. An osteopath would encourage a woman to straighten her spine and would check to see if any pivotal points needed correction. The pelvic tissues will also be under-nourished if there is restriction in the pelvis or the sacrum is compressed.

During labour, an osteopath encourages the woman's natural inclination to move around. This helps normalise the circulation and avoids cramp; it also creates the best physiological situation in which to give birth. Firm pressure at the lumbo-sacral junction can often help to ease painful contractions; other suggestions are to hang from a rope, pole or another person, as seen for instance, in other cultures: Bushwomen used ropes, Siberian women had their shoulders across a bar, Greek women supported each other by the shoulders. Hanging in this way allows the whole spine and the abdomen to lengthen, thereby stretching the lower spine and allowing more abdominal space, all of which seems to inhibit the pain impulses.

Sometimes, after a long and difficult labour, a woman feels a 'dragging down' sensation. To the osteopathic hand, this can give the impression that the whole body continues re-living the downward expulsive force, in some cases for months after the birth. Osteopathic treatment can help re-align the pelvis and bring the spring back into the tissues and this has been found to have a beneficial effect on post-natal depression. Pushing in labour can leave a woman with tight shoulders and ribs; the engorgement thus caused because of interference with lymphatic and venous drainage from the breasts, can create problems with breast feeding. Osteopathic treatment can help free this.

Osteopaths believe that the baby can also benefit from treatment. Even after an easy birth, the occiput at the base of the skull may be compressed or buckled. This can manifest as a floppy, hyperactive, irritable or restless baby. Along with this, there may be compression of the temporal bones, which can result in a number of problems such as crying, restlessness, poor sucking, colic, poor muscle tone, tension, hyper-activity, poor co-ordination or slowness of development during the first year. Again, osteopathic treatment may help. Osteopaths view the process of labour and birth as being important for the baby as it provides a powerful initial stimulus to the cerebro-spinal fluid. They believe that a child born by caesarean section can benefit from treatment which helps invigorate the cranial rhythm. (Not all osteopaths work with babies, usually only those known as 'cranial' osteopaths.)

POLARITY THERAPY

Polarity Therapy is a system of healing developed by Doctor Randolph Stone. German in origin, he lived most of his life in the USA and India where he studied Ayurvedic medicine, naturopathy, nutrition, osteopathy and mysticism. From 1917 to 1973, he spent time studying and researching energy currents of the body which he called 'electro-magnetic energy', similar in idea to the 'prana' of yoga philosophy. This energy field, he believed, corresponds to the elements of air, fire, water and earth which arise from energy centres in the body or 'chakras'. There are endless variations on the inter-relationships of these energy fields, but the movement is always in polarities of positive to negative and back again.

Each element has particular qualities which can either feed or disturb another element. Inhibition or exaggeration of any element causes disharmony and imbalance which reflects on mental, emotional and physical levels. In pregnancy, for instance, Dr Stone believed that the fiery element which relates to digestion and is centred around the umbilicus, is crowded out by the development of the watery element in the womb. Thus, the digestive process is often disturbed towards the latter end of pregnancy as well as at the beginning.

Dr Stone integrated his work on subtle energy flows with his knowledge of osteopathy, physiology, physics and nutrition, creating the wholistic approach known as 'polarity therapy' which incorporates diet, manipulation, exercise and attention to attitude. He taught that the most powerful tools we have to heal are our hands and that the electro-magnetic energy that flows through them in positive and negative polarity can unblock and balance the flow of energy in another person.

Pregnancy may be the first time since puberty a woman has become acutely aware of body processes. Polarity therapy sessions aim to help integrate body/mind awareness and prepare a woman for the demands of labour. Manipulations can be used throughout pregnancy and are particularly useful in the final months to help free congestion, strain and negative emotional states. Polarity therapy includes a simple set of exercises you can do for yourself; one of the most important, particularly for pregnant women, is the squat. Dr Stone said, 'Apana . . . the downward function of energy in nature, is activated by the squatting posture . . . in childbirth this is the active principle which causes the delivery of the baby. It is a current which flows over these abdominal and pelvic muscles and causes them to contract . . . It would be helpful to pregnant mothers to prepare and condition the pelvis for the delivery of the child.'

Nutritional advice is generally based on vegetarian whole-foods, gradually encouraging the pregnant woman to observe and modify her diet for optimum nutrition. A cleansing diet (which can help considerably to offset morning sickness) is sometimes recommended also as a health building diet which contains all the nutriments necessary for healthy growth of mother and baby. It is the elemental, energy giving forces in foods that are emphasised as well as nutritional content. Because of its wholistic nature, polarity therapy provides an opportunity to examine both physical and emotional attitudes in pregnancy and offers the simplicity of relating to one practitioner for many needs.

USEFUL ADDRESSES AND RECOMMENDED READING

Herbal Medicine

National Institute of Medical Herbalists, 41 Hatherly Road, Winchester, Hampshire SO22 6RR.

The General Council and Register of Consultant Herbalists, 18 Elgin Road, Talbot Woods, Bournemouth, Dorset BH4 9ML.

Jean Palaiseul, *Grandmother's Secrets: Her Green Guide to Health from Plants*, Penguin, 1976.
Jethro Kloss, *Back to Eden*, Back to Eden Books, 1971.
M. Grieve, *A Modern Herbal*, Penguin, 1980.
Juliette de Bairacli Levy, *The Natural Rearing of Children*, Faber, 1975.
Dr J. Christopher, *School of Natural Healing*, Bi-World Publications, 1976.

Homeopathy

Society of Homeopaths, 11a Bampton Street, Tiverton, Devon.

British Homeopathic Association, 27a Devonshire Street, London W1N 1RJ.

Hahnemann Society, Humane Education Centre, Avenue Lodge, Bounds Green Road, London N22 4EU.

Homeopathic Development Foundation, Harcourt House, 19a Cavendish Square, London W1M 9AD.

M. Panos and J. Heimlich, *Homeopathic Medicine at Home*, Corgi, 1982.

G. Vithoulkas, *Homeopathy, Medicine of the New Man*, Arco, 1983.
Sarah Richardson, *Homeopathy in Pregnancy and Childhood*, The Society of Homeopaths, 1980.
The Active Birth Movement, *Homeopathy for Pregnancy, Childbirth and Infancy*, 1983.

Bio-Chemic Tissue Salts

Dr W. H. Schussler, *Bio-Chemic Handbook*, New Era, 1978.
Andrew Stanway, *A Guide to Bio-Chemic Tissue Salts*, Van Dyke Books, 1982.

Bach Flower Remedies

The Bach Centre, Mount Vernon, Sotwell, Wallingford, Oxon.

Edward Bach, *Heal Thyself*, The Bach Centre, 1973.
Philip Chancellor, *Handbook of Bach Flower Remedies*, The Bach Centre, 1971.

Acupuncture

British Acupuncture Association, 34 Alderney Street, London SW1V 4EU.

Traditional Acupuncture Society, 11 Grange Park, Stratford-upon-Avon, Warwickshire CV37 6XH.

Register of Traditional Chinese Medicine, 18 Shenley Road, London SE5 8NN.

International Register of Oriental Medicine, Green Hedges House, Green Hedges Avenue, East Grinstead, Sussex RH19 1DZ.

J. R. Worsley, *Talking About Acupuncture*, Element Books, 1982.
Ted Kaptchuk, *The Web That Has No Weaver*, Congdon and Weed, 1984.

Osteopathy

British School of Osteopathy, 1–4 Suffolk Street, London SW1Y 4HG.

European School of Osteopathy, 104 Tonbridge Road, Maidstone, Kent ME16 8SL.

British Naturopathic and Osteopathic Association, 6 Netherhall Gardens, London NW3 5RR.

Polarity Therapy

Polarity Therapy Association, Revelstone, 11 Rowacres, Englishcombe Lane, Bath, Avon BA2 2LM.

The books below are all by Dr Stone and are available from The Polarity Therapy Association:
Health Building
Easy Stretching Postures
Purifying Diet

General Addresses and Reading

For a list of centres belonging to the Natural Health Network write to:

Natural Health Network, Chardstock House, Chard, Somerset TA20 2TL. (Please enclose a stamped addressed envelope.)

Research Institute for Complementary Medicine, 37 Bedford Square, London WC1B 3HW.

Institute for Complementary Medicine, 21 Portland Place, London W1N 3AF.

British Holistic Medical Association, 179 Gloucester Place, London NW1 6DX.

Brian Inglis and Ruth White, *The Alternative Health Guide*, Michael Joseph, 1983.
L. LeShan, *Holistic Health: How to Understand and Use the Revolution in Medicine*, Turnstone Press, 1984.

Helping a woman through labour

INA MAY GASKIN

Any woman, no matter how independent she is at other times, appreciates help while she is in labour. Because every woman's labour is unique, what helps one woman may not be helpful to another. For instance, some mothers appreciate being touched and massaged while in labour, while others cannot stand being touched. Some mothers are better able to relax when they have eye contact with a helper such as a midwife or mate, and some find more strength if they close their eyes and concentrate on their inner reserves.

To really help a mother in labour, attendants must give her full attention and respect. She has no choice but to be extremely sensitive to touch and to the speech, the gesture and movement, the looks, and even the thoughts and attitudes of anyone within her range of hearing and sight. A careless statement ('Is SHE still in labour?' or 'She's TRYING to have natural childbirth') may discourage or distract her when she needs all the concentration and confidence she can muster. When a mother is treated as a background character in the drama of birth, she may be so affected by the presence and the actions of the people who should be helping her, that her labour may even come to a halt. Most midwives who work in hospitals have seen many instances of labours which didn't get anywhere because the mother was in too distracting an atmosphere to relax.

Ideally, the mother's needs are anticipated and met, and she is not put into a position of having to close herself off to the people who are supposed to be helping her. The midwife, partner or doctor recognise that she is like any other mammal when she gives birth, so when they are near her, they adjust their movements and their pace to match hers. If they notice that she is fearful, it will be possible to calm her only if they themselves are calm and centred in their attention.

I recently spoke with a couple who had their first child in a large city hospital, delivered by an obstetrician who tries to give mothers a greater choice in childbirth than is usually allowed. Instead of performing the automatic caesarean section for mothers with breech babies, he allowed low-risk mothers with breech babies to give birth naturally, if they could do so within a reasonable length of time. Although this doctor had good outcomes with his births, he was not popular with the other obstetricians because of his more liberal approach.

Both the husband and the wife told me that they had found it hard to relax enough for her to dilate under the normal conditions of the labour ward. A midwife would come by periodically to check the baby's heartbeat with a large electronic monitor. The husband said she would rapidly twirl on the dial knob to full volume, squeeze a glop of conductant jelly on to the transducer, and then move the unit all over his wife's belly, never remembering from one time to the next where she had heard the heart-beat earlier. If she had trouble locating the heart-beat after a few seconds of trying, she would wack the amplifier smartly with her open palm a few times, producing a sound 'as loud as a bomb', the husband said. At one point, another obstetrician came by and yelled at the couple's doctor because he hadn't yet performed a caesarean. The couple then retreated to the bathroom, hoping to have enough peace there for the natural course of labour to take over. They began to notice some good results after a few minutes; the mother had strong uterine action and began to experience an opening feeling. The only problem was that she could not get really comfortable while sitting on the toilet, because she found it hard to keep her leg from leaning against a heater. The couple, feeling the pressure upon their doctor, knew that they would have to have the baby soon if they were to avoid surgery, so they decided to try taking a walk. The mother had a strong feeling that if she could just get outside for a few minutes, she would be able to open up the last couple of centimetres. They strolled around the hospital a couple of times before a midwife, notified by someone who had seen the couple from the window, came to escort them back to the labour ward. Even so, their strategy had worked, and the mother gave birth easily not long after going back inside.

The course of this couple's labour seems absurd; that the mother actually had to find her own peace and privacy for a while so that nature could proceed, but modern times do sometimes present people with odd choices.

Every first-time mother's labour is an unveiling of a mystery. No one can describe or simulate what labour feels like and no mother is going to know what labour is like until she is in the middle of it for the first time. It never works to tell a mother that labour is going to be easy. At the same time, it doesn't help to scare her. Here is one exchange between a first-time mother and her midwife. The mother was a week or two overdue, with a relatively large baby and was feeling apprehensive, although committed to having a natural childbirth at home, if it turned out to be medically safe.

> *Mother:* 'I have a very low threshold for pain.'
> *Midwife* (humorously): 'That will change. That is one thing you won't say again after the birth.'

This exchange was followed by knowing laughter from the other three midwives present in the room at the time (all had had natural births themselves, so they knew what they were talking about). The idea was not to frighten this mother, who was assured that even though her baby was large and a bit overdue, they were sure that her pelvic measurements were big enough and that she was the kind of person who could get through her labour without anaesthesia. She did have a long, hard labour, but she got through it very well and was justifiably proud of herself.

Pain in childbirth is not a universal experience, but mothers who expect no discomfort may feel cheated by their bodies or by their childbirth educators or midwives. Even mothers who describe their labours as pleasant, usually pass through some moments when they have all they can do to cope. On the other hand, I hesitate to use the word 'pain' very often when talking to a mother during the pre-natal period or in labour, because I am trying to avoid triggering the associations we usually have with the word and with the actual feeling of pain. In the rest of our experience of pain, it serves as a warning to the organism that damage is being done in some way to the tissue of the organism — it's a warning to get one's finger out of the fire or to take that rock off one's toe. With labour, though, a feeling of pain means something different. I am not talking about the sensation that comes with an abrupting placenta or some other catastrophe, in which case we are talking about real pain. I am talking about the use of the word in the sense of 'labour pains', a different situation, even though it may feel equally intense to the mother. The difference is that in normal labour, the feelings of discomfort are not primarily signals to the mother that something is wrong. Discomfort in this instance is a signal that her body is trying to do something which another part of her body is resisting to some degree, but actual damage to the body is not usually involved. The rest of the difference is that she can often lessen the discomfort she feels by paying attention to what it is that her body is trying to do and then helping the process. She then becomes like the surfer who is riding the wave instead of being dashed about by it, and gets to experience the exhilaration that comes with this physical and mental success, even though it requires a lot of muscular exertion.

I like to use the word 'rush' in place of the more usual 'contraction', because I think the first term suggests a better way to deal with the energy of childbirth. We have the expression 'a rush of tenderness' or some other emotion, in which the word is used in much the same sense as the word 'wave' may be used. 'Wave' is also a good word to use for the peaks of energy a woman experiences during labour because it implies the ebb and flow of the process. The words used to communicate with the mother about her labour will tend to influence her attitude and her ability to relax.

Some mothers, however, especially single mothers or those whose mates are not with them while they labour, need steady companionship and coaching in order to relax effectively. The only way to know what each individual mother needs is to pay enough attention to know what really helps her. Helping a mother in labour means letting her discover her own way to move (or not

to move) with the energy of childbirth. If the positions she takes
are effective, but are not those the attendant is used to, it is better
to let her follow her own instincts. Some of the best help an
attendant can give is to keep her informed of even minute details
about her forward progress — how much her cervix has moved
forward or opened since she was last checked, and just when
during her last rush the greatest degree of relaxation took place.

At times, when a mother is having trouble getting used to early
labour, she may need a few general instructions. These are usually
best given between rushes so she is able to absorb what is being
said. Here are a few notes I made of helpful things midwives said
to first-time mothers during labour:

Midwife: 'It's a feeling of acceptance, like sexual acceptance,
of the energy that's coming through you. That's what you
want to strive for.'

'See if you can become really sensitive to it (the rush) and see
what it's trying to tell you to do, see what shape it wants you
to take.' (This was being said to a mother who was holding
back, obviously wishing that the whole thing was already
over.)

'This is not a real hurt, as you would have from being
injured. No damage is being done to your body. In a way,
you have to be willing for this to hurt. If you can accept the
fact that the hurt is from muscle tension, it's no longer so
frightening, and you can then relax more easily.'

Mother: 'How much longer is this going to go on?'
Midwife: 'No one can really tell you that.'

'The reason that kissing is good at a time like this
(approaching transition) is because it keeps the muscles
around your lips and chin relaxed and loose. If you can keep
these muscles relaxed while it is this intense, you don't have
to be in transition so long.'

'It's good to make sounds. Just try to keep them low-pitched
and throaty (demonstrates). You probably aren't going to be
comfortable again until you have the baby.'

'Try to unwrinkle your forehead.'

'This makes you realise how much work it took to get all of us born.'

'It makes you respect your mother in a new way, doesn't it?'

'Approaching transition is something like throwing yourself off a cliff if you are a young bird. You have to trust that you'll know how to fly.'

At times, when the mother is really working hard, the most helpful kind of communication she can get becomes almost a song — a birth song or chant. The mother is usually in need of soothing, and she may also need a boost in courage. Anyone who has been in labour can testify that praise at appropriate times can be very helpful.

Sometimes, when the mother is having a hard time coping, I find myself not saying much — that is, until I'm sure that what I have to say will be helpful. I might confine myself to touching her in comforting ways or looking in her eyes and relaxing (if that is what she wants) when there seems to be nothing helpful to say. I remember one mother, who obviously didn't want to listen to any talk, unless it was going to be directly relevant. She was in a very serious and fearful frame of mind, and I knew she would feel better and more confident if I could think of something she would find funny. The trouble was that she was so serious at the time, it was a long while before I could think of something that could possibly amuse her. Finally, I came up with the one that helped, which was, 'One thing you have to say about it — childbirth is exciting, right?' I knew that she did have a wry sense of humour back in there, and gambled that she might appreciate that. She smiled, the first that I had seen that day and commented that she was pretty tough and could probably do anything. From then on, she noticed that being in a humorous frame of mind actually did make her feel better, as well as tougher and more confident, so it wasn't so hard to think of amusing things to say. Another piece of advice that seemed to help her was, 'You'll always remember this day very clearly, so try to make it the way you'll want to remember it.' I also told her that she could make instantaneous changes in her condition by changing her attitude.

It is necessary to know the mother pretty well in order to know what might appeal to her particular sense of humour. I got one mother to smile during an intense part of her labour by saying, 'It's times like this when you wish there could be some other way you could go about reproduction — like laying eggs or something.'

The best way to deal with fear is to anticipate it. A mother is less likely to totally lose her confidence if she has been told that most every woman, even those who have given birth before, comes to a point in labour when she wonders if it will be possible for her to give birth. Just the knowledge that birth can seem impossible enables her to take the thought less seriously whenever it comes around.

Mothers who are afraid are often helped by knowing that breathing more slowly lessens fear. For some, eye contact with the midwife, who leads a slower pace of breathing, will be enough to restore confidence. Deep, abdominal breathing tends to relax the nerve centres in the solar plexus, reducing the tight feeling that accompanies fear. Sometimes fear needs to be recognised and talked about a little. The mother may need reassurance that she is in no danger. I have helped a few women through labour who became afraid that their being afraid would cause complications to happen. Each one needed to know that while fear can cause certain problems, such as failure to dilate, no bad consequences can come about with a short span of time.

Any mother will tell you that it is awful to be scolded like a child while in labour. It is better to let her try her way, if she wants to do that, and if the result is no progress while she is trying her way, she can learn that for herself. (This leaves her some dignity and increases the attendants' credibility.) Another thought I find myself saying to mothers in labour during the stage of dilation is: 'Try to become as liquid as you can during this rush. Try to turn into a puddle.' This advice may also be needed while the mother is in the pushing stage if she tends to remain excited between her rushes instead of using the periods between each rush to get as rested and relaxed as possible.

The mother who is 'mothered' by her attendants while she labours has an increased chance of being a confident and protective mother after childbirth. During this extremely vulnerable, impressionable and unforgettable few hours of her life, she records tracks of kindness and compassion which she may later draw on when her patience and good humour are tested by her unending responsibilities as a mother. This is the kind of help mothers are grateful for years after the birth of their children.

RECOMMENDED READING

Margot Edwards and Mary Waldorf, *Reclaiming Birth*, The Crossing Press, 1984.

Elizabeth Davis, *Midwifery, Heart and Hands*, John Muir Publications, 1981.

PART THREE

The Future

And is it not time that the wrenching apart of inner and outer worlds was healed, and the *unus mundus* restored, nature understood once more as a living part of the indivisible wholeness of body and spirit? Is not that the vision of the so-called 'New Age' which we are entering, or seeking to create?

Kathleen Raine

Creating a new world

MICHEL ODENT

Homo sapiens had always been a gatherer, a hunter or a fisherman. Then, about 10,000 years ago, homo sapiens discovered his ability to control the reproduction of living things. He created the cultivation of vegetables and the breeding of animals.

Until then the mystery of life was totally dependent upon women. Men were envious and fearful of the power of their female companions. They worshipped goddesses: the 'mother-goddess' and the 'earth-goddess'.

Their control over the reproduction of living creatures helped men become conscious of the power of their male fecundity. This new awareness made possible the most radical change in man-woman relationships. The patriarchal system was born. The mental image of the father became stronger and stronger. Humans started to worship male gods. The monotheist religions appeared and channelled the universal religious instinct towards images of god-fathers.

Male-dominated society grew less and less respectful of life in general, not even stopping at destroying the planet itself.

There have been many stages in the history of the control over life. Perhaps one of the most decisive ones happened in the seventeenth century, when men took over the control of childbirth. Up to that time, childbirth had been solely a women's event. Let us remember, for example, that in 1552 a doctor from Hamburg was sentenced to death by being burnt alive because he had disguised himself as a woman in order to be present at a birth. One century later, Louis XIV could watch the delivery of one of his mistresses thanks to the complicity of the male obstetrician, Jules Clement.

Up to that time, a midwife was a woman who helped other women. She was able to do this thanks to her own experience as a mother, and her specifically feminine sensitivity. But when the male doctor entered the confinement bedroom, his priority was to control the process of the delivery. That's why the first thing he did was to put the labouring woman on her back. The French obstetrician, Mauriceau, is considered to be the pioneer of this practice.

The male doctors encouraged midwifery schools to be set up. From then on the midwife tended to become more and more a technician. She was taught to control the process of delivery in schools which were themselves controlled by doctors. So control was exercised in childbirth at several levels. This tendency to make control a priority in childbirth has increased over the centuries, until it has now reached absurd proportions where childbirth mainly takes place in hospitals in an era of ultrasound and electronics.

In the last twenty years or so, most women giving birth in our modern hospitals have felt the need — and feel more and more deeply the need — to be assisted by the only other possible component of the nuclear family . . . the baby's father. Moreover, it has always been the dream of many men to enter the world of women and participate in childbirth. So now the control of childbirth by men is almost total. It is as if the last bastion against the domination of our world by the masculine brain has been overcome.

So we have to break a vicious circle. First of all, we need another kind of human being: someone who has a much stronger bond to the Earth, or, in other words, to the mother.

Nowadays we understand more and more that the mother-infant bonding is a model for all kinds of attachment. So the first thing to do is to foster the mother-infant relationship. The priority is to stop disturbing the process of delivery, and this must be done at a collective level, by our society as a whole.

When you realise that many labouring women need to be helped by an experienced and motherly female, you can then say that the first change we need is to give childbirth back to women.

For the moment, the priority is certainly not to keep fathers out of the birth place. It is much more commonplace at the present time to marvel at the positive emotions of a couple sharing the experience of childbirth and welcoming the newborn baby, even if it is a way of reinforcing the mental image of the nuclear family as a model. In our maternity unit the participation of the baby's father at birth is almost considered as a rule. However, some midwives in our team dare to say in retrospect that some deliveries would certainly have been much easier with only the assistance of the midwife and that the baby's father is rarely the best 'coach' — to have the possibility of participating is very different from being a 'coach'.

At the present time, the priority is to rediscover the true reasons for midwifery. Midwives have to win back complete autonomy. Midwives could be totally in charge, yet have at their disposal good surgical teams who could be ready to do a caesarean, for example, at any time. And as the midwives take charge of the birthing rooms, so the male doctors must retire from them. Obstetrics is obsolete. Only group pressure by mothers and authentic midwives can take the liberty to explore the most radical choices for the future. Medical men must be at the service of mothers and midwives, instead of controlling them.

Such a venture may be considered unrealistic. But surely it is much more unrealistic to think that our world can survive without such a radical shift.

'I am a woman who carries a child'

YVONNE BAGINSKY

I am a Woman who Carries a Child

I am a woman who carries a child,
A child of three inches who this day
Grows liver, kidney, heart, finger, face, bone,
This day when rain falls and wind blows
From the south, from Harrisburg.

I am a woman who can build a good fire,
Mend tears of cloth or skin,
Who in a summer's growing fills
A winter's worth of jars, baskets, cans, crates, stomachs.

I am woman who sings with children,
Who with care attends each small growth and budding,
Who daily weaves each luminous strand
Into the delicate cloth of family and home.

I am a woman who watches the rain
This day fall upon the soil my fingers cherish,
Sink into the soil that is our life,
Innocent rain, carrying what small death.

I am woman who chooses not to flee,
Whose fear grows heavy in this rain,
Who envelops yet does not protect the tiny embryo
Growing toe, thumb, or small fingernail.

I am a woman who labors in this understanding
So difficult to grasp in its entirety,
We have left no place in this earth
Safe for the growing of seed or child.

I am a woman who carries a child,
Who can never again embrace the rain as it falls
  in total friendship,
Who must learn to distrust the soil and its offerings,
Who must teach children to both love and comprehend,
To stand in their humanity with strength and dignity,
To fashion from their fear
Tools for creation.

I am a woman who carries a child.

by Margie Gaffron
Rebersburg, Pennsylvania

I had been running Birth Rights, a birth information centre for
Scotland, for two years when I first met Dr Helen Caldicott. The
Australian paediatrician was visiting Edinburgh in October 1980
as part of a European lecture tour to alert people to the medical
implications of the escalating nuclear arms race. She had just
given up her own medical work at the Children's Hospital in
Boston, Massachusetts to devote herself full-time to what she saw
as the most serious medical issue ever to face the human race.

I had been involved in medical issues of a different sort for
some time, since the birth of my first child at home in Edinburgh
in 1974. Birth Rights grew out of a second home birth in 1978. My
husband and I, grateful to the National Health Service for the care
we had received, and dismayed at the seemingly universal
ignorance among friends and acquaintances about the NHS
option for home confinement, decided the time was ripe to inform
people about their rights, and support them in their choices.

Few people we met had had births which they could say had
been free of trauma, and many seemed to suffer from residues of
anger, mistrust, fear, or disappointment: the aftermath of uneasy
pregnancies or frustrating birth experiences. As a result of our
two home births, and of the trusting relationships we formed with
doctors and midwives in the course of the two pregnancies, we
felt enhanced as a family. We looked at birth as a gift to all
concerned, a chance, given to most of us only once or twice in a
lifetime, to grow, to be shaken to our very roots by the miracle
of life. And a 'good' birth — one which proceeded organically
from within the family, without interference — seemed the best
possible start for a new human being.

In Edinburgh that October, Helen Caldicott talked about birth and about children; but she also talked about death. In a packed room at Edinburgh University, we heard — many of us for the first time — of how vulnerable we are to radiation, that almost ungraspably lethal emission — tasteless, odourless, invisible — which works its damage on the body's cells over time. We heard that women are particularly vulnerable; exposure to radiation can affect unfertilised eggs. The pregnant woman is even more sensitive; rapidly dividing fetal cells make the unborn baby 200 times more vulnerable to radiation damage than a man in his fifties.

It was just over a year since the near-meltdown of the Three-Mile-Island nuclear power plant in Harrisburg, Pennsylvania. Dr Caldicott talked about the disaster that had so narrowly been averted — the instant deaths, the creeping illnesses, the epidemics of cancer fanning out over the next five decades. 'They say the radioactive iodine will decay in a couple of weeks, but what about the Strontium 90 which lasts for 600 years and gets recycled through the soil, the grass, the milk, the babies, the soil, the grass, the milk? And human breast milk — it's the babies who are twenty times more sensitive to radiation than adults. This is a children's issue.'

Horrifying as the long-term effects of the nuclear energy programme are, these were only the 'pimple on the pumpkin' as far as Dr Caldicott was concerned. The immediate threat to the planet was the build-up of nuclear arms, and the frightening disregard for human life which accompanies this build-up. 'America today has about 30–35,000 hydrogen bombs — enough to overkill every Russian forty times. Russia has about 20,000 hydrogen bombs — enough to overkill every American only twenty times. They have enough, combined, probably, to overkill every person on earth twelve times. It is estimated that in a nuclear war, in 30 days 90 per cent of Americans would be dead. And that would be right for England, for Scotland, for Europe, for Russia.'

This was all disastrous information to those of us who had managed to push increasingly frequent news items about the nuclear arms race safely into the backs of our minds. But the message was not all gloom: we had a role to play. 'The negative masculine principle — competition, warlike games, death and ego and power — has the world in a stranglehold. It is time for the positive feminine principle in both men and women — the principle of caring, protecting, nurturing — to take over.'

Dr Caldicott made a final passionate plea: 'The instinct to protect our young is probably the most powerful instinct of any human being — the instinct for survival. We are the curators of every organism on this earth. We hold it all in the palm of our hand — the children, the trees, the flowers. This is the ultimate in preventative medicine: to eliminate every single nuclear weapon on earth, and close the reactors at once. For if we do not, we are participating in our own suicide, and we're all sick.' I was left feeling deeply shocked, yet also strangely uplifted, committed in the deepest part of myself to some as yet undefined action.

Dr Caldicott stayed at our house that night. As I poured the tea around the kitchen table, I couldn't help voicing an uneasy question which had nagged me all evening. What about birth? Was there any place, in all this desperate battle, for helping people regain control over that ultimate of caring and nurturing experiences? Couldn't the runaway technology she had denounced be reined in at source?

Her answer was quick, and devastating: 'At this point, to talk about birth is displacement activity. When animals are faced with a life-threatening situation, they do something totally irrelevant, and so do we. We write our papers, we go to work, we have the babies, we bake the cakes, and we pretend it's going to go on forever. Does it matter if your kids clean their teeth, or have good food, if we're not going to survive?'

I somehow felt that it did matter, but the visit, and the message, played havoc with my work as a mother, as a journalist, as a birth counsellor. Friends would talk about projects just begun, summer holidays, jobs planned for the end of the year, and I would listen in silent despair, wondering if we would all be here that long. Riding on the top of a double-decker bus through the centre of town, I'd calculate how long it would take me to get to my children's schools if the three-minute warning sound exploded out of that deceptively blue sky. I tormented myself with impossible choices about which school I'd race to — which of my children I'd run to comfort.

The telephone calls to Birth Rights continued to come: pregnant women needing information on the most open-minded hospitals, fathers wanting to know their rights, parents asking to be put in touch with sympathetic midwives. I answered the questions with a heavy conscience. I felt completely paralysed.

In January, I withdrew completely from Birth Rights, and threw my energy into helping launch a new group — Parents for Survival. My colleagues were all childbirth counsellors, NCT teachers, post-natal support leaders; all propelled, like I was, by a kind of anxious panic. Loosely based on Helen Caldicott's own group in the United States — Women for Survival — the group focused on the same kind of nurturing energy which we felt was particularly strong in people who had children. My husband had filmed Dr Caldicott's talk in Edinburgh, and the first priority, it seemed, was to get her message out to as many parents throughout Britain as possible.

The launch-date for the group was 15 March, just after my second child's birthday. One hundred and fifty parents trooped in to the Friends' Meeting House for the showing the video. I looked at all the men and women, some with tiny infants strapped to their chests, most with children tucked up in bed at home: innocent faces, eager, somewhat apprehensive. I turned out the lights as Helen Caldicott began: 'In essence, nuclear reactors are bomb factories.' I waited out the film downstairs in the coffee room; I already knew the transcript by heart.

An hour later I returned, just in time to hear the final plea. The lights went up and I looked out over the grey, shocked faces, knowing what many of these parents would now find impossible to ignore. I also knew my own shock and negativity was over, and I was ready to go back to my birth work. That night, my husband and I decided to make a new film — about home birth.

The issues no longer seemed to undermine each other. How different, in fact, is the concentration of electrical generation into fewer, larger, more mechanised centres from the concentration of births — human generation — into fewer, larger, and more mechanised hospitals? Is talk about 'millirems', 'roentgens', 'overkill' any more mystifying to ordinary people than the barrage of medical terminology — 'endoscopy', 'ultrasound', 'fetal scalp sampling' — now part and parcel of birth? Is it only coincidence that both industries — the nuclear machine and the birth machine — are dominated by men, by competition and power struggles; and that women are their most vulnerable victims?

The nuclear industry, and nuclear war, are only the tip of the iceberg: the most lethal expression of a society characterised by complex levels of exploitation, a society where human skills and values are downgraded, human beings ultimately expendable. Of all experiences which can bring us back in touch with what it is to be human, which can break down generations of conditioning in the skills of domination and control, birth is perhaps the most powerful.

Unfortunately, we are fast loosing control over this experience to the high priests of science. The obstetrician with his bank of monitoring equipment, who chooses to override a woman's instinctive knowledge of how to give birth, is really not so far removed from the nuclear-industry spokesman who advised distraught residents of Harrisburg to 'leave it in the hands of the experts'.

The scientists, the politicians, the bureaucrats who defend nuclear power plants are defending an industry with an inbuilt level of 'acceptable risk': its operation in the United States alone has been calculated to have the potential of causing over 3,000 fatalities, 45,000 early illnesses, and more than 1,500 latent fatal cancers. In the name of progress, technological advance, social benefit, the nuclear experts are paving the way for national, international, perhaps global disaster, an end of civilisation as we know it.

'Acceptable risk' is also a feature of the medical technology now applied to birth: the long-term effects of increasingly administered ultrasound and epidurals have yet to be established; the full range of risks accompanying amniocentesis is rarely spelled out; the extent to which fetal monitoring may adversely affect the progress of labour remains unexplored. In the name of efficiency and safety, the medical experts are paving the way for the end of birth as we know it.

None of us is completely immune to the charisma of the expert. For every woman now squatting to give birth, hundreds of women lie flat on their backs to be delivered. We continue to wonder at the natural swell of love between mother and infant at birth, and insist on making it scientifically credible by calling it 'bonding'. We can still be amazed that a premature baby can do just as well sheltered between its mother's breasts as on a life-support system.

By falling, along with the experts, for the glitter of technology we are all in danger of forgetting how to use our human skills to determine what is possible, our human judgement to decide what is permissible. As the American antinuclear activist Rosalie Bertell puts it, 'We are all fragile, already damaged, and not too careful human beings. Our ability to withstand abuse can not and must not be calculated in the same terms as wear and tear on a mechanical system.' What technology can chalk up to acceptable risk involves our bodies, our babies, our births, our deaths.

We have come a long way since Helen Caldicott's talk in 1980. That was before the deployment of Cruise missiles, the breakdown of SALT II talks, the radioactive contamination of beaches around Windscale. But it was also before public enquiries, here and in the United States halted, if only temporarily, the building of new nuclear power plants. It was before the explosive growth of CND, before the widespread use of nonviolent direct action, and before Greenham Common.

Since that time, British birth has also suffered a massive technological onslaught: amniocentesis for women over 35 is rarely questioned; ultrasound is becoming routine; epidurals are blandly encouraged and acquiesced to. Yet these past four years have also seen alternative birth centres springing up throughout the country; Radical Midwives clamouring to rescue their age-old birthing skills from the machines which threaten to supplant them; active birth postures adopted by growing numbers of mothers and an increase in the number of women giving birth at home.

The balance is indeed finely drawn. If, in Helen Caldicott's words, we hold the life of every organism in the palm of our hand, we must fight to wrest control over that life from the hands of those who have so irresponsibly abused their power. Whether we work to reclaim our food from agricultural toxins, our waters from nuclear waste, our births from mechanical hands, or, ultimately, our deaths from the nuclear war machine, the struggle is one. Our refusal to allow the issues to become separate is perhaps the most powerful expression of that positive feminine principle which may prove to be our strongest weapon.

Epilogue

The Tibetan Buddhist 'Shambhala Prophecy'

We are now entering a time of extreme danger in which two great powers — called Lalös, the barbarians — are locked in mutual hostility. One is in the centre of the Eurasian land mass, the other is in the West, and they have, for all their enmity, a great deal in common, including the fact they they have both developed and are manufacturing and deploying weapons of unfathomable death and devastation.

So the future of the planet is in question. And it is at this time that the kingdom of the Shambhala begins to emerge. This kingdom is hard to detect because it is not a geo-political entity; it exists in the hearts and minds of the 'Shambhala warriors'. For that matter, you can't even tell a Shambhala warrior by looking at her or him: they wear no insignias, badges or uniforms; they carry no banners; they have no barricades on which to climb or behind which to rest or re-group, no turf to call their own. Ever and always they do their work on the terrain of the Lalös themselves.

Then there comes a time, which we are approaching, when physical and moral courage is required of these Shambhala warriors, for they must go right into the centres and corridors of power, into the very citadels and pockets where these weapons (in the broadest sense of the term) are kept, to dismantle them. Now is the time that the Shambhala warriors must train for this work. And how do they train? They train in the use of two weapons: compassion (karuna) and insight (prajna) into the inter-relatedness of all reality.

As told to Joanna Macy by Choegyal Rinpoche.

Useful addresses

THE BIRTH CENTRE NETWORK

For addresses of other Birth Centres, names and addresses of affiliated teachers and those teaching yoga for pregnancy please contact:

The West London Birth Centre, 7 Waldemar Avenue, London W13.

For information about the Birth Teachers' Course run by the Birth Centre contact:

The Reading Birth Centre, 71 De Beauvoir Road, Reading RG1 5NR.

(Please enclose a stamped addressed envelope with all enquiries.)

OTHER ORGANISATIONS

Active Birth Movement, 18 Laurier Road, London, NW5.

Association of Breastfeeding Mothers, 131 Mayhow Road, London SE26 4HZ.

Association for Improvements in the Maternity Services, 163 Liverpool Road, London N1 0RF.
The Ipswich group of AIMS has compiled a 'Directory of Maternity and Post-Natal Care Organisations' price £1.10 available from: Amanda Wade, 76 Suffolk Road, Ipswich, Suffolk.

Association of Post-natal Illness, 7 Gowan Avenue, London SW6.

Association of Radical Midwives, Lakefield, 8a The Drive, London SW20.

Caesarean Section Support Group, 44 Lantree Crescent, Trumpington, Cambridge.

The Dick-Read School for Natural Childbirth, 14 Pitt Street, London W8 4NY.

Foresight, (The Association for the Promotion of Pre-Conceptual Care) The Old Vicarage, Church Lane, Witley, Godalming, Surrey GU8 5PN.

La Leche League, Box 3424, London WC1 6XX.

Maternity Defence Fund, 33 Castle Street, Henley-in-Arden, Warwickshire.

The Miscarriage Association, Dolphin Cottage, 4 Ashfield Terrace, Thorpe, Wakefield, West Yorks WF3 3DD.

The National Childbirth Trust, 9 Queensborough Terrace, London W2 3TB.

The Pre-Eclamptic Toxaemia Society, 88 Plumberow, Lee Chapel North, Basildon, Essex SS15 5LQ.

Society to Support Home Confinements, 17 Laburnum Avenue, Durham DH4 HA.

The Stillbirth Association, 15a Christchurch Hill, London NW3 1JY.

Further Reading

(Books not already referred to or recommended in the text)

Suzanne Arms, *Immaculate Deception*, Bantam, 1975.

S. Borg and J. Lasker, *When Pregnancy Fails*, Routledge & Kegan Paul, 1983.

Fritjof Capra, *The Turning Point*, Fontana, 1983.

Grantley Dick-Read, *Childbirth Without Fear*, revised and edited by Helen Wessel and Harlan F. Ellis, Harper & Row, 1984.

Barbara Ehrenreich and Deirdre English, *For Her Own Good*, Pluto Press, 1979.

Marilyn Ferguson, *The Aquarian Conspiracy*, Granada, 1982.

Doris Haire, *The Cultural Warping of Childbirth*, ICEA, 1972 (available from ICEA, PO Box 20048, Minneapolis, MN 55426 USA).

Sheila Kitzinger, *The Experience of Childbirth*, Penguin, 1970.

Ann Oakley, *From Here To Maternity: Becoming a Mother*, Penguin, 1979.

Ann Oakley, *Women Confined*, Martin Robertson, 1980.

Ann Oakley, Ann McPherson and Helen Roberts, *Miscarriage*, Fontana, 1984.

Ann Oakley, *The Captured Womb*, Basil Blackwell, 1985.

Angela Phillips, Nicky Lean and Barbara Jacobs, *Your Body, Your Baby, Your Life*, Pandora Press, 1983.

Angela Phillips and Jill Rakusen, *Our Bodies, Our Selves*, Penguin, 1978.

H. Pizer and C. Palinski, *Coping With A Miscarriage*, Jill Norman, 1981.

Adrienne Rich, *Of Woman Born: Motherhood As An Experience And An Institution*, Virago, 1977.

Barbara Rothman, *In Labour: Women and Power In The Birthplace*, Junction Books, 1982.

Penny and Andrew Stanway, *Breast Is Best*, Pan, 1978.

Vivienne Welburn, *Post-natal Depression*, Fontana, 1980.

Index